Agatha Christie's
MURDER IN THE MAKING

Mousetrap II ?

A reunion dinner - The survivors
of (Revolution ?) (that ?)

(Aircrew + Passengers lost in desert)

1 Man - Gale crashes — A lawyer?
Elderly?   Marooned?   Felix Ceylin?
type? 1   Or a Richardson

A murder — Here — One of them
is a murderer — one of them is
a victim. —
        Don't know v. of ———

End of Scene — 2 in the prospectus
Victim, and 3?

        (Really murderer —)

Possibility of house in street Soho hired for party - waiters
hired for jobs!)

        one man is waiter - brings
drinks to guests - Later enters
as guest - with moustache.
                        P.T.O

*From Notebook 4 a tantalising glimpse of a project, never realised,
from the 1960s. See* Unused Ideas Three.

Agatha Christie's
MURDER IN THE MAKING

<o>

*Stories and Secrets
from her Archive*

JOHN CURRAN

HarperCollins*Publishers*

HarperCollins*Publishers*
77–85 Fulham Palace Road
Hammersmith, London W6 8JB
www.harpercollins.co.uk

This edition published for The Book People
by HarperCollins*Publishers* 2011

1

ISBN 978-0-00-739676-4

Printed and bound in Great Britain by Clays Ltd, St Ives plc

MIX
Paper from
responsible sources
FSC
www.fsc.org
FSC® C007454

For
Mathew, Lucy and Mahler,
without whom . . .

Contents

Acknowledgements		9
Preface		11
Introduction		21
1	Rule of Three	31
2	The First Decade 1920–1929	67
	Unused Ideas – One	117
3	Favourite Stories and 'The Man Who Knew'	122
4	The Second Decade 1930–1939	137
	Unused Ideas – Two	177
5	'How I Created Hercule Poirot'	182
6	The Third Decade 1940–1949	190
	Unused Ideas – Three	229
7	Miss Marple and 'The Case of the Caretaker's Wife'	234
8	The Fourth Decade 1950–1959	260
	Unused Ideas – Four	319
9	Agatha Christie and Poison	323

10 The Fifth Decade 1960–1969   330
    Unused Ideas – Five   361

11 The Dark Lady . . .   366

12 The Sixth Decade 1970–1976   372
    Unused Ideas – Six   403

13 Agatha Christie's Booklists   408

Appendix 1: Agatha Christie Chronology   415
Appendix 2: Alphabetical List of Agatha
    Christie Titles   422
Index of Titles   425

Acknowledgements

Although my name alone appears on the title-page there were many others who made significant contributions to *Murder in the Making*.

As reflected in the Dedication, my gratitude to Mathew Prichard and his wife, Lucy, is boundless. Without their contribution *Murder in the Making* would not exist.

My editors, David Brawn and Steve Gove.

My brother and sister-in-law, Brendan and Virginia, for my home-from-home.

Joseph and Francis, who helped with the proof-reading.

Patricia, Noel, Brian and Ann Donnelly, hosts par excellence.

Robyn Brown, National Trust General Manager of Greenway House, where it all began.

Dr Robin Whelpton for his advice on matters chemical.

Elaine Wiltshire for double-checking.

David, Daniel and Pavla of Goldsboro Books.

Thanks also to Katie Lusty and Torbay Library Services; Elizabeth Wilson of HarperCollins Archive; Moira Reilly, Alice Moss and Laura Mell, publicists extraordinaire; Tony Medawar, my friend and fellow Christie admirer; and Eurion Brown, Peter Coleman, Karl Pike, John Ryan, John Timon and Andy Trott.

Of the many books written about Agatha Christie, the following have been most helpful:

Barnard, Robert, *A Talent to Deceive* (1980)

Gerald, Michael, *The Poisonous Pen of Agatha Christie* (1993)

Morgan, Janet, *Agatha Christie* (1984)

Osborne, Charles, *The Life and Crimes of Agatha Christie* (1982)

Sanders, Dennis and Lovallo, Len, *The Agatha Christie Companion* (1984)

Sova, Dawn B., *Agatha Christie A to Z* (1996)

Thompson, Laura, *Agatha Christie, An English Mystery* (2007)

Victoria Station, March 1931

Although she is by now an experienced traveller, the sights, sounds and even smells of the great railway station never fail to excite her. This is the start of her journey and she takes a moment to savour the sense of anticipation that bustling railway stations have always engendered in her – harassed and luggage-laden passengers hurrying along platforms, imperious-looking porters issuing instructions and shouting to invisible colleagues, the great trains snorting and bellowing clouds of smoke. She walks purposefully along the continental platform and hails a porter. As soon as she is installed in her seat she has an opportunity to observe, at her leisure, her fellow passengers. She can't help speculating about the life of these strangers with whom she is to share a few hours in close proximity. This covert observation has, by now, become almost an occupational hazard and provided she is left to her own devising it's all potential material. Now let's see . . .

The moth-eaten looking man sitting opposite . . . studying his railway timetable and jotting down the details as he turns the pages could be . . . an office worker planning his holiday? a Civil Servant checking a business trip? a salesman plotting his sales route? His only luggage is a smallish case . . . probably for his samples . . . too small for encyclopaedias . . . brushes, perhaps, or . . . pens or . . . hosiery?

And that very handsome young man opposite . . . reading . . .
what, exactly? It's not a book . . . or a magazine . . . it seems
to be typed pages, loosely bound, printed on only one side of
the page and laid out very specifically. And he is studying it
intensely and underlining sections of it . . . a business report?
A manuscript perhaps and he's correcting it? No . . . the cor-
rections seem too regular. Ah, I've got it – it's a script and he's
marking his lines . . . he's an actor and that makes sense . . .
matinee-idol good looks.

The older, haughty-looking woman in the far corner . . .
seems to be waiting for someone, as evidenced both by her exas-
perated demeanour and by the continual checking of her wrist-
watch and her scanning of the platform for . . . her husband?
No . . . no wedding ring . . . a friend, maybe . . . a travelling
companion?

A harassed-looking older woman, struggling with a fox
terrier on a lead and carrying a suitcase, a handbag, an
umbrella and an assortment of magazines, hurries along the
platform. In response to an imperious gesture she clambers
into the carriage, managing to drop the magazines as she
does so. Any lingering doubt as to her status is removed by
the recriminations which follow.

Yes, definitely a companion . . . almost certainly a paid
companion . . . nobody else would accept that sort of abuse.

At last, to the accompaniment of final shouts and whistles,
the train glides out of the station and passengers settle down
for the journey. As London begins to disappear her thoughts
turn to the reunion ahead of her in a few days. Although
married six months ago she has not seen her husband for
almost four of those months. And despite a constant flow
of letters in both directions she is anxious that, when they

finally meet again, there should be no awkwardness. She knows that the best remedy for worry is work and she can easily and unobtrusively do some here where she sits.

And goodness knows, there is no shortage of potential material; just look around this carriage . . . and I want to get down that idea about Ruth Draper . . . very clever performance . . . complete transformation in a few seconds . . . must take lots of practice and endless rehearsals . . . which also reminds me . . .

Reaching into her bag, she produces a small, black-covered notebook. She opens it, idly noting that Rosalind has already tried to appropriate it by the simple expedient of writing her name and address on the inside cover – 'Rosalind Christie, Ashfield, Torquay, Devon'. A further search produces a fountain pen. Unscrewing the top of the pen, she opens the notebook, flattens the pages and begins to read what she has already written.

Ideas 1931
Book
Poirot and a crime
a closed circle – one of them did it – he knows which – but
now . . .
Could Why Didn't they ask Evans fit in?

Hmm . . . can't really remember much about this 'closed circle' . . . and 'Poirot and a crime' is not much help . . . probably full of ideas at the beginning of the year. Evans, Evans . . . that rings a bell although I don't think I settled on any particular idea . . . although haven't I got an Evans in Sittaford? . . . Let's see . . .

She turns the page and continues reading, noting the under-lined qualification at the beginning.

Tentative
Old lady (or man) sends for P – in a state of coma when he arrives
Last words – Poirot is left to find out
Evans (maid)
Also Evans (gardener)
and Evans – a baker or butcher or tradesman . . .

Oh, yes, of course . . . the last words of someone who is dying and they make no sense . . . not even to me at the moment, I must admit . . . but distinct possi-bilities here . . . infinite ones, in fact. I could have a lot of fun with this. Should it be another case for Miss M? . . . it sounds village-y, and Miss M would know about maids and gardeners and tradesmen. Although I haven't given Poirot an airing since . . . let's see . . . Blue Train, I think . . . and that was at least three years ago. Yes, that was his last case . . . of course End House will remedy that next . . . what did Edmund tell me . . . next February I think . . . Anyway, didn't I have a blood-covered butcher in one of those Big Four episodes . . . and a baker seems an unlikely possibility . . . a gardener, perhaps. But would it carry a book or should I use it as just an element of a plot . . . or a short story maybe . . . although it would look great as a title: 'Why Didn't They Ask Evans?'

She leaves 'Evans' for a moment, looks up and stares absent-mindedly at the passing countryside. Outside snow is still lying on many of the fields, a fleeting reminder of the snow-bound setting of yet-to-be-published *The Sittaford Mystery*. She returns to her notebook and turns the page.

14

*Yes, here we are . . . I knew I jotted down a note somewhere . . .
this one I do remember . . .*

Idea for book
Murder utterly motiveless
Because dead man and murderer
Unacquainted –
Reason – a rehearsal

*I'm sure this is really original but it needs careful treatment.
Let's leave that for the moment . . . not sure where to go from
there . . . tricky set-up but I think the idea is promising . . .
worth thinking about it carefully . . .*

She looks speculatively again at the final word of the note
and then glances across at the good-looking man opposite,
still ostensibly studying his script.

*My good-looking friend is examining his reflection in the
window . . . he knows the young girl opposite is watching
him . . . seems to enjoy it . . . used to people watching him . . .
matinee-idol good looks . . . matinee . . . actor . . . rehearsal.
How about an actor for the murder-as-rehearsal idea? Seems
to make sense . . . but victim or murderer? Mmm . . . possibilities here although I'm not sure of carrying off a theatre
milieu. Maybe just an actor and his social circle . . .*

She turns another page and looks reminiscently at what she
has previously written.

Man stabbed in room – everyone there – behind screen –
gagged first.
Man induced to hide in other man's rooms (his wife coming
there) has tea first (drugged)

Hmmm, yes, that one we all wrote . . . was it last year? . . . the body found behind the screen when the blood flowed out from beneath it . . . lots of people in the room. Blood on the Screen or Under the Screen or something . . . Trouble with those combined efforts . . . you have to remember that someone else is going to take over after you so you can't do everything, or even anything, you want . . . Dorothy always wants it all very structured and organised . . . I can't really work under those circumstances and I think I can do something else with that same basic idea . . .

Man hides in chest – (but bores hole to see through) has previously had a dinner with friend . . .

Must finish this off . . . Edmund is sure The Strand *will take it . . . which would be nice . . . and I have most of it sketched here . . . just a matter of writing it up. But I want to get Ruth Draper down on paper.*

She flicks through a few pages until she finds a blank one, unscrews the top of her pen, writes and firmly underlines:

<u>Book</u>
Man Killed – says Jane Wilkinson (actress) beautiful amoral
– 'Only way is for me to kill him'
Carlotta Adams – her imitations – (including Jane) 'Would do anything for money'
Crime discovered – either victim says it was Jane – or man servant saw her – or girl secretary saw her
However, Jane has alibi – quite unbreakable – dinner
Carlotta Adams also dies – before Poirot can see her – a simple poison

Right, that's my basic situation. Now I wonder if I could work in the 'Evans' dying words idea, if the victim says Jane's name . . . and I could call one of the servants Evans . . . must be careful about Poirot not getting to see Carlotta before she dies . . . now, some more detail . . .

An actress Jane W comes to see Poirot – engaged to Duke of Merton
Martin Squire – pleasant hearty young fellow – an admirer of Miss Wilkinson's – he is seen next evening having supper with Carlotta
Lord Mountcarlin
Other man (Duke? Millionaire?)
Bryan Martin actor in films with her
Lord Mountcarlin's nephew Ronnie West (debonair Peter Wimseyish)
Miss Carroll Margaret Carroll middle-aged woman
A Miss Clifford

Not convinced about some of those names but I can remedy that later . . . 'Evans' is still a possibility but I'm not sure in which capacity . . . and I need some more suspects . . . what about the old reliable, the butler? or maybe a maid of Carlotta's? And I think I'd better have Japp, especially if I set it in London . . . which is the most likely possibility if I have theatres and actors and actresses and rehearsals . . . he could be the official investigator. Rehearsals . . . now, I wonder . . . should I combine Ruth Draper and the rehearsal idea . . . or are they each good enough to carry a book on their own? I think they are . . .

Japp comes to see Poirot – threats – P says quietly 'Who heard them?' – J hedges? But perfect alibi – party Amersham

She pauses briefly and considers what she has written, reflecting on possible opening scenes. Turning the page she continues covering the smaller-than-usual pages in flowing, black handwriting.

Now, the actual events from the beginning . . .

Sequence
At theatre – CA's performance – H's reflections. Is JW really such a good actress? Looks round – JW – her eyes sparkling with enthusiasm. Supper at Savoy – Jane at next table – CA there also . . .
Enter Bryan (and CA) JW has gone into bedroom . . .

Next JW herself – her account – the telephone call . . .

With Jenny Driver – called for her – 8.30 – and took her out for evening . . .

Immersed mentally in the West End of night clubs and theatres and hat shops and dinner parties, she fails to notice the train slowing down until it jerks to a stop and her pen stabs the page. Glancing up briefly, she notes the approach of the ticket collector and reaches into her handbag to retrieve her ticket. Anxious to return to Jane and Carlotta and Miss Carroll, she begins a new page.

She is relieved? or disappointed. P asks if he can see Miss Carroll . . .

Her pen falters and she shakes it impatiently; a large splash of black ink obliterates most of the page.

Oh, what a mess . . . how can I mop it up? . . . no, I'll just tear it out completely and start again . . . luckily, it's a new page and I won't lose the back . . .

'Tickets, please.'

Distracted, she tears the page from the notebook and produces her ticket, noting idly that the official has a button missing from his uniform.

'Thank you, Ma'am.'

Now, where was I? . . . Poirot was about to question Jenny . . . no, Miss Carroll . . . and he was talking to . . . let me check . . .

She unfurls the discarded, blotted page and studies it.

he is relieved

. . . who is? . . . was he not talking to . . . Oh, I see what's happened . . . I didn't remove it completely . . . there's still some of the first word left in the notebook . . . makes quite a difference . . . now, I wonder . . .

She stares out the carriage window but instead of snow-covered countryside she sees Poirot, clutching a letter with a torn edge, gesticulating and explaining excitedly to Hastings, who merely looks bewildered, completely missing the vital point. She picks up her pen once more and while the idea is fresh in her mind dashes down her inspiration – an inspiration that will hang the murderer of Lord Edgware.

P looking at letter –
He <u>had</u> to tear it – you see?
I see nothing . . .
Letter . . . suggesting the letter was <u>She</u> . . .

19

INTRODUCTION

'If one idea in particular seems attractive, and you feel you could do something with it, then you toss it around, play tricks with it, work it up, tone it down, and gradually get it into shape.'

Introduction to Passenger to Frankfurt

The 73 notebooks reposed in an unpretentious brown cardboard box at the bottom of a cupboard; notebooks in various shapes, sizes, colours and states of preservation, covered with sprawling and often illegible handwriting in pencil, fountain pen and biro; no chronology, no order, no method; but a splendid profusion of imagination.

This was my introduction to the Notebooks of Agatha Christie on a November evening in 2005 as I stood upstairs in Greenway House, her former Devon home. Downstairs Mathew Prichard, her grandson, sat in the library surrounded by the books from his grandmother's childhood as well as numerous examples of her own literary output. At Mathew's invitation I was spending the weekend in Greenway House, and I passed most of those few days in a small room at the top of the stairs which contained the archive of Agatha Christie's literary life. It was a breathtaking and absorbing miscellany of signed first editions and much-read paperbacks, typescripts and manuscripts, letters and contracts, theatre programmes and film posters, audio and video tapes, film and television scripts; and 73 notebooks.

Hours after I laid eyes on the notebooks for the first time I was still immersed in the fascinating behind-the-scenes look at the plotting of the best detective novels of the century. Every Notebook contained fresh surprises – Miss Marple in *Death on the Nile*; Mrs Oliver in *They Came to Baghdad*; a different ending for *Crooked House*; the 'lost' chapter of *The Mysterious Affair at Styles*; an altered killer in *A Murder is Announced*. Scattered among these revelations were notes for projected stage adaptations and possible short story expansions, along with the outline for a novel to follow *Postern of Fate*, and the discovery of a new timeline for *Sleeping Murder*.

Appearance

The Notebooks of Agatha Christie are a unique and priceless literary heritage. But viewed solely as physical objects they resemble a pile of exercise books, similar to those gathered by teachers at the end of class in schools the world over. Red and blue and green and grey exercise books, coverless copybooks ruled with wide-spaced blue lines, small black pocket-sized notebooks: The Minerva, The Marvel, The Kingsway, The Victoria, The Lion Brand, The Challenge, The Mayfair.

Some years before her death Rosalind Hicks, Agatha Christie's daughter, arranged that the contents of the Notebooks be listed and in this process each was allocated a number from 1 through to 73; this numbering is completely arbitrary and a lower number does not indicate an earlier year or a more important Notebook.

The number of pages used in each Notebook varies greatly – Notebook 35 has 220 pages of notes while Notebook 72 has a mere five. Notebook 63 has notes on over 150 pages but Notebook 42 uses only 20. The average lies somewhere between 100 and 120.

Contents

In a career spanning more than 55 years and two world wars, the loss of some Notebooks is inevitable, but the reassuring fact is that it seems to have happened so seldom. From the 1920s we have notes only for *The Mysterious Affair at Styles, The Man in the Brown Suit, The Secret of Chimneys* and *The Mystery of the Blue Train.* For the collection *Partners in Crime,* there are only the sketchiest of notes and for *The Murder of Roger Ackroyd* there remains only an incomplete list of characters. From the prolific 1930s onwards, however, the only missing book titles are *Murder on the Orient Express, Cards on the Table* and, apart from a passing reference, *Murder is Easy.* And although there are notes on most of Christie's stage work, including unknown, unperformed and uncompleted stage and radio plays, only two pages each are devoted to her most famous play and her greatest, *Three Blind Mice* (as it was before it became *The Mousetrap*) and *Witness for the Prosecution* respectively.

Not all the Notebooks are concerned with Christie's literary output. Notebooks 11, 40 and 55 consist solely of chemical formulae, probably from her days as a student dispenser; Notebook 71 contains French homework; Notebook 73 is completely blank. Moreover, she often used them for making random personal notes, sometimes on the inside covers. There is a list of 'furniture for 48 [Sheffield Terrace]' in Notebook 59; Notebook 67 has reminders to ring up Collins and make a hair appointment; Notebook 68 has a list of train times from Stockport to Torquay.

In only five instances is a Notebook devoted to a single title. Notebooks 26 and 42 are entirely dedicated to *Third Girl;* Notebook 68 concerns only *Peril at End House;* Notebook 2 is *A Caribbean Mystery;* Notebook 46 contains nothing but extensive historical background and a rough outline for

Death Comes as the End. In some cases the notes are sketchy, consisting of little more than a list of characters – for example *Death on the Nile* in Notebook 30. Other titles have copious notes – *They Came to Baghdad* has 100 pages, while *Five Little Pigs* and *One, Two, Buckle my Shoe* each have 75 pages.

Chronology

Although there are 73 Notebooks, complete (day/month/year) dates are given only on six occasions, and they are all from the last ten years of Christie's life. In the case of incomplete dates it is sometimes possible to work out the year from the publication date of the title in question, but sometimes this is almost impossible, because . . .

First, use of the Notebooks was utterly random. Christie opened a Notebook (or, as she says herself, any of half a dozen contemporaneous ones), found the next blank page, even one between two already filled pages, and began to write. And to compound this unpredictability, in almost all cases she turned the Notebook over and, with admirable economy, wrote from the back also.

Second, in many cases jottings for a book may have preceded publication by many years. The earliest notes for *The Unexpected Guest* are headed '1951' in Notebook 31, in other words seven years before its first performance; the germ of *Endless Night* first appears, six years before publication, on a page of Notebook 4 dated 1961.

Third, the pages following a clearly dated page cannot be assumed to have been written at the same time. For example:

page 1 of Notebook 3 reads 'General Projects 1955'
page 9 reads 'Nov. 5th 1965' (there were ten books in the
    intervening period)
page 12 reads '1963'

page 21 reads 'Nov. 6 1965 Cont.'
page 28 is headed 'Notes on Passenger to Frankfort [sic]
   1970'
page 36 reads 'Oct. 1972'
page 72 reads 'Book Nov. 1972'

In the space of 70 pages we have moved through 17 years
and as many novels and, between pages 9 and 21, skipped
back and forth between 1963 and 1965.

Finally, because many of the pages contain notes for stories that were never completed, there are no publication
dates as a guideline. Deductions can sometimes be made
from the notes immediately preceding and following, but as
we have seen, this method is not entirely flawless.

Handwriting and transcription

Before describing the handwriting in the Notebooks, it is only
fair to emphasise that these were notes and jottings and there
was no reason to make an effort to maintain a certain standard, as no one but Christie herself was ever intended to read
them. These were personal journals and not written for any
purpose other than to clarify her thoughts. For her first ten
years of productivity and at her creative peak her handwriting
is almost indecipherable. Whether in fountain pen, biro or
pencil, it looks, in many cases, like shorthand and it is debatable whether even she could read some sections of it. I have
no doubt that the reason for this near-illegibility was that,
during these hugely prolific years, her fertile brain teemed
with ideas for books and stories. It was a case of getting them
on to paper as fast as possible, and clarity of presentation was
a secondary consideration. Although in most cases it is safe
to assert that as we get older our handwriting deteriorates, in
the case of Agatha Christie the opposite is the case, so that by

the early 1950s and, for example, 1953's *After the Funeral* in Notebook 53, the notes could be read relatively easily.

Solely in the interests of legibility, when transcribing material from the Notebooks I have removed some capital letters, brackets and dashes and in some cases have separated a paragraph of words, broken only by dashes, into separate sentences. All remaining question marks, underlinings and dashes, as well as some grammatical errors, are reproduced as they appear in the Notebooks.

If I have omitted text from within extracts I indicate this by the use of dots.

Misspellings have not been corrected but marked as [sic].

Square brackets are used for editorial clarification or remarks.

Dates of publication of works by Christie refer to the UK edition. They have been taken, for the most part, from contemporary catalogues in Collins archives. Traditionally, Crime Club titles were published on the first Monday of the month and in the few instances where actual dates were not available, I have used this guideline. In general, publication dates are included only with the first mention of each title in the Decade introductions. They are not included with later references, unless the timescale is relevant.

At the beginning of each chapter I have included a list of titles whose solutions are revealed within. It proved impossible to discuss a title intelligently, or to compare it to the Notebooks, unless I disclosed some endings. And in many cases the notes mention the vital name or plot device anyway. Christie's creative ruthlessness in deciding her killer is a vital part of her genius and to try circumventing this with ambiguous verbal gymnastics cannot do her justice.

Since the publication of *Agatha Christie's Secret Notebooks* I have received many enquiries regarding access to the Notebooks. Although it is not possible for the public to read the Notebooks, two of them are on public display in Devon, England. One can be seen in Torquay Museum and a second in Paignton Library and Information Centre.

The quotations at the beginning of each chapter are from Agatha Christie's *Autobiography*.

In *Agatha Christie's Secret Notebooks* my aim was to examine how a unique body of work, produced over a 50-year period, came into being. I analysed the creative process of the Queen of Crime and showed how the chaotic scribbles in a copybook were transformed into a body of detective fiction that set the standard for the time and, as it transpired, for all time. A brief resumé at this point will aid an understanding of later chapters.

In February 1955, on the BBC radio programme *Close-Up*, Agatha Christie admitted, when asked about her process of working, that 'the disappointing truth is that I haven't much method'. But although she had no particular method, no definite system, we discover that the apparently indiscriminate jotting and plotting in the Notebooks *is* her method. This randomness is how she worked, how she created, how she wrote. She thrived mentally on chaos, it stimulated her more than neat order; rigidity stifled her creative process. She used the Notebooks as a combination of sounding board and literary sketchpad where she devised and developed; selected and rejected; sharpened and polished; revisited and recycled.

One system of creation that she used, especially during the prolific years, was the listing of a series of scenes, sketching what she wanted each to include and allocating to each individual scene a number or a letter. She would subsequently reorder those letters to suit the purposes of the plot in a pre-computer version of 'cut and paste'.

She reused plot devices throughout her career; and she recycled short stories into novellas and novels – she often speculates in the Notebooks about the expansion or adaptation of an earlier title. The Notebooks demonstrate how, even if she discarded an idea for now, she left everything there to be considered again at a later stage. And when she did that, as she wrote in her *Autobiography*, 'What it's all about I can't remember now; but it often stimulates me.'

Many of Christie's best plots did not necessarily spring from a single devastating idea. She considered all possibilities when she plotted and did not confine herself to one idea, no matter how good it may have seemed. She rattled off possibilities and variations on the basic idea so that, for instance, in very few cases is the identity of the murderer settled from the start of the plotting. An example from the notes for *Mrs McGinty's Dead*, as she considers the possible identity both of the killer from the past and from the present, illustrates this:

1. A. False – elderly Cranes – with daughter (girl – Evelyn)
   B. Real – Robin – son with mother son
2. A. False Invalid mother (or not invalid) and son
   B. Real – dull wife of snob A.P. (Carter) Dau[ghter]
3. A. False artistic woman with son
   B. Real middle-aged wife – dull couple – or flashy Carters (daughter invalid)
4. A. False widow – soon to marry rich man
5. [A] False man with dogs – stepson – different name
   [B] Real – invalid mother and daughter – dau[ghter] does it

Throughout the Notebooks murder methods, motives, settings and even the detective are apt to change between the early notes and the published book; names, in particular, change, sometimes radically. I try, where possible, to identify which character Christie may have had in mind when this occurs.

In *Agatha Christie's Secret Notebooks* I examined over 25 novels, almost a dozen short stories and the genesis of all 13 of *The Labours of Hercules*; I also included some stage scripts and presented two 'new' Hercule Poirot investigations. *Agatha Christie's Murder in the Making* includes the rest of her novels, as well as an 'unknown' stage script. And, unlike *Agatha Christie's Secret Notebooks*, this new volume contains some more personal glimpses – her reading lists, her own account of the creation of Hercule Poirot, a fascinating letter to *The Times*. As well as a new version of a Miss Marple short story I also include, from either end of her career, the original denouement of *The Mysterious Affair at Styles* and her notes for a final, unwritten novel.

If any further proof were needed of the universal and timeless appeal of Agatha Christie, the appearance of *Agatha Christie's Secret Notebooks* provided it. Since its appearance I have received correspondence from Christie devotees the world over: from Australia, Russia, Croatia, Brazil, Argentina and Italy as well as the UK, the USA and Ireland; I have been interviewed for magazines, radio and TV in France, Portugal, Turkey, the USA, Iceland, Finland, Spain and Brazil as well as the UK and Ireland; I have been invited to Tokyo, Helsinki, Istanbul and New York, and to literary festivals throughout the UK and Ireland. And the book itself has been translated into 17 languages including Vietnamese and Croatian.

As a certain Belgian might say, 'It gives one furiously to think, does it not . . .?'

1

Rule of Three

'One of the pleasures in writing detective stories is that there are so many types to choose from: the light-hearted thriller . . . the intricate detective story . . . and what I can only describe as the detective story that has a kind of passion behind it . . .'

◄○►

SOLUTIONS REVEALED

The A.B.C. Murders • *After the Funeral* • *Appointment with Death* • *The Body in the Library* • *Curtain* • *Death in the Clouds* • *Death on the Nile* • *Evil under the Sun* • *Endless Night* • *Hercule Poirot's Christmas* • *The Hollow* • *Lord Edgware Dies* • *The Man in the Brown Suit;* • 'The Man in the Mist' • 'The Market Basing Mystery' • *The Mousetrap* • *The Murder at the Vicarage* • 'Murder in the Mews' • *The Murder of Roger Ackroyd* • *Murder on the Orient Express* • *The Mysterious Affair at Styles* • *One, Two, Buckle my Shoe* • *Ordeal by Innocence* • *A Pocket Full of Rye* • *Sparkling Cyanide* • *Taken at the Flood* • *They Came to Baghdad* • *They Do It with Mirrors* • *Three Act Tragedy* • 'The Unbreakable Alibi' • 'Witness for the Prosecution'

◄○►

'Surely you won't let Agatha Christie fool you again. That would be "again" – wouldn't it?' Thus read the advertisement, at the back of many of her early Crime Club books, for the latest titles from the Queen of Crime. The first in the series to appear, bearing the now-famous hooded gunman logo, was Philip MacDonald's *The Noose* in May 1930; Agatha Christie's first Crime Club title, *The Murder at the Vicarage*, followed in October of that year. By then Collins had already published, between 1926 and 1929, five Christie titles – *The Murder of Roger Ackroyd, The Big Four, The Mystery of the Blue Train, The Seven Dials Mystery* and *Partners in Crime* – in their general fiction list. As soon as The Crime Club was founded, Agatha Christie's was an obvious name to grace the list and over the next 50 years she proved to be one of the most prolific authors – and by far the most successful – to appear under its imprint. This author/publisher relationship continued throughout her writing life, almost all of her titles appearing with the accompaniment of the hooded gunman.[1]

As the back of the dustjacket on the first edition of *The Murder at the Vicarage* states, 'The Crime Club has been formed so that all interested in Detective Fiction may, at NO COST TO THEMSELVES, be kept advised of the best new Detective Novels before they are published.' By 1932 and *Peril at End House*, The Crime Club was boasting that 'Over 25,000 have joined already. The list includes doctors, clergymen, lawyers, University Dons, civil servants, business men;

---

1 Odhams Press first published *The Hound of Death* in 1933 and Collins reissued it in 1936 as a Crime Club title. Collins published two short story collections – *The Listerdale Mystery* and *Parker Pyne Investigates* – in 1934 but not as Crime Club titles, as the contents were not devoted exclusively to crime. For the same reason, although HarperCollins (as it had then become) published *Problem at Pollensa Bay* (1991) and *While the Light Lasts* (1997), neither appeared under the Crime Club imprint; of course, after 1994 The Crime Club no longer existed.

THE MURDER AT THE VICARAGE
AGATHA CHRISTIE

Published for

THE CRIME CLUB LTD.
by

W. COLLINS SONS & CO LTD

LONDON

This is the first edition title page of The Murder at the Vicarage,
the first Agatha Christie title to appear under The Crime Club imprint on
13th October 1930.

it includes two millionaires, three world-famous statesmen, thirty-two knights, eleven peers of the realm, two princes of royal blood and one princess.'

And the advertisement on the first edition wrapper of *The A.B.C. Murders* (1936) clearly states the Club's aims and objectives:

> The object of the Crime Club is to provide that vast section of the British Public which likes a good detective story with a continual supply of first-class books by the finest writers of detective fiction. The Panel of five experts selects the good and eliminates the bad, and ensures that every book published under the Crime Club mark is a clean and intriguing example of this class of literature. Crime Club books are not mere thrillers. They are restricted to works in which there is a definite crime problem, an honest detective process, with a credible and logical solution. Members of the Crime Club receive the Crime Club News issued at intervals.

As the above statement suggests, not for nothing was the 1930s known as the Golden Age of detective fiction. In that era the creation and enjoyment of a detective story was a serious business for reader, writer and publisher. Both reader and writer took the elaborate conventions seriously. The civilised outrage that followed the publication of *The Murder of Roger Ackroyd* in 1926 showed what a serious breach of the rules its solution was considered at the time. So, while in many ways observing the so-called 'rules', and consolidating the image of a safe, cosy and comforting type of fiction, Agatha Christie also constantly challenged those 'rules' and, by regularly and mischievously tweaking, bending, and breaking them, subverted the expectations of her readers and critics. She was both the mould creator and mould breaker, who delighted in effectively saying to her fans, 'Here is the comforting read that you expect when you pick up my new book but because I respect your intelligence and my own professionalism, I intend to fool you.'

But how did she fool her readers while at the same time retaining her vice-like grip on their admiration and loyalty? In order to understand how she managed this feat it is necessary to take a closer look at 'The Rules'.

THE RULES OF DETECTIVE FICTION – POE, KNOX, VAN DINE

Edgar Allan Poe: inventor of the detective story

In April 1841 the American periodical *Graham's Magazine* published Edgar Allan Poe's 'The Murders in the Rue Morgue' and introduced a new literary form – the detective story. Together with four more of Poe's stories, 'The Murders in the Rue Morgue' established the unwritten ground-rules that distinguish detective fiction from other forms of crime writing – the thriller, the suspense story, the adventure story. Among the many motifs introduced by Poe in these stories were:

* The brilliant amateur detective
* The less-than-brilliant narrator-friend
* The wrongly suspected person
* The sealed room
* The unexpected solution
* The 'armchair detective' and the application of pure reasoning
* The interpretation of a code
* The trail of false clues laid by the murderer

* The unmasking of the least likely suspect
* Psychological deduction
* The most obvious solution

All of Poe's pioneering initiatives were exploited by subsequent generations of crime writers and although many of those writers introduced variations on and combinations of them, no other writer ever established so many influential concepts. Christie, as we shall see, exploited them to the full.

The first, and most important, of the Poe stories, 'The Murders in the Rue Morgue', incorporated the first five ideas above. The murder of a mother and daughter in a room locked from the inside is investigated by Chevalier C. Auguste Dupin, who, by logical deduction, arrives at a most unexpected solution, thereby proving the innocence of an arrested man; the story is narrated by his unnamed associate.

Although Poe is not one of the writers she mentions in her *Autobiography* as being an influence, Agatha Christie took his template of a murder and its investigation when she began to write *The Mysterious Affair at Styles*, 75 years later.

The brilliant amateur detective

If we take 'amateur' to mean someone outside the official police force, then Hercule Poirot is the pre-eminent example. With the creation of Miss Marple, Christie remains the only writer to create two famous detective figures. Although not as well known, the characters Tommy and Tuppence, Parker Pyne, Mr Satterthwaite and Mr Quin also come into this category.

The less-than-brilliant narrator-friend

Poirot's early chronicler, Captain Arthur Hastings, appeared in nine novels (if we include the 1927 episodic novel *The Big Four*) and 26 short stories. After *Dumb Witness* in 1937,

Christie dispensed with his services, though she allowed him a nostalgic swan song in *Curtain*, published in 1975. But she also experimented with other narrators, often with dramatic results – *The Man in the Brown Suit*, *The Murder of Roger Ackroyd*, *Endless Night*. The decision to send Hastings to Argentina may have had less to do with his mental ability than with the restrictions he imposed on his creator: his narration meant that only events at which he was present could be recounted. Signs of this growing unease can be seen in the use of third-person narrative at the beginning of *Dumb Witness* and the interspersing of third-person scenes throughout *The A.B.C. Murders*, published the year before Hastings' banishment. Miss Marple has no permanent Hastings-like companion.

The wrongly suspected person

This is the basis of some of Christie's finest titles, among them the novels *Five Little Pigs*, *Sad Cypress*, *Mrs McGinty's Dead* and *Ordeal by Innocence*, and the short story 'Witness for the Prosecution'. The wrongly suspected may be still on trial as in *Sad Cypress* or already convicted as in *Mrs McGinty's Dead*. In more extreme cases – *Five Little Pigs*, *Ordeal by Innocence* – they have already paid the ultimate price, although in each case ill-health, rather than the hangman, is the cause of death. And being Agatha Christie, she also played a variation on this theme in 'Witness for the Prosecution' when the vindicated suspect is shown to be the guilty party after all.

The sealed room

The fascination with this ploy lies in the seeming impossibility of the crime. Not only has the detective – and the reader – to work out 'Who' but also 'How'. The crime may be committed in a room with all the doors and windows locked from the inside, making the murderer's escape seemingly impossible; or in a room that is under constant observation;

or the corpse may be discovered in a garden of unmarked snow or on a beach of unmarked sand. Although this was not a favourite Christie ploy she experimented with it on a few occasions, but in each case – *Murder in Mesopotamia, Hercule Poirot's Christmas,* 'Dead Man's Mirror', 'The Dream' – the sealed-room element was merely an aspect of the story and not its main focus.

The unexpected solution

Throughout her career this was the perennial province of Agatha Christie and the novels *Murder on the Orient Express, Endless Night* and *And Then There Were None,* as well as the short story 'Witness for the Prosecution', are the more dramatic examples. But mere unexpectedness is not sufficient; it must be fairly clued and prepared. The unmasking of, for example, the under-housemaid's wheelchair-bound cousin from Australia, of whom the reader has never heard, may be unexpected but it is hardly fair. The unexpected murderer is dealt with below.

The 'armchair detective' and the application of pure reasoning

In 1842, Poe's story 'The Mystery of Marie Roget' was an example both of 'faction', the fictionalisation of a true event, and of 'armchair detection', an exercise in pure reasoning. Although set in Paris, the story is actually an account, complete with newspaper reports, of the murder, in New York some years earlier, of Mary Cecilia Rogers. In this story Dupin seeks to arrive at a solution based on close examination of newspaper reports of the relevant facts, without visiting the scene of the crime. The clearest equivalent in Christie is *The Thirteen Problems,* the Marple collection in which a group of people meets regularly to solve a series of mysteries including murder, robbery, forgery and smuggling. Miss Marple also solves the murders in *The Mirror Crack'd from Side to Side* basing her solution on the observations of others, and visiting the scene of the crime only at the conclusion of the book; she undertakes a similar challenge in *4.50 from Paddington* when Lucy Eyelesbarrow acts as her eyes and ears. Poirot solves 'The Mystery of Hunter's Lodge', in *Poirot Investigates*, without leaving his sick-bed; and in *The Clocks*, making what amounts to a cameo appearance, he bases his deductions on the reports of Colin Lamb. For the novels of Christie's most prolific and ingenious period (roughly 1930 to 1950), the application of pure reasoning applies. From the mid 1950s onwards there was a loosening of the form – *Destination Unknown, Cat among the Pigeons, The Pale Horse, Endless Night* – and she wrote fewer formal detective stories. But as late as 1964 and *A Caribbean Mystery* she was still defying her readers to interpret a daring and blatant clue.

The interpretation of a code

Poe's 'The Gold Bug', not a Dupin story, appeared in 1843, and could be considered the least important of his contributions to the detective genre. It involves the solution to a cipher in an effort to find a treasure. A variation on this can be found in the Christie short stories 'The Case of the Missing Will' and 'Strange Jest', both of which involve the interpretation of a deceased person's last cryptic wishes. Although the code concept was only a minor part of Christie's output it is the subject of the short story 'The Four Suspects' in *The Thirteen Problems*. On a more elaborate canvas, the interpretation of a code could be seen as the basis of *The A.B.C. Murders*; and it is the starting-point of Christie's final novel, *Postern of Fate*.

The Trail of false clues laid by the murderer

'Thou Art the Man', published in 1844, is not as well known as the other Poe stories but it includes at least two influential concepts, the trail of false clues and the unmasking of the most unlikely suspect. Although a minor theme in many Christie novels, the idea of a murderer leaving a trail of false clues is a major plot device in *The A.B.C. Murders* and *Murder is Easy*; and in *Towards Zero* it is taken to new heights of triple-bluff ingenuity.

The unmasking of the least likely suspect
Like its counterpart above, the unexpected solution, this was a career-long theme for Christie and appears at its most stunning in *The Murder of Roger Ackroyd*, *Hercule Poirot's Christmas*, *Crooked House* and *Curtain*. The double-bluff, a regular feature of Christie's output from her first novel onwards, also comes into this category.

Psychological deduction
Poe's 'The Purloined Letter' pioneered the ideas of psychological deduction and the 'obvious' solution. In this type of story, the deductions depend as much on knowledge of the human heart as on interpretation of the physical clues. In Poe's story Dupin's psychological interpretation of the suspect allows him to deduce the whereabouts of the missing letter of the title. The Foreword to Christie's *Cards on the Table* explains that the deductions in that book will be entirely psychological due to the lack of physical clues apart from the bridge scorecards. And *Appointment with Death*, set in distant Petra, sees Poirot dependent almost entirely on the psychological approach. *Five Little Pigs* and *The Hollow* each have similar emotional and psychological content, although both novels also involve physical clues.

The most obvious solution
Poe's employment of the 'obvious solution' of hiding in plain sight (using a letter-rack as the hiding place of a

letter) is adopted, though not as a solution, by Christie in 'The Nemean Lion', the first of *The Labours of Hercules*. The solutions to, for example, *The Murder at the Vicarage, Death on the Nile, Evil under the Sun* and *The Hollow*, among others, all unmask the most obvious culprits even though it seems that they have been cleared early in the story and have been dismissed by both detective and reader. In her *Autobiography*, Christie writes: 'The whole point of a *good* detective story is that it must be somebody obvious but at the same time, for some reason, you would find that it was *not* obvious, that he could not possibly have done it. Though really, of course, he *had* done it.'

So, Christie's output adhered to most of the conditions of Poe's initial model, while simultaneously expanding and experimenting with them. Although Poe created the template for later writers of detective fiction to follow, early in the twentieth century two practitioners formalised the 'rules' for the construction of successful detective fiction. But these formalisations, by S.S. Van Dine and Ronald Knox, writing almost simultaneously on opposite sides of the Atlantic, merely acted as a challenge to Agatha Christie's ingenuity.

S.S. Van Dine's 'Twenty Rules for Writing Detective Stories'

Willard Huntington Wright (1888–1939) was an American literary figure and art critic who, between 1929 and 1939, wrote a dozen detective novels under the pen name S.S. Van Dine. Featuring his detective creation Philo Vance, they were phenomenally successful and popular at the time but are almost completely – and deservedly, many would add – forgotten nowadays. Vance is an intensely irritating creation,

with an encyclopaedic knowledge of seemingly every subject under the sun and with a correspondingly condescend-
ing manner of communication. In *The American Magazine*
for September 1928 Wright published his 'Twenty Rules
for Writing Detective Stories'. Christie knew of S.S. Van
Dine; some of his novels can still be seen on the shelves of
Greenway House and she mentioned him in Notebook 41
(see *Agatha Christie's Secret Notebooks*), although it is doubtful
if she was aware of his Rules until long after they were written. Van Dine's Rules are as follows:

1. The reader must have equal opportunity with the
   detective for solving the mystery.
2. No willful tricks or deceptions may be placed on the
   reader other than those played by the criminal on the
   detective.
3. There must be no love interest.
4. The detective himself, or one of the official investigators,
   should never turn out to be the culprit.
5. The culprit must be determined by logical deduction –
   not by accident, coincidence or unmotivated confession.
6. The detective novel must have a detective in it.
7. There simply must be a corpse in a detective novel.
8. The problem of the crime must be solved by strictly
   naturalistic means.
9. There must be but one detective.
10. The culprit must turn out to be a person who has
    played a more or less prominent part in the story.
11. A servant must not be chosen as the culprit.
12. There must be but one culprit no matter how many
    murders are committed.
13. Secret societies have no place in a detective story.
14. The method of murder, and the means of detecting it,
    must be rational and scientific.

15. The truth of the problem must be at all times apparent provided the reader is shrewd enough to see it.
16. A detective novel should contain no long descriptive passages, no literary dallying with side issues, no subtly worked-out character analyses, and no 'atmospheric' preoccupations.
17. A professional criminal must never be shouldered with the guilt in a detective novel.
18. A crime in a detective story must never turn out to be an accident or a suicide.
19. The motives for all the crimes in detective stories should be personal.
20. A list of devices, which no self-respecting detective story writer should avail himself of including, among others:

* The bogus séance to force a confession
* The unmasking of a twin or look-alike
* The cipher/code-letter
* The hypodermic syringe and the knockout drops
* The comparison of cigarette butts.

Ronald Knox's Detective Story Decalogue

Monsignor Ronald Knox (1888–1957) was a priest and classical scholar who wrote six detective novels between 1925 and 1937. He created the insurance investigator detective Miles Bredon, and considered the detective story such a serious game between writer and reader that in some of his novels he provided page references to his clues. When he edited a collection of short stories, *The Best Detective Stories of 1928*, his Introduction included a 'Detective Story Decalogue'. These distilled the essence of a detective story, as distinct from the thriller, into ten cogent sentences:

1. The criminal must be someone mentioned in the early part of the story, but must not be anyone whose thoughts the reader has been allowed to follow.
2. All supernatural agencies are ruled out as a matter of course.
3. Not more than one secret room or passage is allowable.
4. No hitherto undiscovered poisons may be used, nor any appliance which will need long scientific explanation at the end.
5. No Chinamen must figure in the story.
6. No accident must ever help the detective, nor must he ever have an unaccountable intuition that proves to be right.
7. The detective must not himself commit the crime.
8. The detective must not light on any clues that are not instantly disclosed to the reader.
9. The stupid friend of the detective, the Watson, must not conceal any thoughts that pass through his mind; his intelligence must be slightly, but very slightly, below that of the average reader.
10. Twin brothers, and doubles generally, must not appear unless we have been duly prepared for them.

But as will be seen from a survey of Christie's output, many of the Rules laid down by both Knox and Van Dine were ingeniously ignored and often gleefully broken by the Queen of Crime. Her infringement was, in most cases, instinctive rather than premeditated; and her skill was such that she managed to do so while still remaining faithful to the basic tenets of detective fiction.

Agatha Christie's Rule of Three

In order to examine these Rules, and Christie's approach to them, I have grouped together Rules common to both lists and have divided them into categories:

* Fairness
* The crime
* The detective
* The murderer
* The murder method
* To be avoided

Fairness

Both lists are very concerned with Fairness to the reader in the provision of information necessary to the solution, and with good reason; this is the essence of detective fiction and the element that distinguishes it from other branches of crime writing. Van Dine 1 and Knox 8 are, essentially, the same rule while Van Dine 2, 5, 15 and Knox 9 elaborate this concept.

Van Dine 1. The reader must have equal opportunity with the detective for solving the mystery.

Knox 8. The detective must not light on any clues that are not instantly disclosed to the reader.

Christie did not break these essentially identical rules, mainly because she did not need to. She was quite happy to provide the clue, firm in the knowledge that, in the words of her great contemporary R. Austin Freeman, 'the reader would mislead himself'. After all, how many readers will properly interpret the clue of the torn letter in *Lord Edgware Dies*, or the bottle of nail polish in *Death on the Nile*, or the 'shepherd, not the shepherdess' in *A Murder is Announced*? Or who will correctly appreciate the significance of the smashed bottle in *Evil under the Sun*, or the initialled handkerchief in *Murder on the Orient Express*, or the smell of turpentine in *After the Funeral*?

Knox 9. The stupid friend of the detective, the Watson, must not conceal any thoughts that pass through his mind; his intelligence must be slightly, but very slightly, below that of the average reader.

Hastings has been dubbed 'the stupidest of Watsons' and there are times when we wonder how Poirot endured his intellectual company. And, of course, Agatha Christie herself tired of him and banished him to Argentina in 1937 after *Dumb Witness*, although he was to return for *Curtain: Poirot's Last Case*, written during the Second World War but not published until 1975. It can be argued that the intelligence of the Watson character *has* to be below average because it is necessary for the Great Detective to explain his deductions to the reader *through* the Watson character. If the Watson were as clever as the detective there would be no need for an explanation at all. If Poirot were to look at the scene of the crime and announce, 'We must look for a left-handed female from Scotland with red hair and a limp,' and Hastings were to reply, 'Yes, I see what you mean,' the reader would feel, justifiably, more than a little exasperated. And, of course, this Rule overlaps with Knox 1 (see below) in the case of *The Murder of Roger Ackroyd* because Dr Sheppard in that famous case was acting as Poirot's Watson.

Van Dine 2. No willful tricks or deceptions may be placed on the reader other than those played by the criminal on the detective.

This Rule seems to negate the whole purpose of a good detective novel. Surely the challenge is the struggle between reader and writer. In essence, the writer says: 'I present you with a challenge to spot the culprit before I am ready to reveal him/her. To make it easier for you, I will give you hints and clues along the way but I still defy you to anticipate my solution. However, I give you fair warning that I will use every trick in my writer's repertoire to fool you but I still promise to abide by the fair play rule.' As Dorothy L. Sayers said in the aftermath of the Roger Ackroyd controversy, 'It is the reader's business to suspect *everybody*.'

Into this category come Christie's greatest conjuring tricks, including *The Murder of Roger Ackroyd* and *Endless Night*. In both these novels the reader is fooled into accepting the bona fides of a character who is taken for granted but not 'seen' in the same way that all the other protagonists are. The narrator is a 'given' whose presence and veracity the reader accepts unquestioningly. And, indeed, the narrator's veracity in each case is above reproach. They do not actually *lie* at any stage. There are certainly some ambiguous statements and judicious omissions but their significance is obvious only on a re-reading, when the secret is known. In Chapter 27 of *The Murder of Roger Ackroyd* Dr Sheppard himself states:

> I am rather pleased with myself as a writer. What could be neater, for instance, than the following? *'The letters were brought in at twenty minutes to nine. It was just on ten minutes to nine when I left him, the letter still unread. I hesitated with my hand on the door-handle, looking back and wondering if there was anything I had left undone.'* All true, you see. But suppose I had put a row of stars after that first sentence! Would somebody then have wondered what exactly happened in that blank ten minutes?

All true; but not one reader in a thousand will stop to examine the details, especially not in the more innocent era of the 1920s, when the local doctor had a status just below that of the Creator.

Michael Rogers, in *Endless Night*, is also scrupulously fair in his account of his life. He tells us the truth but, as with Dr Sheppard, not the whole truth. But if we re-read Chapter 6, which recounts a telling conversation with his mother about 'his plan', what a new significance it all takes on when we know the truth. The 'plan', and even 'the girl', are no longer what we had originally supposed. This novel has much in common with *The Mysterious Affair at Styles* and *Death on the Nile*, as well as with *The Man in the Brown Suit* and *The Murder of Roger Ackroyd*. In the first two titles, two lovers collude, as in *Endless Night*, in the murder of an inconvenient wife, stage a dramatic quarrel and have seemingly foolproof alibis; *The Mysterious Affair at Styles* also features a poisoning which happens in the absence of the conspirators. In the latter two titles, the narrator (a diarist in *The Man in the Brown Suit*) is exposed as the villain.

Van Dine 5. The culprit must be determined by logical deduction – not by accident, coincidence or unmotivated confession.

An example of confession (albeit not unmotivated) as a solution in Christie's output is *And Then There Were None*. Here the entire explanation is given in the form of a confession. In this most ingenious novel, Agatha Christie set herself an almost insoluble problem – how to kill off the entire ten characters of the book and yet have an explanation at the end. The only solution would seem to be the one that she actually adopted – a confession. Confessions do feature in other novels, for example *Lord Edgware Dies*, *Why Didn't They*

Ask Evans? and *Crooked House,* but only as confirmation of what has already been revealed, while *Curtain: Poirot's Last Case* contains one of the most shocking confessions in literary history . . .

Van Dine 15. The truth of the problem must be at all times apparent – provided the reader is shrewd enough to see it.

Although tautological, this is intended as an elaboration of the earlier Rules regarding fairness to the reader. One of the clearest examples of this in the Christie output is *Lord Edgware Dies* where a very audacious plot is, in retrospect, glaringly obvious with all the clues staring the reader in the face. Other blindingly evident clues include the final words – '*Evil Eye . . . Eye . . . Eye . . .*' – of Chapter 23 of *A Caribbean Mystery*; or the description of Lewis Serrocold emerging from the study in Chapter 7 of *They Do It with Mirrors*; or the thoughts of Ruth Lessing in Chapter 2 of *Sparkling Cyanide* after her meeting with Victor; or, most controversially of all, Dr Sheppard's leave-taking of Roger Ackroyd in Chapter 4 of *The Murder of Roger Ackroyd.*

Knox 6. No accident must ever help the detective, nor must he ever have an unaccountable intuition that proves to be right.

There are, unfortunately, a few examples in Christie's oeuvre of 'deductions' not based on any tangible evidence. It must be conceded that they can only be accounted for by intuition. How, for example, does Miss Marple alight on Dr Quimper in *4.50 from Paddington?* And only the 'Divine Revelation' forbidden by The Detection Club Oath can explain how Poirot knows that Lady Westholme from *Appointment with Death* spent time in prison in her early life.

The crime

The crime itself did not feature strongly in the Rules, although Christie enjoyed the challenge of Van Dine 18 below.

Van Dine 7. There simply must be a corpse in a detective novel.

The first detective novel, Wilkie Collins' *The Moonstone* (1878), concerns a robbery rather than a murder, but a mysterious death is the sine qua non of most detective novels. Although she broke this Rule often in her short story output, Christie never short-changed her readers in novel form, generously providing a multitude of corpses in *And Then There Were None, Death Comes as the End* and *Endless Night.*

Van Dine 18. A crime in a detective story must never turn out to be an accident or a suicide.

The rejection of this Rule could mean a huge disappointment for a reader who discovers, after 250 pages, that the death under investigation is not a crime at all. See how cleverly Agatha Christie overcomes this. In *Taken at the Flood*, none of the deaths is what it first seems. The seeming murder of 'Enoch Arden' is an accident, the death of Major Porter is suicide and the seeming suicide of Rosaleen Cloade is murder. In one brilliant plot she effortlessly breaks both aspects of Van Dine's Rule. In the Poirot cases 'The Market Basing Mystery' and 'Murder in the Mews' – both essentially the same story, the latter being a more elaborate version, 15 years later, of the former – we have not murder disguised to look like suicide but suicide disguised to look like murder. But there is another twist; the real murder plan is to get someone else hanged (and therefore murdered) for a crime they did not commit. Both suicide scenes are subtly altered to give an impression exactly opposite to the reality.

Van Dine 19. The motives for all the crimes in detective stories should be personal.

This Rule essentially outlawed murder committed for ideological reasons, specifically political motivation. Van Dine goes on to suggest that this should be confined to secret-service stories and this type of plot is indeed a feature of some of Christie's international thriller novels – *They Came to Baghdad, Destination Unknown, Passenger to Frankfurt* – as well as some of the early titles – *The Secret Adversary, The Secret of Chimneys* – but it is not a feature of her classical detective stories. But into which category does the motive for the first murder in *Three Act Tragedy* fall?

The detective

The supposedly all-important figure of the detective occupied both writers: Van Dine 4 and Knox 7 are identical, although Van Dine added further embellishments in Rules 6 and 9. Some of Christie's greatest triumphs involve these Rules; she has joyously shattered all of them.

Van Dine 4. The detective himself, or one of the official investigators, should never turn out to be the criminal.

Knox 7. The detective must not himself commit the crime.

From the very beginning of the detective novel the unmasking of the official investigator was considered a valid ploy. *The Mystery of the Yellow Room* (1907) by Gaston

Leroux, creator of *The Phantom of the Opera*, is credited by Agatha Christie herself as being one of the two detective novels that she had actually read before embarking on *The Mysterious Affair at Styles* and contains one of the earliest examples of the criminal investigator. In *The Clocks*, Poirot, talking about his *magnum opus* on detective fiction, is unstinting in his praise for this groundbreaking novel. Some of Christie's most deftly plotted books featured this ploy. *Hercule Poirot's Christmas* was chosen by Robert Barnard in his *Agatha Christie: A Talent to Deceive* (1980) as one of the three best novels of Dame Agatha's career, and indeed it is a classic English detective story of the type considered synonymous with the Christie school of whodunit, in other words a snowbound country mansion with a group of suspects and among them a killer. While her intentions when originally plotting this novel were completely different from those realised in the book we now know (see *Agatha Christie's Secret Notebooks*), the solution is breathtaking in its daring and simplicity. We are given numerous clues to the true identity of Simeon Lee's killer – the good looks, the habit of stroking the jaw, the subterfuge with the piece of rubber, the insistence on the family 'on the other side of the blanket', the daring exchange with Pilar in the chapter 'December 24th'. But, like the presence of a narrator, Superintendent Sugden is not really seen by the reader, just accepted. With his unmasking, an ingenious (if somewhat unlikely) plot is revealed. An early foreshadowing of this ploy can also be found in 'The Man in the Mist' in *Partners in Crime*.

The Mousetrap, in both its stage and novella versions, and its earlier incarnation as the radio play *Three Blind Mice*, all unmask the investigator as the villain. Sergeant Trotter arrives like a deus ex machina in Monkswell Manor and is accepted unquestioningly both by its snowbound inhabitants and by the audience. In fairness, it should be said that although we think he is a policeman, he is actually an imposter, although the overall effect is the same. In the late 1940s and early 1950s the policeman, like the village doctor, was perceived as uncorrupted and incorruptible. Nowadays, unfortunately, we know differently and modern audiences are more likely to spot this type of villain than their more innocent counterparts of an earlier age.

In *Curtain: Poirot's Last Case*, Agatha Christie played her last and greatest trick of all on her readers; and they loved her all the more for it. This is the ultimate sleight of hand from the supreme prestidigitator in the crime-writing pantheon. Who but Agatha Christie would have thought of, and then carried out, this almost sacrilegious trick? After 55 years of partnership, she unmasks Poirot as the killer. Certainly the book is contrived (which detective story is not?), but only the most churlish of readers would complain after such a dazzling culmination of two careers.

Van Dine 6. The detective novel must have a detective in it.

This is a perfectly reasonable Rule. But Agatha Christie made a career out of breaking the Rules, reasonable or otherwise, and she managed to demolish this one also. The most famous and best-selling crime novel of all time, *And Then There Were None*, has no detective. An epilogue is set at Scotland Yard where Inspector Maine and Sir Thomas Legge, the Assistant Commissioner, discuss the mass slaughter on the island but can offer no explanation that covers all the facts. It is left to a confession (breaking yet another Rule) to pinpoint the guilty party. *Death Comes as the End* is another example of a detective novel with no detective. Set as it is in Ancient Egypt 4,000 years ago, the absence of a detective is not remarkable. Clues also are necessarily in short supply; the fingerprints, cigarette ash and telephone alibis beloved of writers and readers alike are notable only by their absence.

Van Dine 9. There must be but one detective.

In the sense that Poirot and Miss Marple never meet between the covers of any of her books Agatha Christie abided by this Rule. But in many novels they work in close collaboration with the official investigators. And in other titles there is an unofficial coming-together of, effectively, suspects in order to solve the crime. In *Three Act Tragedy*, *Death in the Clouds* and *The A.B.C. Murders* Poirot agrees to co-operate with some of those under suspicion in order to arrive at the truth. And in all three cases one of his group of collaborators is unmasked in the last chapter. Coincidentally or otherwise, these novels were all published in the same 12-month period between January 1935 and January 1936.

The murderer

The other important figure, the murderer, also exercised both rule-makers. But Christie had broken most of these Rules before either Knox or Van Dine sat down to compose them.

Knox 1. The criminal must be someone mentioned in the early part of the story, but must not be anyone whose thoughts the reader has been allowed to follow.

While adhering to the former part of this injunction, the circumvention of the latter became almost a motif throughout Agatha Christie's writing life. As early as 1924 with *The Man in the Brown Suit* she neatly and unobtrusively breaks this rule. Throughout the book we are presented with passages from Sir Eustace Pedler's diary in which he shares his thoughts with the reader, before his eventual unmasking as the villain of the piece. The most famous, or infamous, example is, of course, *The Murder of Roger Ackroyd*. This title, her first for the publisher Collins, caused a major stir on its first appearance with its revelation of the narrator as a cold-blooded killer and blackmailer. The book immediately ensured her fame and success and it is safe to assert that, even if she had never written another word, her name would still be remembered today in recognition of this stunning conjuring trick. Forty years later she replayed it but in such a different guise that most of her readers were not aware of the repetition. While a doctor in a small 1920s village narrates *The Murder of Roger Ackroyd*, a young, working-class, charming ne'er-do-well narrates *Endless Night*. But it is essentially the same sleight of hand at work. (See also 'Fairness' above.)

More subtly, we share the thoughts of a group of characters, which includes the killer, in *And Then There Were None*, but without identifying which thoughts belong to which character (Chapter 11). And in *The A.B.C. Murders* we think we are sharing the thoughts of a serial killer when, in fact, he is the innocent dupe of the real killer. Less overtly, we are given an insight into the minds of the killer in *Five Little Pigs*, *Towards Zero* and *Sparkling Cyanide*.

Van Dine 10. The culprit must turn out to be a person who has played a more or less prominent part in the story.

Never one to cheat her readers, this is one of the Rules that Christie did not break, or not in the way that Van Dine intended. She never unmasked the second cousin of the under-housemaid as the killer in the last chapter. But adhering to the hidden-in-plain-sight ploy, the more prominent a part a character played the more suspicious should the reader be.

Van Dine 11. A servant must not be chosen as the culprit.

This is not mere social prejudice (although there is plenty of that in the work of Van Dine himself) but a practical solution to the problem of the unmasking, in the last chapter, of a member of the domestic staff whose presence in the novel was fleeting at best. Consider how Christie overcame this stricture. Kirsten Lindstrom in *Ordeal by Innocence* is, strictly speaking, a domestic servant but her significance to the Argyle family can be interpreted as placing her outside this category. But it is as a servant that we meet, and continue to perceive, her. This same consideration applies to Miss Gilchrist in *After the Funeral*; witness the telling scene at the denouement when she bitterly recriminates the Abernethie family. Gladys, in *A Pocket Full of Rye*, is a clearer example of domestic servitude. Indeed, it is her status as such that makes her a necessary part of Lance's murderous plan. It is her job to poison the breakfast marmalade while Lance is demonstrably miles away, thereby giving him an impeccable alibi. But it is also a fact that, in defence of Christie's oft-criticised attitude to domestic servants, it is the subsequent death of Gladys that causes Miss Marple to arrive at Yewtree Lodge to avenge the death of a foolish and gullible former maid.[2] And the closing pages of the book, as Miss Marple reads a letter from Gladys written just before her murder, are very affecting. The same plot device, and much of the same plot, can

---

2 Lest it be thought that Christie was alone in this attitude to servants, in Chapter 12 of Anthony Berkeley's *The Piccadilly Murder* (1929) a character muses: 'For the first time he realised that one very seldom does look a waiter or waitress directly in the face, unless with the object of learning whom to summon later.' Twenty-five years later, in Chapter 5 of Harry Carmichael's *Death Times Three* (1954), the detective John Piper 'was trying to remember what the maid Tessa looked like. His recollections were hazy . . . just a female in cap and apron . . .'

be seen in the earlier short story 'The Tuesday Night Club' in *The Thirteen Problems*.

Van Dine 17. A professional criminal must never be shouldered with the guilt in a detective novel.

This Rule was adhered to and, apart from brief forays into organised crime in *The Big Four*, *The Secret of Chimneys* and *At Bertram's Hotel*, no use is made of a professional criminal in Christie's solutions.

Van Dine 12. There must be but one culprit no matter how many murders are committed.

Murderous alliances are a feature of Christie's fiction beginning with *The Mysterious Affair at Styles* and continuing with *The Murder at the Vicarage*, *Death on the Nile*, *One, Two, Buckle my Shoe*, *Evil under the Sun*, *The Body in the Library*, *Sparkling Cyanide* and *Endless Night*, all of which feature murderous couples. *Cat among the Pigeons* and, to a lesser degree, *Taken at the Flood*, feature more than one killer working independently of each other; *The Hollow* features an unusual and morally questionable, collusion; and, of course, *Murder on the Orient Express* features the ultimate conspiracy.

The murder method

Christie never resorted to elaborate mechanical or scientific means to explain her ingenuity, and much of her popularity and accessibility lies in her adherence to this simplicity. Many of her last-chapter surprises can be explained in a few sentences. Once you have grasped the essential fact that the corpse identified as A is, in fact, Corpse B and vice versa everything else falls into place; when you realise that all twelve suspects conspired to murder one victim all confusion disappears; when it dawns that the name Evelyn can mean a male or a female little further explanation is necessary.

Van Dine 14. The method of murder, and the means of detecting it, must be rational and scientific.

Knox 4. No hitherto undiscovered poisons may be used, nor any appliance which will need long scientific explanation at the end.

While Christie uses poisons as a means of killing characters more than any of her contemporaries, she uses only those that are scientifically known. But, that said, thanks to her training as a dispenser, she had more knowledge of the subject than many of her fellow writers and was familiar with unusual poisons and the more unusual properties of the common ones. Her first novel, *The Mysterious Affair at Styles*, depends for its surprise solution on knowledge of the properties of strychnine, but this is not unreasonable as the reader is fully aware of the poison used. In fact, there is a graphic description of the death of Mrs Inglethorpe and a discussion of the effects of, and the chemical formula for, strychnine. Taxine in *A Pocket Full of Rye*, ricin in 'The House of Lurking Death' from *Partners in Crime*, thallium in *The Pale Horse* and physostigmine in *Crooked House* are just some of the unusual poisons featuring in Christie. Fictitious drugs such as Serenite in *A Caribbean Mystery*, Calmo in *The Mirror Crack'd from Side to Side* and Benvo in *Passenger to Frankfurt* also feature, but as the plot does not turn on their usage, they merely bend rather than break Knox's Rule.

To be avoided

Some of these items are mere personal prejudice; there is no good reason why cigarettes or twins, for instance, cannot be a clue, or even a main plot device, provided that the reader has been properly prepared for them. With all of these the important point is the originality of the approach in utilising them – and this Christie had in full measure and overflowing.

Van Dine 13. Secret societies have no place in a detective story.

Many readers, including probably the author herself, would wish that *The Big Four* had never found its way between hard covers. Cobbled together at the lowest point in her life (after the death of her mother, the request for a divorce from her husband and her subsequent disappearance) with the help of her brother-in-law, Campbell Christie, this collection of short stories that had earlier appeared in various magazines was turned into a novel by judicious editing. The 'secret society' bent on world domination that it features was, mercifully, a one-off aberration on Christie's part. *The Seven Dials Mystery* features an equally preposterous secret society, albeit one with a Christie twist. Throughout the novel we are told of the existence of this society and the reader assumes the worst. At the eventual and literal unmasking we discover that it is actually working for the eradication, rather than the promotion, of crime, and its membership includes Superintendent Battle. *The Pale Horse*, one of the best books of the 1960s, features a mysterious organisation, Murder Inc., that seems to specialise in remote killing, but a rational and horribly plausible method of murder is revealed in the closing chapters.

Knox 5. No Chinamen must figure in the story.

This comment is not as racist as it may first appear. At the time of its writing Orientals in fiction were perceived as the personification of everything undesirable and came under the general heading of 'The Yellow Peril'. A more lengthy discussion of the subject can be found in Colin Watson's *Snobbery with Violence* (1971), an investigation of the social attitudes reflected in British crime fiction of the twentieth century, but suffice it to say that the white-slave trade, torture and other 'unspeakable acts' were the accepted fictional norms at the time for any character of Oriental extraction. This Rule was included to raise the literary horizon above that of the average opium den. Apart from *The Big Four*, and the more politically correct Poirot case 'The Lost Mine' in 1923, no 'Chinamen' play a part in any of Christie's detective novels. Unfortunately, she succumbs to stereotype in *The Big Four* where, as well as some cringe-inducing scenes with Oriental characters and 'speech', the chief villain, 'the greatest criminal brain of all time', is Chinese. But these stories had appeared some years earlier, pre-dating Knox.

Knox 3. Not more than one secret room or passage is allowable.

This Rule is taken to mean that no solution may *turn* on the existence of a secret passage. It was designed to eliminate the possibility of an exasperated reader hurling his detective novel across the room as the detective explains how the killer gained access to his closely guarded victim through such a passage, the existence of which was unknown up to that point. Christie is not above introducing the odd secret passage almost as a challenge to the cliché, but their very introduction long before the solution is in keeping with the tenet of this Rule. *The Secret of Chimneys, Three Act Tragedy* and 'The Adventure of Johnny Waverley' all feature, but openly and not covertly, a secret room or passage. The play *Spider's Web* features a sliding panel with a concealed cavity; but its use pokes gentle fun at this convention.

Knox 10. Twin brothers, and doubles generally, must not appear unless we have been duly prepared for them.

This Rule was formalised in an effort to avoid the disclosure that Suspect A, who had a cast-iron alibi for the night of the crime, was the guilty party because his alibi was provided by a hitherto unheard-of twin brother. Tongue firmly planted in literary cheek, Christie cocks a snook at this convention in 'The Unbreakable Alibi' in *Partners in Crime*. This is her take on the alibi-breaking stories of her contemporary Freeman Wills Crofts. And look at the ingenious double-bluff of *Lord Edgware Dies. The Big Four* also has an episode featuring a twin – one Achille Poirot . . .

Van Dine 20. A list of devices, which no self-respecting detective story writer should avail himself of . . .

The bogus séance to force a confession
At the end of *Peril at End House* Poirot arranges something very like a séance in End House, but it is really a variation on his usual 'all-the-suspects-in-the-drawing-room' ploy – although he does manage to elicit a confession. At the other end of a story is the séance in *The Sittaford Mystery*, where such an event is cleverly stage-managed in order to set a plot in motion.

The unmasking of a twin or look-alike
In *Partners in Crime*, Christie has Tommy and Tuppence tweak this Rule in 'The Unbreakable Alibi'.

The cipher/code-letter

In *The Thirteen Problems* Christie features a very clever version of the code-letter in 'The Four Suspects' and in the last book she wrote, *Postern of Fate*, Tommy and Tuppence find a hidden message that begins their final case.

The comparison of cigarette butts

'Murder in the Mews' features not just this idea but also the clue of the cigarette smoke, or, more accurately, the absence of cigarette smoke.

Knox 2. All supernatural agencies are ruled out as a matter of course.

Van Dine 8. The problem of the crime must be solved by strictly naturalistic means.

These two Rules are, in effect, the same and are more strictly adhered to, but Christie still sails close to the wind on various occasions, especially in her short story output. The virtually unknown radio play *Personal Call* has a supernatural twist at the last minute just when the listener thinks that everything has been satisfactorily, and rationally, explained. *Dumb Witness* features the Tripp sisters, quasi-spiritualists, but apart from her collection *The Hound of Death*, which has a supernatural rather than a detective theme, most of Chritie's stories are firmly rooted in the natural, albeit sometimes evil, real world. *The Pale Horse* makes much of black magic and murder-by-suggestion but, like 'The Voice in the Dark' from *The Mysterious Mr Quin* and its seeming ghostly presence, all is explained away in rational terms.

Van Dine 3. There must be no love interest.

Although Van Dine managed this in his own books (thereby reducing them to semi-animated Cluedo), this Rule has been ignored by most successful practitioners. It is in the highest degree unlikely that, in the course of a 250-page novel, the 'love interest' can be completely excised while some semblance of verisimilitude is retained. Admittedly, Van Dine may have been thinking of some of the excesses of the Romantic suspense school, when matters of the heart take precedence over matters of the intellect; or when the reader can safely spot the culprit by pairing off the suspects until only one remains. Christie, as usual, turned this rule to her advantage. In some novels we confidently expect certain characters to walk up the aisle after the book finishes but, instead, one or more of them end up walking to the scaffold. In *Death in the Clouds*, Jane Grey gets as big a shock as the reader when the charming Norman Gale is unmasked as a cold-blooded murderer. In *Taken at the Flood*, Lynn is left pining after the ruthless David Hunter and in *They Came to Baghdad*, Victoria is left to seek a replacement for the shy Edward. In some Christie novels the 'love interest' or, more accurately, the emotional element and personal interplay between the characters, is not just present but of a much higher standard than is usual in her works. For example, in *Five Little Pigs*, *The Hollow* and *Nemesis* it is the emotional entanglements that set the plot in motion and provide the motivation; in each case it is thwarted love that motivates the killer.

Van Dine 16. A detective novel should contain no long descriptive passages, no literary dallying with side-issues, no subtly worked-out character analyses, and no 'atmospheric' preoccupations.

This Rule merely mirrors the time in which it was written. And it must be admitted that it would be no bad matter to reintroduce it to some present-day practitioners. Many examples of current detective fiction are shamelessly over-written and never seem to use ten words when a hundred will do. That said, character analysis and atmosphere can play an important part in the solution. In *The Moving Finger*, it is only when Miss Marple looks beyond the 'atmosphere' of fear in Lymstock that the solutions both to the explanation of the poison-pen letters and the identity of the murderer become clear. In *Cards on the Table* the only physical clues are the bridge scorecards and Poirot has to depend largely on the character of the bridge-players, as shown by these scorecards, to arrive at the truth. In *Five Little Pigs*, an investigation into the murder committed 16 years earlier has to rely almost solely on the evidence and accounts of the suspects. Character reading and analysis play an important part in this procedure. In *The Hollow*, it is from his study of the characters staying for the weekend at The Hollow that Poirot uncovers the truth of the crime. Apart from the gun there is nothing in the way of physical clues for him to analyse.

RULE OF THREE: SUMMARY

The Knox Decalogue is by far the more reasonable of the two sets of Rules. Written somewhat tongue-in-cheek – 'Not more than one secret room or passage is allowable' – it is less repetitive and restrictive and shows less personal prejudice than does its American counterpart. A strict adherence to Van Dine's Rules would have resulted in an arid, uninspired and ultimately predictable genre. It would have meant forgoing (much of) the daring brilliance of Christie, the inventive logic of Ellery Queen, the audacious ingenuity of John

Dickson Carr or the formidable intelligence of Dorothy L. Sayers. In later years it would have precluded the witty cunning of Edmund Crispin, the erudite originality of Michael Innes or the boundary-pushing output of Julian Symons. Van Dine's list is repetitive and, in many instances, a reflection of his personal bias – no long descriptive passages, no literary dallying with side-issues, no subtly worked-out character analyses, no 'atmospheric' preoccupations. It is somewhat ironic that while the compilers of both lists are largely forgotten nowadays, the writer who managed to break most of their carefully considered Rules remains the best-selling and most popular writer in history.

And so, from *The Mysterious Affair at Styles* in 1920 until *Sleeping Murder* in 1976, Agatha Christie produced at least one book a year and for nearly twenty of those years she produced two titles. The slogan 'A Christie for Christmas' was a fixture in Collins's publishing list and in 1935 it became clear that the name of Agatha Christie was to be a perennial best seller. That year, with *Three Act Tragedy*, she reached the magic figure of 10,000 hardback copies sold in the first year. And this trebled over the next ten years. By the time of her fiftieth title, *A Murder is Announced*, she matched it with sales of 50,000; and never looked back. And all of this without the media circus that is now part and parcel of the book trade – no radio or TV interviews, no signing sessions, no question-and-answer panels and virtually no public appearances.

Although mutually advantageous, the relationship between Christie and her publisher was by no means without its rockier moments, usually about jacket design or blurb. The proposed design for *The Labours of Hercules* horrified her ('Poirot going naked to the bath'), she considered that an announcement in 'Crime Club News' about 1939's *Ten Little*

Niggers – its title later amended to the more acceptable *And Then There Were None* – revealed too much of the plot (see *Agatha Christie's Secret Notebooks*), and in September 1967 she sent Sir William ('Billy') Collins a blistering letter for not having received her so-called advance copies of *Endless Night* before she saw them herself on sale at the airport. And as late as 1968 she wrote her own blurb for *By the Pricking of my Thumbs.*

Thanks to her phenomenal sales and prodigious output, she became a personal friend of Sir William and his wife, Pierre, and conducted much of her correspondence through the years directly with him. They were regular visitors to Greenway, her Devon retreat, and Sir William was one of those who spoke at her memorial service in May 1976. A measure of the respect in which he held her can be gauged from his closing remarks, when he said that 'the world is better because she lived in it'.

The First Decade 1920–1929

'It was while I was working in the dispensary that I first conceived the idea of writing a detective story.'

◄○►

SOLUTIONS REVEALED

The Mysterious Affair at Styles • *The Mystery of the Blue Train*

◄○►

The Mysterious Affair at Styles was published in the USA at the end of 1920 and in the UK on 21 January 1921. It is a classic country-house whodunit of the sort that would eventually become synonymous with the name of Agatha Christie. Ironically, over the following decade she wrote only one more 'English' domestic whodunit, *The Murder of Roger Ackroyd* (1926). The other two whodunits of this decade are set abroad – *The Murder on the Links* (1923) is set in Deauville, France and *The Mystery of the Blue Train* (1928) has a similar South of France background. With the exception of the last title, which Christie, according to her *Autobiography*, 'always hated' and had 'never been proud of', they are first-class examples of the classic detective story then entering its Golden Age. Each title, with the same exception, displays the gifts that would later make Agatha Christie the Queen of Crime – uncomplicated language briskly telling a cleverly constructed story, easily recognisable and clearly delineated characters, inventive plots with all the necessary clues given to the reader, and an unexpected killer unmasked in the last chapter. These hallmarks would continue to be a feature of Christie's books until the twilight of her career, half a century later.

The rest of her novels of the 1920s consist of thrillers, both domestic – *The Secret Adversary* (1922), *The Secret of Chimneys* (1925) and *The Seven Dials Mystery* (1929) – and international – *The Man in the Brown Suit* (1924). While none of these titles are first-rate Christie, they all exhibit some elements that would appear in later titles. *The Secret Adversary*, the first Tommy and Tuppence adventure, unmasks the least likely suspect while *The Man in the Brown Suit* is an early experiment with the famous Roger Ackroyd conjuring trick. *The Seven Dials Mystery* subverts reader expectation of the 'secret society' plot device and *The Secret of Chimneys*, a light-hearted mixture of missing jewels, international intrigue, incriminating letters, blackmail and murder in a high society setting, shows early experimentation with impersonation and false identity.

Throughout the 1920s Christie's short story output was impressive. She published three such collections in the decade. The contents of *Poirot Investigates* (1924) first appeared in *The Sketch*, in a commissioned series of short stories, starting in March 1923 with 'The Affair at the Victory Ball'. By the end of that year two dozen stories had appeared and 50 years later the remainder of these stories had their first UK book appearance in *Poirot's Early Cases*. In 1953 Christie dedicated *A Pocket Full of Rye* to the editor of *The Sketch*, 'Bruce Ingram, who liked and published my first short stories.' In 1927, at a low point in Christie's life, after the death of her mother and her own disappearance, *The Big Four* was published. This episodic Poirot novel, consisting of a series of connected short stories all of which had appeared in *The Sketch* during 1924, can also be considered a low point in the career of Hercule Poirot as he battles with a gang of international criminals intent on world domination. The last collection of the decade is the hugely entertaining *Partners in Crime* (1929). These Tommy and Tuppence adventures, most of which had appeared in *The Sketch* also during 1924, were pastiches of many of the crime writers of the time – 'The Man in the Mist' (G.K. Chesterton), 'The Case of the Missing Lady' (Conan Doyle), 'The Crackler' (Edgar Wallace) – and, while light-hearted in tone, contain many clever ideas.

Apart from her crime and detective stories, tales of the supernatural, romance and fantasy all appeared under her name in many of the multitude of magazines that filled the bookstalls. Many of the stories later published in the collections *The Mysterious Mr Quin, The Hound of Death* and *The Listerdale Mystery* were written and first published in the 1920s. And, of course, it was during the 1920s that Miss Marple made her first appearance, in the short story 'The Tuesday Night Club', published in *The Royal Magazine* in December 1927. With the exception of the final entry, 'Death by Drowning', the stories that appear in *The Thirteen Problems* were all written in the 1920s and appeared in two batches, the first six between December 1927 and May 1928, and the second between December 1929 and May 1930. In 1924 her first poetry collection *The Road of Dreams* was published. And it seems likely that her own stage adaptation of *The Secret of Chimneys* was begun in the late 1920s, as was the unpublished and unperformed script of the macabre short story 'The Last Séance'.

The other important career decision taken in 1923 was to employ the services of a literary agent, Edmund Cork. The first task undertaken by Cork was to extricate Christie from a very one-sided contract with The Bodley Head Ltd and negotiate a more favourable arrangement with Collins, the publisher with which she was destined to remain for the rest of her life; as, indeed, she did with Edmund Cork.

Three of the best short stories Christie ever wrote were

published during this decade. In January 1925 'Traitor Hands', later to achieve immortality as the play, and subsequent film, *Witness for the Prosecution*, appeared in *Flynn's Weekly*. The much-anthologised 'Accident' was published in the *Daily Express* in 1929; this was later adapted by other hands into the one-act play *Tea for Three*. And 'Philomel Cottage', which spawned five screen versions as *Love from a Stranger*, appeared in *The Grand* in November 1924.

Finally, the first stage and screen version of her work appeared during the 1920s. *Alibi*, adapted for the stage by Michael Morton from *The Murder of Roger Ackroyd*, opened in May 1928 while the same year saw the opening of films of *The Secret Adversary* – as *Die Abenteuer G.m.b.h.* – and *The Passing of Mr Quinn*, based loosely on the short story 'The Coming of Mr Quin'.

This hugely prolific decade shows Christie gaining an international reputation while experimenting with form and structure within, and outside, the detective genre. Although her first novel was very definitely a detective story, her output for the following nine years returned only three times to the form in which she was eventually to gain immortality.

The Mysterious Affair at Styles
21 January 1921

Arthur Hastings goes to Styles Court, the home of his friend John Cavendish, to recuperate during the First World War. He senses tension in the household and this is confirmed when his hostess, John's stepmother, is poisoned. Luckily, a Belgian refugee staying nearby is an old friend, a retired policeman called Hercule Poirot.

In her *Autobiography* Agatha Christie gives a detailed account of the genesis of *The Mysterious Affair at Styles*. By now, the main facts are well known: the immortal challenge – 'I bet you can't write a good detective story' – from her sister Madge, the Belgian refugees from the First World War in Torquay who inspired Poirot's nationality, Christie's knowledge of poisons from her work in the local dispensary, her intermittent work on the book and its eventual completion, at the encouragement of her mother, during a two-week seclusion in the Moorland Hotel. This was not her first literary effort, nor was she the first member of her family with literary aspirations. Both her mother and sister Madge wrote, and Madge actually had a play, *The Claimant*, produced in the West End before Agatha did. Agatha had already written a 'long dreary novel' (her own words in a 1955 radio broadcast) and some short stories and sketches. While the story of the bet is realistic, it is clear that this alone would not be stimulus enough to plot, sketch and write a successful book. There was obviously an innate gift and a facility with the written word.

Although she began writing the novel in 1916 (*The Mysterious Affair at Styles* is actually set in 1917), it was not published for another four years. And its publication was to demand consistent determination on its author's part as more than one publisher declined the manuscript. Eventually, in 1919, John Lane, co-founder of The Bodley Head Ltd, asked to meet her with a view to publication. But, even then, the struggle was far from over.

The contract, dated 1 January 1920, that John Lane offered her took advantage of Agatha Christie's publishing naivety. She explains in her *Autobiography* that she was 'in no frame of mind to study agreements or even think about them'. Her delight at the prospect of publication, combined with the conviction that she was not going to pursue a writing career, persuaded her to sign. Remarkably, the actual contract is for

The Mysterious Affair of (rather than 'at') *Styles*. She was to get 10 per cent only after 2,000 copies were sold in the UK and she was contracted to produce five more titles. This clause was to lead to much correspondence over the following years.

Later, as her productivity, success and popularity increased and she realised what she had signed, she insisted that if she *offered* a book she was fulfilling her side of the contract whether or not The Bodley Head accepted it. When they expressed doubt as to whether *Poirot Investigates*, as a volume of short stories rather than a novel, should be considered part of the six-book contract, the by now confident writer pointed out that she had offered them the non-crime *Vision*, described in Janet Morgan's *Agatha Christie: A Biography* as a 'fantasy', as her third title. The fact that her publisher had refused it was, as far as she was concerned, their choice. It is quite possible that if John Lane had not tried to take advantage of his literary discovery she might have stayed longer with The Bodley Head. But the prickly surviving correspondence shows that those early years of her career were a sharp learning curve in the ways of publishers – and that Agatha Christie was a star pupil. Within a relatively short space of time she is transformed from an awed and inexperienced neophyte perched nervously on the edge of a chair in John Lane's office to a confident and business-like professional with a resolute interest in every aspect of her books – jacket design, marketing, royalties, serialisation, translation and cinema rights.

The readers' reports on the *Styles* manuscript were, despite some misgivings, promising. One gets right to the commercial considerations: 'Despite its manifest shortcomings, Lane could very likely sell the novel. . . . There is a certain freshness about it.' A second report is more enthusiastic: 'It is altogether rather well told and well written.' And another speculates on her potential future 'if she goes on writing detective stories and she evidently has quite a talent for them'.

The readers were much taken with the character of Poirot – 'the exuberant personality of M. Poirot who is a very welcome variation on the "detective" of romance'; 'a jolly little man in the person of has-been famous Belgian detective'. Although Poirot might take issue with the use of the description 'has-been', it was clear that his presence was a factor in the manuscript's acceptance. In a report dated 7 October 1919 one very perceptive reader remarked, 'but the account of the trial of John Cavendish makes me suspect the hand of a woman'. Because her name on the manuscript appears as A.M. Christie, another reader refers to 'Mr. Christie'.

Despite these favourable readers' reports, there were further delays and after a serialisation in *The Weekly Times* – the first time a 'first' novel had been chosen – beginning in February 1920, Christie wrote to Mr Willett at The Bodley Head in October that year wondering if her book was 'ever coming out' and pointing out that she had almost finished her second one. This resulted in her receiving the projected cover design, which she approved. Eventually, *The Mysterious Affair at Styles* was published later that year in the USA. And, almost five years after she began it, Agatha Christie's first book went on sale in the UK on 21 January 1921. Even after its appearance there was much correspondence about statements and incorrect calculations of royalties as well as cover designs. In fairness to John Lane and The Bodley Head, cover design and blurbs also featured regularly throughout her career in her correspondence with Collins.

As we have seen, one of the readers' reports mentioned the John Cavendish trial. In the original manuscript, Poirot's explanation of the crime is given in the form of his evidence in the witness box during the trial. In her *Autobiography* Christie describes John Lane's verdict on her manuscript, including his opinion that this courtroom scene did not convince and his request that she amend it. She agreed to a rewrite and although the explanation of the crime itself remains the same, instead of giving it in the course of the judicial process, Poirot holds forth in the drawing room of Styles in the kind of scene that was to be replicated in many later books.

Incredibly, almost a century later – it was written, in all probability, in 1916 – the deleted scene has survived in the pages of Notebook 37, which also contains two brief and somewhat enigmatic notes about the novel. Equally incredible is the illegibility of the handwriting. It was written in pencil, with much crossing out and many insertions. This is difficult enough, but an added complication lies in the fact that Christie often replaced the deleted words with alternatives, squeezed in, sometimes at an angle, above the original. And although the explanation of the crime is, in essence, the same as the published version, the published text was of limited help. The wording is often different and some names have changed. Of the Notebooks, this exercise in transcription was the most challenging of all. The fact that it is Agatha Christie's and Hercule Poirot's first case made the extra effort worthwhile.

In the version that follows I have amended the usual Christie punctuation of dashes to full stops and commas, and I have added quotation marks throughout. I use square brackets where an obvious, or necessary, word is missing in the original; a few illegible words have been omitted. Footnotes have been used to draw attention to points of particular interest.

The Mysterious Affair at Styles

The story so far . . .

When wealthy Emily Inglethorp, owner of Styles Court, remarries, her new husband Alfred is viewed by her stepsons, John and Lawrence, and her faithful retainer, Evelyn Howard, as a fortune-hunter. John's wife, Mary, is perceived as being over-friendly with the enigmatic Dr Bauerstein, a German and an expert on poisons. Also staying at Styles Court, while working in the dispensary of the local hospital, is Emily's protégée Cynthia Murdoch. Then Evelyn walks out after a bitter row. On the night of 17 July Emily dies from strychnine poisoning while her family watches helplessly. Hercule Poirot, called in by his friend Arthur Hastings, agrees to investigate and pays close attention to Emily's bedroom. And then John Cavendish is arrested . . .

Poirot returned late that night.[3] I did not see him until the following morning. He was beaming and greeted me with the utmost affection.

'Ah, my friend – all is well – all will now march.'

---

3 Chapter 11 ends with the words '"Well," said Mary, "I expect he will be back before dinner." But night fell and Poirot had not returned.' I suggest that it is at this point that the Notebook 37 extract would have appeared.

Notebook 37 showing the beginning of the deleted chapter from The Mysterious Affair at Styles.

'Why,' I exclaimed, 'You don't mean to say you have got—'

'Yes, Hastings, yes – I have found the missing link.[4] Hush . . .'

On Monday the hearing was resumed[5] and Sir E.H.W. [Ernest Heavywether] opened the case for the defence. Never, he said, in the course of his experience had a murder charge rested on slighter evidence. Let them take the evidence against John Cavendish and sift it impartially.

What was the main thing against him? That the powdered strychnine had been found in his drawer. But that drawer was an unlocked one and he submitted that there was no evidence to show that it was the prisoner who placed it there. It was, in fact, a wicked and malicious effort on the part of some other person to bring the crime home to the prisoner. He went on to state that the Prosecution had been unable to prove to any degree that it was the prisoner who had ordered the beard from Messrs Parksons. As for the quarrel with his mother and his financial constraints – both had been most grossly exaggerated.

His learned friend had stated that if [the] prisoner had been an honest man he would have come forward at the inquest and explained that it was he and not his step-father who had been the participator in that quarrel. That view was based upon a misapprehension. The prisoner, on returning to the house in the evening, had been told at once[6] that his mother had now had a violent dispute with her husband. Was it likely, was it probable, he asked the jury, that he should connect the two? It would never enter his head that anyone could ever mistake his voice for that of

---

4　Chapter 12 is called 'The Last Link'. In the preceding chapter
　　Poirot refers several times to 'the last link' in his chain of evidence.

5　John Cavendish's trial began on 15 September (Agatha Christie's
　　birthday), two months after the poisoning of Emily Inglethorp.

6　The 'authoritatively told' of the published version is written over
　　the original 'told at once' in Notebook 37.

Mr. A[lfred] Inglethorp. As for the construction that [the] prisoner had destroyed a will – this mere idea was absurd. [The] prisoner had presented at the Bar and, being well versed in legal matters, knew that the will formerly made in his favour was revoked automatically. He had never heard a more ridiculous suggestion! He would, however, call evidence which would show who *did* destroy the will, and with what motive.

Finally, he would point out to the jury that there was evidence against other persons besides John Cavendish. He did not wish to accuse Mr. Lawrence Cavendish in any way; nevertheless, the evidence against *him* was quite as strong – if not stronger – than that against his brother.

Just at that point, a note was handed to him. As he read it, his eyes brightened, his burly figure seemed to swell and double its size.

'Gentlemen of the jury,' he said, and there was a new ring in his voice, 'this has been a murder of peculiar cunning and complexity. I will first call the prisoner. He shall tell you his own story and I am sure you will agree with me that he *cannot* be guilty. Then I will call a Belgian gentleman, a very famous member of the Belgian police force in past years, who has interested himself in the case and who has important proofs that it was *not* the prisoner who committed this crime. I call the prisoner.'

John in the box acquitted himself well. His manner, quiet and direct, was all in his favour.[7] At the end of his examination he paused and said, 'I should like to say one thing. I utterly refute and disapprove of Sir Ernest Heavywether's insinuation about my brother Lawrence. My brother, I am convinced, had no more to do with this crime than I had.'

Sir Ernest, remaining seated, noted with a sharp eye that

---

7 None of the questioning of John Cavendish by Sir Ernest appears in Notebook 37.

John's protest had made a favourable effect upon the jury. Mr Bunthorne cross-examined.[8]

'You say that you never thought it possible that *your* quarrel with your mother was identical with the one spoken of at the inquest – is not that very surprising?'

'No, I do not think so – I knew that my mother and Mr Inglethorp had quarrelled. It never occurred to me that they had mistaken my voice for his.'

'Not even when the servant Dorcas repeated certain fragments of this conversation which you *must* have recognised?'

'No, we were both angry and said many things in the heat of the moment which we did not really mean and which we did not recollect afterwards. I could not have told you which exact words I used.'

Mr Bunthorne sniffed incredulously.

'About this note which you have produced so opportunely, is the handwriting not familiar to you?'

'No.'

'Do you not think it bears a marked resemblance to your own handwriting?'

'No – I don't think so.'

'I put it to you that it *is* your own handwriting.'

'No.'

'I put it to you that, anxious to prove an alibi, you conceived the idea of a fictitious appointment and wrote this note to yourself in order to bear out your statement.'

'No.'

'I put it to you that at the time you claim to have been waiting about in Marldon Wood,[9] you were really in Styles

---

8 Mr Philips KC appears for the Crown in the published version.

9 Although *The Mysterious Affair at Styles* is set in Essex, there is an area called Marldon near Torbay, where Christie was living when she wrote the novel. The reference was replaced in the published novel by 'a solitary and unfrequented spot'..

St Mary, in the chemist's shop, buying strychnine in the name of Alfred Inglethorp.'

'No – that is a lie.'

That completed Mr Bunthorne's CE [cross examination]. He sat down and Sir Ernest, rising, announced that his next witness would be M. Hercule Poirot.

Poirot strutted into the witness box like a bantam cock.[10] The little man was transformed; he was foppishly attired and his face beamed with self confidence and complacency. After a few preliminaries Sir Ernest asked: 'Having been called in by Mr. Cavendish what was your first procedure?'

'I examined Mrs Inglethorp's bedroom and found certain . . .?'

'Will you tell us what these were?'

'Yes.'

With a flourish Poirot drew out his little notebook.

'Voila,' he announced, 'There were in the room five points of importance.[11] I discovered, amongst other things, a brown stain on the carpet near the window and a fragment of green material which was caught on the bolt of the communicating door between that room and the room adjoining, which was occupied by Miss Cynthia Paton.'[12]

'What did you do with the fragment of green material?'

---

10 The alternate, but crossed out, version in Notebook 37 reads, 'entered the box and was duly sworn. The little man was transformed.'

11 In Chapter 4, Poirot notes 'six points of interest': a coffee cup that was ground into powder; a despatch-case with a key in the lock; a stain on the floor; a fragment of some dark green fabric; and a large splash of candle grease on the floor. At first he withholds the sixth item, but later in the chapter he adds the bromide-powder box.

12 The surname is changed to Murdoch in the published version, although in some editions the name is spelt with a 'K' on the floor-plan in Chapter 3.

'I handed it over to the police, who, however, did not consider it of importance.'

'Do you agree?'

'I disagree with that most utterly.'

'You consider the fragment important?'

'Of the first importance.'

'But I believe,' interposed the judge, 'that no-one in the house had a green garment in their possession.'

'I believe so, Mr Le Juge,' agreed Poirot facing in his direction. 'And so at first, I confess, that disconcerted me – until I hit upon the explanation.'

Everybody was listening eagerly.

'What is your explanation?'

'That fragment of green was torn from the sleeve of a member of the household.'

'But no-one had a green dress.'

'No, Mr Le Juge, this fragment is a fragment torn from a green land armlet.'

With a frown the judge turned to Sir Ernest.

'Did anyone in that house wear an armlet?'

'Yes, my lord. Mrs Cavendish, the prisoner's wife.'

There was a sudden exclamation and the judge commented sharply that unless there was absolute silence he would have the court cleared. He then leaned forward to the witness.

'Am I to understand that you allege Mrs Cavendish to have entered the room?'

'Yes, Mr Le Juge.'

'But the door was bolted on the inside.'

'Pardon, Mr Le Juge, we have only one person's word for that – that of Mrs Cavendish herself. You will remember that it was *Mrs Cavendish* who had tried that door and found it locked.'

'Was not her door locked when you examined the room?'

'Yes, but during the afternoon she would have had ample opportunity to draw the bolt.'[13]

'But Mr *Lawrence* Cavendish has claimed that he *saw* it.'

There was a momentary hesitation on Poirot's part before he replied.

'Mr. Lawrence Cavendish was mistaken.'

Poirot continued calmly:

'I found, on the floor, a large splash of candle grease, which upon questioning the servants, I found had not been there the day before. The presence of the candle grease on the floor, the fact that the door opened quite noiselessly (a proof that it had recently been oiled) and the fragment of the green armlet in the door led me at once to the conclusion that the room had been entered through that door and that Mrs Cavendish was the person who had done so. Moreover, at the inquest Mrs Cavendish declared that she had heard the fall of the table in her own room. I took an early opportunity of testing that statement by stationing my friend Mr Hastings[14] in the left wing just outside Mrs Cavendish's door. I myself, in company with the police, went to [the] deceased's room and whilst there I, apparently accidentally, knocked over the table in question but found, as I had suspected, that [it made] no sound at all. This confirmed my view that Mrs Cavendish was not speaking the truth when she declared that she had been in her room at the time of the tragedy. In fact, I was more than ever convinced that, far from being in her own room, Mrs Cavendish was actually in the *deceased's* room when the table fell. I found that no one had actually *seen* her leave her room.

---

13 At this point in Notebook 37 there is a reference to 'Other Book', possibly referring to another Notebook, no longer extant.

14 Hastings is Mr Hastings throughout *The Mysterious Affair at Styles*; he did not become Captain until *The Murder on the Links*.

The first that anyone could tell me was that she was in Miss Paton's room shaking her awake. Everyone presumed that she had come from her own room – but I can find no one who *saw* her do so.'

The judge was much interested. 'I understand. Then your explanation is that it was *Mrs* Cavendish and not the prisoner who destroyed the will.'

Poirot shook his head.

'No,' he said quickly, 'That was not the reason for Mrs Cavendish's presence. There is only one person who *could* have destroyed the will.'

'And that is?'

'Mrs Inglethorp herself.'

'*What?* The will she had made that very afternoon?'

'Yes – it must have been her. Because by no other means can you account for the fact that on the hottest day of the year [Mrs Inglethorp] ordered a fire to be lighted in her room.'

The judge objected. 'She was feeling ill . . .'

'Mr Le Juge, the temperature that day was 86 in the shade. There was only one reason for which Mrs Inglethorp could want a fire – namely to destroy some document. You will remember that in consequence of the war economies practised at Styles, no waste paper was thrown away and that the kitchen fire was allowed to go out after lunch. There was, consequently, no means at hand for the destroying of bulky documents such as a will. This confirms to me at once that there was some paper which Mrs Inglethorp was anxious to destroy and it must necessarily be of a bulk which made it difficult to destroy by merely setting a match to it. The idea of a will had occurred to me before I set foot in the house, so papers burned in the grate did not surprise me. I did not, of course, at that time know that the will in question had only been made the previous afternoon and I will admit that when I learnt this fact, I fell into a grievous error. I deduced that Mrs Inglethorp's determination to destroy this will came as a direct consequence of the quarrel and that consequently the quarrel took place, contrary to belief, *after* the making of the will.

'When, however, I was forced to reluctantly abandon this hypothesis – since the various interviews were absolutely steady on the question of time – I was obliged to cast around for another. And I found it in the form of the letter which Dorcas describes her mistress as holding in her hand. Also you will notice the difference of attitude. At 3.30 Dorcas overhears her mistress saying angrily that "scandal will not deter her." "You have brought it on yourself" were her words. But at 4.30, when Dorcas brings in the tea, although the actual words she used were almost the same, the meaning is quite different. Mrs Inglethorp is now in a clearly distressed condition. She is wondering what to do. She speaks with dread of the scandal and publicity. Her outlook is quite different. We can only explain this psychologically by presuming [that] her first sentiments applied to the scandal between John Cavendish and his wife and did not in any way touch herself – but that in the second case the scandal affected herself.

'This, then, is the position: At 3.30 she quarrels with her son and threatens to denounce him to his wife who, although they neither of them realise it, overhears part of the conversation. At 4 o'clock, in consequence of a conversation at lunch time on the making of wills by marriage, Mrs Inglethorp makes a will in favour of her husband, witnessed by her gardener. At 4.30 Dorcas finds her mistress in a terrible state, a slip of paper in her hand. And she then orders the fire in her room to be lighted in order that she can destroy the will she only made half an hour ago. Later she writes to Mr Wells, her lawyer, asking him to call on her tomorrow as she has some important business to transact.

Now what occurred between 4 o'clock and 4.30[15] to cause such a complete revolution of sentiments? As far as we know, she was quite alone during the time. Nobody entered or left the boudoir. What happened then? One can only guess but I have an idea that my guess is fairly correct.

'Late in the evening Mrs Inglethorp asked Dorcas for some stamps and my thinking is this. Finding she had no stamps in her desk she went along to that of her husband which stood at the opposite corner. The desk was locked but one of the keys on her bunch fitted it. She accordingly opened the desk and searched for stamps – it was then she found the slip of paper which wreaked such havoc! On the other hand Mrs Cavendish believed that the slip of paper to which her mother [in-law] clung so tenaciously was a written proof of her husband's infidelity. She demanded it. These were Mrs Inglethorp's words in reply:

'"No, [it is out of the] question." We know that she was speaking the truth. Mrs Cavendish however, believed she was merely shielding her step-son. She is a very resolute woman and she was wildly jealous of her husband and she determined to get hold of that paper at all costs and made her plans accordingly. She had chanced to find the key of Mrs Inglethorp's dispatch case which had been lost that morning. She had meant to return it but it had probably slipped her memory. Now, however, she deliberately retained it since she knew Mrs Inglethorp kept all important papers in that particular case. Therefore, rising about 4 o'clock she made her way through Miss Paton's room, which she had previously unlocked on the other side.'

---

15 These timings are 30 minutes earlier than those in Chapter 12 of the novel.

'But Miss Paton would surely have been awakened by anyone passing through her room.'

'Not if she were drugged.'

'Drugged?'

'Yes – for Miss Paton to have slept through all the turmoil in that next room was incredible. Two things were possible: either she was lying (which I did not believe) or her sleep was not a natural one. With this idea in view I examined all the coffee cups most carefully, taking a sample from each and analysing. But, to my disappointment, they yielded no result. Six persons had taken coffee and six cups were found. But I had been guilty of a very grave oversight. I had overlooked the fact that Dr Bauerstein had been there that night. That changed the face of the whole affair. *Seven, not* six people had taken coffee. There was, then, a cup missing. The servants would not observe this since it was the housemaid Annie who had taken the coffee tray in and she had brought in seven cups, unaware that Mr Inglethorp never took coffee. Dorcas who cleared them away found five cups and she suspected the sixth [of] being Mrs Inglethorp's. One cup, then, had disappeared and it was Mademoiselle Cynthia's, I knew, because she did not take sugar in her coffee, whereas all the others did and the cups I had found had all contained sugar. My attention was attracted by the maid Annie's story about some "salt" on the cocoa tray which she took nightly into Mrs Inglethorp's room. I accordingly took a sample of that cocoa and sent it to be analysed.'

'But,' objected the judge, 'this has already been done by Dr Bauerstein – with a negative result – and the analysis reported no strychnine present.'

'There was no strychnine present. The analysts were simply asked to report whether the contents showed if there were or were not strychnine present and they reported accordingly. But I had it tested for a *narcotic*.'

'For *a narcotic?*'

'Yes, Mr Le Juge. You will remember that Dr Bauerstein was unable to account for the delay before the symptoms manifested themselves. But a narcotic, taken with strychnine, will delay the symptoms some hours. Here is the analyst's report proving beyond a doubt that a narcotic *was* present.'

The report was handed to the judge who read it with great interest and it was then passed on to the jury.

'We congratulate you on your acumen. The case is becoming much clearer. The drugged cocoa, taken on top of the poisoned coffee, amply accounts for the delay which puzzled the doctor.'

'Exactly, Mr Le Juge. Although you have made one little error; the coffee, to the best of my belief was *not* poisoned.'

'What proof have you of that?'

'None whatever. But I can prove this – that poisoned or not, Mrs Inglethorp never drank it.'

'Explain yourself.'

'You remember that I referred to a brown stain on the carpet near the window? It remained in my mind, that stain, for it was still damp. Something had been spilt there, therefore, not more than twelve hours ago. Moreover there was a distinct odour of coffee clinging to the nap of the carpet and I found there two long splinters of china. I later reconstructed what had happened perfectly, for, not two minutes before I had laid down my small despatch case on the little table by the window and, the top of the table being loose, the case had been toppled off onto the floor onto the *exact spot where the stain was.* This, then, was what had happened. Mrs Inglethorp, on coming up to bed had laid her untasted coffee down on the table – the table had tipped up and [precipitated] the coffee onto the floor – spilling it and smashing the cup. What had Mrs Inglethorp done? She had picked up the pieces and laid them on the table beside her bed and, feeling in need of a stimulant of some kind, had heated up her cocoa[16] and drank it off before going to bed. Now, I was in a dilemma. The cocoa contained no strychnine. The coffee had not been drunk. Yet Mrs Inglethorp had been poisoned and the poison must have been administered sometime between the hours of seven and nine. But what else had Mrs Inglethorp taken which would have effectively masked the taste of the poison?'

'Nothing.'

'Yes – Mr Le Juge – she had taken her *medicine*.'

'Her medicine – but . . .'

'One moment – the medicine, by a [coincidence] already contained strychnine and had a bitter taste in consequence. The poison might have been introduced into the medicine. But I had my reasons for believing that it was done another way. I will recall to your memory that I also discovered a box which had at one time contained bromide powders. Also, if you will permit it, I will read out to you an extract – marked in pencil – out of a book on dispensing which I noticed at the dispensary of the Red Cross Hospital at Tadminster. The following is the extract . . .'[17]

'But, surely a bromide was not prescribed with the tonic?'

'No, Mr Le Juge. But you will recall that I mentioned an empty box of bromide powders. One of the powders introduced into the full bottle of medicine would effectively precipitate the strychnine and cause it to be taken in

---

16 In her *Autobiography* Christie describes the trouble she had with the formidable Miss Howse at The Bodley Head, who insisted on the spelling 'coco' rather than, as here, 'cocoa'. The first edition uses the former, and incorrect, 'coco'.

17 There are two blank lines in Notebook 37 at this point, presumably in order to check the chemical details as they appear in Chapter 12.

the last dose. You may observe that the "Shake the bottle" label always found on bottles containing poison has been removed. Now, the person who usually poured out the medicine was extremely careful to leave the sediment at the bottom undisturbed.'

A fresh buzz of excitement broke out and was sternly silenced by the judge.

'I can produce a rather important piece of evidence in support of that contention, because on reviewing the case, I came to the conclusion[18] that the murder had been *intended* to take place the night before. For in the natural course of events Mrs I[nglethorp] *would* have taken the last dose on the previous evening but, being in a hurry to see to the Fashion Fete she was arranging, she omitted to do so. The following day she went out to luncheon, so that she took the actual last dose *24 hours later* than had been anticipated by the murderer. As a proof that it was expected the night before, I will mention that the bell in Mrs Inglethorp's room was found cut on Monday evening, this being when Miss Paton was spending the night with friends. Consequently Mrs Inglethorp would be quite cut off from the rest of the house and would have been unable to arouse them, thereby making sure that medical aid would not reach her until too late.'

'Ingenious theory – but have you no proof?'

Poirot smiled curiously.

'Yes, Mr Le Juge – I have a proof. I admit that up to some hours ago, I merely *knew* what I have just said, without being able to *prove* it. But in the last few hours I have obtained a sure and certain proof, the missing link in the chain, a link *in the murderer's own hand,* the one slip he made. You will remember

---

18 The alternative version in Notebook 37 is 'all the evidence points to the . . .'

Notebook 37 showing the end of the deleted chapter from The Mysterious Affair at Styles. *See Footnote 19.*

the slip of paper held in Mrs Inglethorp's hand? That slip of paper has been found. For on the morning of the tragedy the murderer entered the dead woman's room and forced the lock of the despatch case. Its importance can be guessed at from the immense risks the murderer took. There was one risk he did not take – and that was the risk of keeping it on his own person – he had no time or opportunity to destroy it. There was only one thing left for him to do.'

'What was that?'

'To hide it. He did hide it and so cleverly that, though I have searched for two months it is not until today that I found it. Voila, ici le prize.'

With a flourish Poirot drew out three long slips of paper.

'It has been torn – but it can easily be pieced together. It is a complete and damning proof.[19] Had it been a little clearer in its terms it is possible that Mrs Inglethorp would not have died. But as it was, while opening her eyes to *who*, it left her in the dark as to *how*. Read it, Mr Le Juge. For it is an unfinished letter from the murderer, Alfred Inglethorp, to his lover and accomplice, Evelyn Howard.'

━━━━━━━━━━◄○►━━━━━━━━━━

And there, like Alfred Inglethorp's pieced-together letter at the end of Chapter 12, Notebook 37 breaks off, despite the fact that the following pages are blank. We know from the published version that Alfred Inglethorp and Evelyn Howard are subsequently arrested for the murder, John and Mary Cavendish are reconciled, Cynthia and Lawrence announce their engagement, while Dr Bauerstein is shown to be more interested in spying than in poisoning. The book closes with

---

19 Notebook 37 reads: 'damning (2) and complete (1)', which I interpret as a reminder to reverse the adjectives; it is followed by 'for it is a letter from the [murderer]', which is crossed out and reinstated in the last sentence.

Poirot's hope that this investigation will not be his last with 'mon ami' Hastings.

The reviews on publication were as enthusiastic as the pre-publication reports for John Lane. *The Times* called it 'a brilliant story' and the *Sunday Times* found it 'very well contrived'. *The Daily News* considered it 'a skilful tale and a talented first book', while the *Evening News* thought it 'a wonderful triumph' and described Christie as 'a distinguished addition to the list of writers in this [genre]'. 'Well written, well proportioned and full of surprises' was the verdict of *The British Weekly*.

Poirot's dramatic evidence in the course of the trial resembles a similar scene at the denouement of Leroux's *The Mystery of the Yellow Room* (1907), where the detective, Rouletabille, gives his remarkable and conclusive evidence from the witness box. Had John Lane but known it, in demanding the alteration to the denouement of the novel he unwittingly paved the way for a half century of drawing-room elucidations stage-managed by both Poirot and Miss Marple. And although this explanation, in both courtroom and drawing room, is essentially the same, the unlikelihood of a witness being allowed to give evidence in this manner is self-evident. In other ways also *The Mysterious Affair at Styles* presaged what was to become typical Christie territory – an extended family, a country house, a poisoning drama, a twisting plot, and a dramatic and unexpected final revelation.

It is not a very extended family, however. Of Mrs Inglethorp's family, there is a husband, two stepsons, one daughter-in-law, a family friend, a companion and a visiting doctor; there is the usual domestic staff although none of them is ever a serious consideration as a suspect. In other words, there are only seven suspects, which makes the disclosure of a surprise murderer more difficult. This very limited circle makes Christie's achievement in her first novel even more impressive. The usual clichéd view of Christie is that all of her novels are set in country houses and/or country villages. Statistically, this is inaccurate. Less than 30 (i.e. little over a third) of her titles are set in such surroundings, and the figure drops dramatically if you discount those set completely in a country house, as distinct from a village. But as Christie herself said, you have to set a book where people live.

Some ideas that feature in *The Mysterious Affair at Styles* would appear again throughout Christie's career. The dying Emily Inglethorp calls out the name of her husband, 'Alfred . . . Alfred', before she finally succumbs. Is the use of his name an accusation, an invocation, a plea, a farewell; or is it entirely meaningless? Similar situations occur in several novels over the next 30 years. One novel, *Why Didn't They Ask Evans?*, is built entirely around the dying words of the man found at the foot of the cliffs. In *Death Comes as the End*, the dying Satipy calls the name of the earlier victim, 'Nofret'; as John Christow lies dying at the edge of the Angkatells' swimming pool, in *The Hollow*, he calls out the name of his lover, 'Henrietta.' An extended version of the idea is found in *A Murder is Announced* when the last words of the soon-to-be-murdered Amy Murgatroyd, 'she wasn't there', contain a vital clue and are subjected to close examination by Miss Marple. Both *Murder in Mesopotamia* – 'the window' – and *Ordeal by Innocence* – 'the cup was empty' and 'the dove on the mast' – give clues to the method of murder. And the agent Carmichael utters the enigmatic 'Lucifer . . . Basrah' before he expires in Victoria's room in *They Came to Baghdad*.

The idea of a character looking over a shoulder and seeing someone or something significant makes its first appearance in Christie's work when Lawrence looks horrified at something he notices in Mrs Inglethorp's room on the night of her death. The alert reader should be able to tell what it is. This ploy is a Christie favourite and she enjoyed ringing the changes on the possible explanations. She predicated at least two novels – *The Mirror Crack'd from Side to Side* and *A Caribbean Mystery* – almost entirely on this, and it makes noteworthy appearances in *The Man in the Brown Suit*, *Appointment with Death* and *Death Comes as the End*, as well as a handful of short stories.

In the 1930 stage play *Black Coffee*,[20] the only original script to feature Hercule Poirot, the hiding-place of the papers containing the missing formula is the same as the one devised by Alfred Inglethorp. And in an exchange very reminiscent of a similar one in *The Mysterious Affair at Styles*, it is a chance remark by Hastings that leads Poirot to this realisation.

In common with many crime stories of the period there are two floor-plans and no less than three reproductions of handwriting. Each has a part to play in the eventual solution. And here also we see for the first time Poirot's remedy for steadying his nerves and encouraging precision in thought: the building of card-houses. At crucial points in both *Lord Edgware Dies* and *Three Act Tragedy* he adopts a similar strategy, each time with equally triumphant results. The important argument overheard by Mary Cavendish through an open window in Chapter 6 foreshadows a similar and equally important case of eavesdropping in *Five Little Pigs*.

In his 1953 survey of detective fiction, *Blood in their Ink*, Sutherland Scott describes *The Mysterious Affair at Styles* as 'one of the finest "firsts" ever written'. Countless Christie readers over almost a century would enthusiastically agree.

---

20 The original title of which was to have been *After Dinner.*

The Secret of Chimneys
12 June 1925

————————◄○►————————

A shooting party weekend at the country house
Chimneys conceals the presence of international
diplomats negotiating lucrative oil concessions with the
kingdom of Herzoslovakia. When a dead body is found,
Superintendent Battle's subsequent investigation
uncovers international jewel thieves, impersonation
and kidnapping as well as murder.

————————◄○►————————

'These were easy to write, not requiring too much plotting or planning.' In her *Autobiography*, Agatha Christie makes only this fleeting reference to *The Secret of Chimneys*, first published in the summer of 1925 as the last of the six books she had contracted to produce for John Lane when they accepted *The Mysterious Affair at Styles*. In this 'easy to write' category she also included *The Seven Dials Mystery*, published in 1929, and, indeed, the later title features many of the same characters as the earlier.

The Secret of Chimneys is not a formal detective story but a light-hearted thriller, a form to which she returned throughout her writing career with *The Man in the Brown Suit, The Seven Dials Mystery, Why Didn't they ask Evans?* and *They Came to Baghdad. The Secret of Chimneys* has all the ingredients of a good thriller of the period – missing jewels, a mysterious manuscript, compromising letters, oil concessions, a foreign throne, villains, heroes, and mysterious and beautiful women. It has distinct echoes of *The Prisoner of Zenda*, Anthony Hope's immortal swashbuckling novel that Tuppence recalls with affection in Chapter 2 of *Postern of Fate* – 'one's first introduction, really, to the romantic novel. The romance of Prince Flavia. The King of Ruritania, Rudolph Rassendyll . . .' Christie organised these classic elements into a labyrinthine plot and also managed to incorporate a whodunit element.

The story begins in Africa, a country Christie had recently visited on her world tour in the company of her husband Archie. The protagonist, the somewhat mysterious Anthony Cade, undertakes to deliver a package to an address in London. This seemingly straightforward mission proves difficult and dangerous and before he can complete it he meets the beautiful Virginia Revel, who also has a commission for him – to dispose of the inconveniently dead body of her blackmailer. This achieved, they meet again at Chimneys, the country estate of Lord Caterham and his daughter Lady Eileen 'Bundle' Brent. From this point on, we are in more 'normal' Christie territory, the country house with a group of temporarily isolated characters – and one of them a murderer.

That said, it must be admitted that a hefty suspension of disbelief is called for if some aspects of the plot are to be accepted. We are asked to believe that a young woman will pay a blackmailer a large sum of money (£40 in 1930 has the purchasing power today of roughly £1,500) for an indiscretion that she did not commit, just for the experience of being blackmailed (Chapter 7), and that two chapters later when the blackmailer is found inconveniently, and unconvincingly, dead in her sitting room, she asks the first person who turns up on her doorstep (literally) to dispose of the body, while she blithely goes away for the weekend. By its nature this type of thriller is light-hearted, but *The Secret of Chimneys* demands much indulgence on the part of the reader.

The hand of Christie the detective novelist is evident in elements of the narration. Throughout the book the reliability of Anthony Cade is constantly in doubt and as early as Chapter 1 he jokes with his tourist group (and, by extension, the reader) about his real name. This is taken as part of his general banter but, as events unfold, he is revealed to be speaking nothing less than the truth. For the rest of the book Christie makes vague statements about Cade and when we are given his thoughts they are, in retrospect, ambiguous.

Anthony looked up sharply.
'Herzoslovakia?' he said with a curious ring in his voice. [Chapter 1]

'. . . was it likely that any of them would recognise him now if they were to meet him face to face?' [Chapter 5]

'No connexion with Prince Michael's death, is there?'
His hand was quite steady. So were his eyes. [Chapter 18]

'The part of Prince Nicholas of Herzoslovakia.'
The matchbox fell from Anthony's hand, but his amazement was fully equalled by that of Battle. [Chapter 19]

'I'm really a king in disguise, you know' [Chapter 23]

And how many readers will wonder about the curious scene at the end of Chapter 16 when Anchoukoff, the manservant, tells him he 'will serve him to the death' and Anthony ponders on 'the instincts these fellows have'? Anthony's motives remain unclear until the final chapter, and the reader, despite the hints contained in the above quotations, is unlikely to divine his true identity and purpose.

There are references, unconscious or otherwise, to other Christie titles. The rueful comments in Chapter 5 when Anthony remarks, 'I know all about publishers – they sit on manuscripts and hatch 'em like eggs. It will be at least a year before the thing is published,' echo Christie's own experiences with John Lane and the publication of *The Mysterious Affair at Styles* five years earlier. The ploy of leaving a dead body in a railway left-luggage office, adopted by Cade in Chapter 9, was used in the 1923 Poirot short story 'The Adventure of the Clapham Cook'. Lord Caterham's description of the finding of the body in Chapter 10 distinctly foreshadows a similar scene almost 20 years later in *The Body in the Library* when Colonel Bantry shares his unwelcome experience. And Virginia Revel's throwaway comments about governesses and companions in Chapter 22 – 'It's awful but I never really look at them properly. Do you?' – would become the basis of more than a few future Christie plots, among them *Death in the Clouds*, *After the Funeral* and *Appointment with Death*. The same chapter is called 'The Red Signal', also the title of a short story from *The Hound of Death* (see Chapter 3). Both this chapter and the short story share a common theme.

There are a dozen pages of notes in Notebook 65 for the novel, consisting mainly of a list of chapters and their possible content with no surprises or plot variations. But the other incarnation of *The Secret of Chimneys* makes for more interesting reading. Until recently this title was one of the few Christies not adapted for stage, screen or radio. Or so it was thought, until it emerged that the novel was actually, very early in her career, Christie's first stage adaptation. The history of the play is, appropriately, mysterious. It was scheduled to appear at the Embassy Theatre in London in December 1931 but was replaced at the last moment by a play called *Mary Broome*, a twenty-year-old comedy by one Allan Monkhouse. The Embassy Theatre no longer exists and research has failed to discover a definitive reason for the last-minute cancellation and substitution. Almost a year before the proposed staging of *Chimneys*, Christie was writing from Ashfield in Torquay to her new husband, Max

Mallowan, who was on an archaeological dig. Rather than clarifying the sequence of events, these letters make the cancellation of the play even more mystifying:

> Tuesday [16 December 1930] Very exciting – I heard this morning an aged play of mine is going to be done at the Embassy Theatre for a fortnight with a chance of being given West End production by the Reandco [the production company]. Of course nothing may come of it but it's exciting anyway. Shall have to go to town for a rehearsal or two end of November.

> Dec. 23rd [1930] Chimneys is coming on here but nobody will say when. I fancy they want something in Act I altered and didn't wish to do it themselves.

> Dec. 31st [1930] If Chimneys is put on 23rd I shall stay for the first night. If it's a week later I shan't wait for it. I don't want to miss Nineveh and I shall have seen rehearsals, I suppose.

A copy of the script was lodged with the Lord Chamberlain on 19 November 1931 and approved within the week, and rehearsals were under way. But it was discovered that, due possibly to an administrative oversight, the licence to produce the play had expired on 10 October 1931. Why it was not simply renewed in order to allow the play to proceed is not clear but it may have been due to financial considerations, because at the end of February 1932 the theatre closed, to reopen two months later under new management, the former company Reandco (Alec Rea and Co.) having sold its interest. But it must be admitted that this theory is speculative.

Whatever happened during the final preparations, Christie herself was clearly unaware of any problems and was as surprised and as puzzled as anyone at the outcome. The last two references to the play appear in letters written during her journey home, via the Orient Express, in late 1931 from visiting Max in Nineveh. The dating of the letters is tentative, for she was as slipshod about dating letters as she was about dating Notebooks.

[Mid November 1931] I am horribly disappointed. Just seen in the Times that Chimneys begins Dec. 1st so I shall just miss it. Really is disappointing

[Early December 1931] Am now at the Tokatlian [Hotel in Istanbul] and have looked at Times of Dec 7th. And 'Mary Broome' is at the Embassy!! So perhaps I shall see Chimneys after all? Or did it go off after a week?

And that was the last that was heard of *Chimneys* for over 70 years, until a copy of the manuscript appeared, equally mysteriously, on the desk of the Artistic Director of the Vertigo Theatre in Calgary, Canada. So, almost three-quarters of a century after its projected debut, the premiere of *Chimneys* took place on 11 October 2003. And in June 2006, UK audiences had the opportunity to see this 'lost' Agatha Christie play, when it was presented at the Pitlochry Theatre Festival.

It is not known when exactly or, indeed, why Christie decided to adapt this novel for the stage. The use of the word 'aged' in the first letter quoted above would seem to indicate that it was undertaken long before interest was shown in staging it. The adaptation was probably done during late 1927/early 1928; a surviving typescript is dated July 1928. This would tally with the notes for the play; they are contained in the Notebook that has very brief, cryptic notes for some of the stories in *The Thirteen Problems*, the first of which appeared in December 1927. Nor does *The Secret of Chimneys* lend itself easily, or, it must be said, convincingly, to adaptation. If Christie decided in the late 1920s to dramatise one of her titles, one possible reason for choosing *The Secret of Chimneys* may have been her reluctance to put Poirot on the stage. She dropped him from four adaptations in later years – *Murder on the Nile, Appointment with Death, The Hollow* and *Go Back for Murder* (*Five Little Pigs*). The only play thus far to feature him was the original script, *Black Coffee*, staged the year before the proposed presentation of *Chimneys*. Yet, if she had wanted to adapt an earlier title, surely *The Mysterious Affair at Styles* or even *The Murder on the Links* would have been easier, set as they are largely in a single location and therefore requiring only one stage setting?

Perhaps with this in mind, the adaptation of *The Secret of Chimneys* is set entirely in Chimneys. This necessitated dropping large swathes of the novel (including the early scenes in Africa and the disposal, by Anthony, of Virginia's blackmailer) or redrafting these scenes for delivery as speeches by various characters. This tends to make for a clumsy Act I, demanding much concentration from the audience as they are made aware of the back-story; but it is necessary in order to retain the plot. The second and third Acts are more smooth-running and, at times, quite sinister, with the stage in darkness and a figure with a torch making his way quietly across the set. There are also sly references, to be picked up by alert Christie aficionados, to 'retiring and growing vegetable marrows' and to the local town of Market Basing, a recurrent Christie location.

The solution propounded in the stage version is the earliest example of Christie altering her own earlier explanation. She was to do this throughout her career. On the stage she gave extra twists to *And Then There Were None, Appointment with Death* and *Witness for the Prosecution*; on the page, to 'The Incident of the Dog's Ball'/*Dumb Witness*, 'Yellow Iris'/*Sparkling Cyanide* and 'The Second Gong'/'Dead Man's Mirror'. In *Chimneys* she makes even more drastic alterations to the solution of the original; the character unmasked as the villain at the end of the novel does not even appear in the stage adaptation.

Some correspondence between Christie and Edmund Cork, her agent, in the summer of 1951 would seem to indicate that there were hopes of a revival, or to be strictly accurate, a debut of the play, due to the topicality of 'recent developments in the oil business'; this is a reference to one of the elements of the plot, the question of oil concessions. But further developments in connection with a staging of the play, if any, remain unknown and it is clear that until Calgary in 2003 the script remained an 'unknown' Christie. The remote possibility that the script preceded the novel, which might have explained the unlikely choice of title for adaptation, is refuted by the reference in the opening pages of notes by the use of the phrase 'Incidents likely to retain'.

There are amendments to the original novel in view of the fact that the entire play is set in Chimneys. As the play opens a weekend house party, arranged in order to conceal a more important international meeting, is about to begin, and by the opening of Act I, Scene ii the murder has been committed. And, in a major change from the novel, Anthony Cade and Virginia Revel are the ones to find the body, although they say nothing and allow the discovery to be made the following morning. In a scene very reminiscent of a similar one in *Spider's Web*, Cade and Virginia examine the dead body and find the gun with Virginia's name; in view of the danger in which this would place her, they agree to remain quiet about their discovery. In effect, Act II opens at Chapter 10 of the book and from there on both follow much the same plan.

A major divergence is the omission of the scenes involving the discovery and disposal, by Cade, of the blackmailer's body. In fact, the entire blackmail scenario is substantially different. But whether written or staged, it is an unconvincing

PERSONS OF THE PLAY

----------◦◦◦----------

TREDWELL

MONSIEUR LEMAITRE

AN OLD LADY

LORD CATERHAM

LADY EILEEN BRENT (BUNDLE)

THE HONOURABLE GEORGE LOMAX

BILL EVERSLEIGH

ANTHONY CADE

VIRGINIA REVEL

THE STRANGER

SUPERINTENDENT BATTLE C.I.D.

HERMAN ISAACSTEIN

BORIS ANDRASSY

MONSIEUR X.

S C E N E S

----------◦◦◦----------

A C T I.

SCENE I.   The Council Chamber at Chimneys.
                (A September afternoon)

SCENE II.   The same.
                (11.30 that night)

A C T II.

SCENE: The Library at Chimneys.
                (The following morning)

A C T III.

SCENE I.   Same as Act I.
                (The same night)

SCENE II.   The same.
                (The following evening)

*The Cast of Characters and Scenes of the Play from a 1928 script
of Chimneys.*

red herring and it could have been omitted entirely from the script without any loss. Other changes incorporated into the stage version include the fact that Virginia has no previous connection with Herzoslovakia, an aspect of the book that signally fails to convince. The secret passage from Chimneys to Wyvern Abbey is not mentioned, the character Hiram Fish has been dropped and the hiding place of the jewels is different from, and not as well clued as, that in the novel.

The notes for *Chimneys* are all contained in Notebook 67. It is a tiny, pocket-diary sized notebook and the handwriting is correspondingly small and frequently illegible. In addition to the very rough notes for some of *The Thirteen Problems* the Notebook contains sketches of some Mr Quin short stories, as well as notes for a dramatisation of the Quin story 'The Dead Harlequin'. Overall, the notes for *Chimneys* do not differ greatly from the final version of the play, but substantial changes have been made from the original novel.

The first page reads:

People
Lord Caterham
Bundle
Lomax
Bill
Virginia
Tredwell
Antony
Prince Michael

Now what happens?

Incidents likely to retain – V[irginia] blackmailed

Idea of play
Crown jewels of Herzoslovakia stolen from assassinated King and Queen during house party at Chimneys – hidden there.

And twenty-five pages later she is amending her cast of characters:

Lord C
George
Bill
Tredwell
Battle
Inspector
Isaacstein
Bundle
Virginia
Antony
Lemaitre
Boris

The entire action of the play moves between the Library and the Council Chamber of Chimneys. The opening scene, which does not have an exact equivalent in the novel, introduces us to Lord Caterham, Bundle and George Lomax, the immensely discreet civil servant, arranging a top-level meeting that is to masquerade as a weekend shooting party. Chapter 16 of the novel has a brief reference to visitors being shown over the house and it is with such a brief scene that the play opens, as outlined below:

Act I Scene I – The Council Chamber

Lord C[aterham] in shabby clothes – Tredwell showing party over. 'This is the . . . .' A guest comes back for his hat tips Lord C. Bundle comes – 'First bit [of honest money] ever earned by the Brents.' She and Lord C – he complains of political party Lomax has dragged him into. Bundle says

why does he do it? George arrives and B goes. Explanation
etc. about Cade – the Memoirs – Streptiltich . . . the Press
– the strain of public life etc. Mention of diamond – King
Victor – stolen by the Queen, 3rd rate actress – more like a
comic opera – she killed in revolution

Despite the crossing-out and amended heading of this
extract, the following passage appears in the script as Act I,
Scene ii. It corresponds to Chapter 9 of the novel, although
there it takes place in Virginia's house. I have broken up the
extract and added punctuation to aid clarity.

Scene II – The Same (Evening)

Act II Scene I

That evening Antony arrives first – then V. He says about a
poacher – shots – They do go to bed early – no light except
in your window . . . – not this side of the house. Then she
talks about the man – his queer manner – didn't ask for
money – wanted to find out. Then discovery of body – she
screams. He stops her – takes her to chair.
'It's all right my dear, it's all right.'
'I'm quite all right.'
'You marvellous creature – anyone else would have fainted.'
'I want to look.'
He goes, coming back with revolver.
'Yes – stay.'
He asks her to look.
'You are marvellous'
'Have you ever seen him before?'
'Have I – Oh! Why, it's the man – he's different. He had
horn-rimmed glasses – spoke broken English.'
'This man wasn't . . . He was educated at Eton and Oxford'
'How do you know?'

'Oh, I know all right. I've – I've seen his pictures in the
newspapers'
'Have you ever had a pistol?'
'No'
'It's [an] automatic.' Shows her.
'It's got my name on it.'
'Did you tell anyone – anyone see come down here?
'Go up to bed.'
'Shouldn't I shut the window after you?'
'No – no . . .'
'But . . .'
'No tell tale footprints'
V goes. A. comes round – examines body. A little earth – he
sweeps it up – wipes fingerprints from handles inside. Then
goes out, looking at pistol.

Christie reorganises her earlier listing of acts and scenes,
although the sequence is somewhat confused:

Act II Scene I – The Library

[Act II] Scene II – The Council Chamber

Act III

Act II Scene I – The same (evening)
Scene II – The Library (next morning)

Act III The Council Chamber (that evening)
[Scene] II The same – the following evening

[Act II] Scene II The library next morning

Bundle and her father (the police and doctor)
Then begins – splutters – I've got Battle. Battle comes in,
asks for information. Scene much as before – plenty of rope
– gets him to look at body next door – watches him through

crack – Antony slips out unnoticed

And the third act is sketched twice, the second time in a more elaborate version:

Act III Scene I The following evening

Assembled in library – George and Battle read code letter – Richmond – they wait – struggle in darkness. Lights go up – Antony holding Lemaitre – always suspected this fellow – colleague from the Surete

Act III That evening ~~Battle and George~~

Virginia, Lord C, Bundle go to bed. Lights out – George and Battle – the cipher – George 3 – man in armour. They [struggle] – door opens – the window – shadows. Suddenly outbreak of activity – they roll over and over – the man in armour clangs down. Suddenly door opens – Lord C. switches on light – others behind him. Battle in front of window – Antony on top of Lemaitre – 'I've got you.'

As the above extract might suggest, *The Secret of Chimneys* is, both as novel and play, a hugely enjoyable but preposterous romp. Overall it is littered with loose ends, unlikely motivations and unconvincing characters. Characters drop notes with significant information; jewel thieves act with uncharacteristic homicidal responses; blackmail victims react with glee at a new 'experience' and bodies are disposed of with everyday nonchalance. And virtually nobody is who or what they seem. Why does Virginia not recognise Anthony if, as is reported in Chapters 15 and 24, she lived for two years in Herzoslovakia? Would someone really mistake a bundle of letters for the manuscript of a book? Would Battle accept Cade's bona-fides so easily? It is difficult not to have a certain amount of sympathy with the pompous George Lomax and to sympathise deeply with the unfortunate Lord Caterham.

There are glimpses of the Christie to come in the final surprise revelation and the double-bluff with King Victor (in a novel about a disputed kingdom, why use this name for a character unconnected with the throne?), but her earlier thriller, *The Man in the Brown Suit*, and the later book with some of the *Chimneys* characters, *The Seven Dials Mystery*, are, if not more credible, at least far less incredible.

The Mystery of the Blue Train
29 March 1928

The elegant train is the setting for the murder of wealthy American Ruth Kettering. Fellow passenger Katherine Grey assists Hercule Poirot as he investigates the murder and the disappearance of the fabulous jewel, the Heart of Fire, among the wealthy inhabitants of the French Riviera.

The Mystery of the Blue Train was written at the lowest point in Christie's life. In her *Autobiography* she writes, 'Really, how that wretched book came to be written I don't know.' Following her disappearance and her subsequent separation from Archie Christie, she went to Tenerife with her daughter Rosalind and her secretary, Carlo Fisher, to finish the book she had already started. Rosalind constantly interrupted the writing of it, as she was a child not given to entertaining herself and demanded attention from her preoccupied mother.

The writing of this book also represented an important

milestone in the career of Agatha Christie. She realised that she had advanced from amateur to professional status and now she had to write whether she wanted to or not. 'I was driven desperately on by the desire, indeed the necessity, to write another book and make money.' But 'I had no joy in writing, no élan. I had worked out the plot – a conventional plot, partly adapted from one of my other stories . . . I have always hated *The Mystery of the Blue Train* but I got it written and sent it off to the publishers. It sold just as well as my last book had done. So I had to content myself with that – though I cannot say I have ever been proud of it.' Most Christie fans would agree with her.

The short story to which she refers is 'The Plymouth Express', a minor entry in the Poirot canon, published in April 1923. It is a perfectly acceptable short story but it is debatable that it merited expansion into a novel. Frequently in the Notebooks she toys with the idea of expanding, inter alia, 'The Third Floor Flat' and 'The Rajah's Emerald'; why she opted for 'The Plymouth Express' remains a mystery. It is indeed a conventional plot and lacks both the ingenuity and glamour of her later train mystery, *Murder on the Orient Express*.

Extra complications in the shape of the history of the Heart of Fire are added in the novel and the inclusion of a new character, Katherine Grey, is significant. Katherine lives in St Mary Mead, although she does not know a certain Miss Jane Marple, who had made her detective debut some three months earlier in 'The Tuesday Night Club', the first of *The Thirteen Problems*. A quiet, determined, sensible young woman seeing the world for the first time, Katherine is a sympathetic character who captivates Poirot. And it is not fanciful to see her as a wish fulfilment for Christie herself.

The notes for *The Mystery of the Blue Train* are in Notebooks 1 and 54. Notebook 1 has a mere five pages but Notebook 54 has over 80, although the entries on each page are relatively short. They all reflect accurately the finished novel; no variations are considered and nor are there any ideas that did not make it into the published book, possibly because Christie was expanding a short story. For some reason the notes begin at Chapter 4 and then, 20 pages into Notebook 54, we find a listing of the earlier chapters, suggesting that the notes for those chapters had been destroyed.

I include a dozen pages from towards the end of Notebook 54. They contain Poirot's explanation of the crimes, a passage so close to the published version in Chapter 35 that it merits reproduction in full, although the published version is more elaborate. Nowhere else in the plotting of her books is there anything else like this. Her flowing handwriting covers the pages, elucidating a complex plot with a minimum of deletion. Much of the following passage is almost exactly as Agatha Christie wrote it in Tenerife in 1927; it appears in the Notebook almost without punctuation, but I have added only enough to make it readable. The single most concentrated example of continuous text in the Notebooks, it is an impressive example of Christie's fluency, clarity and readability – the factors that still play such an important part in her continuing popularity.

'Explanations? Mais oui, I will give them to you. It began with 1 point – the disfigured face, usually a question of identity; but not this time. The murdered woman <u>was</u> undoubtedly Ruth Kettering and I put it aside.'

'When did you first begin to suspect the maid?'

'I did not for some time – one trifling [point] – the note case – her mistress not on such terms as would make it likely – it awakened a doubt. She had only been with her mistress two months yet I could not connect her to the crime since she had been left behind in Paris. But once having a doubt I began to question that statement – how did we know? By the evidence of your secretary, Major Knighton, a completely outside and impartial testimony, and by the dead woman's own ~~confession~~ testimony to the conductor. I put that latter point aside for the moment because a very curious idea was growing up in my mind. Instead, I concentrated on the first point – at first sight it seemed conclusive but it led me to consider Major Knighton and at once certain points occurred to me. To begin with he, also, had only been with you for a period of 2 months and his initial was also K. Supposing – just supposing – that it was <u>his</u> notecase. If Ada Mason and he were working together and she recognised it, would she not act precisely as she had done? At first taken aback, she quickly ~~fell in with him~~ gave herself time to think and then suggested a plausible explanation that fell in with the idea of DK's guilt. That was not the original idea – the Comte de la Roche was to be the stalking horse – but after I had left the hotel she came to you and said she was quite convinced on thinking it over that the man was DK – why the sudden certainty? Clearly because she had had time to consult with someone and had received instructions – who could have given her these instructions? Major Knighton. And then came another slight incident – Knighton happened to mention that he has been at Lady Clanraven's when there had been a jewel robbery there. That might mean nothing or on the other hand it might mean a great deal. And so the links of the chain –'

'But I don't understand. Who was the man in the train?'

'There <u>was</u> no man – don't you see the cleverness of it all? Whose words have we for it, that there was a man. Only Ada Mason's – and we believe in Ada Mason because of Knighton's testimony.'

'And what Ruth said . . .'

'I am coming to that – yes – Mrs. Kettering's own testimony. But Mrs Kettering's testimony is that of a dead woman, who cannot come forward to dispute it.'

'You mean the conductor lied?'

'Not knowingly – the woman who spoke to him he believed in all good faith to be Mrs Kettering.'

'Do you mean that it wasn't her?'

'I mean that the woman who spoke to the conductor was the maid, dressed in her mistress's clothes – ~~wearing her~~ very distinctive clothes remember – more noticeable than the woman herself – the little red hat jammed down over the eyes – the long mink coat – the bunch of auburn curls each side of the face. Do you not know, however, that it is a commonplace nowadays how like one woman is to another in her street clothes.'

'But he must have noticed the change?'

'Not necessarily, ~~he saw~~ The maid handed him the tickets – he hadn't seen the mistress until he came to make up the bed. That was the first time he had a good look at her and that was the reason for disfiguring the face – he would probably have noticed that the dead woman was not the same as the woman he had talked to. ~~M. Grey would~~ The dining room attendants might have noticed and M. Grey of course would have, but by ordering a dinner basket that danger was avoided.'

'Then – where was Ruth?'

P[oirot] paused a minute and then said very quietly 'Mrs Kettering's dead body was rolled up in the rug on the floor in the adjoining compartment.'

'My God!'

'It is easily understood. Major Knighton was in Paris – on your business. He boarded the train somewhere on its way round the *ceinture* – he spoke perhaps of bringing some message from you – then he draws her attention to something out of the window slips the cord round her neck and pulls . . . .It is over in a minute. They ~~roll up~~ put the body in the adjoining compartment of which the door into

113

the corridor is locked. Major Knighton hops off the train again – with the jewel case. Since the crime is not supposed to be committed until several hours later he is perfectly safe and his evidence and the supposed Mrs. Kettering's words to the conductor will prove an alibi for her.

At the Gare de Lyon Ada Mason gets a dinner basket – then locks the door of her compartment – hurriedly changes into her mistress's clothing – making up to resemble her and adjusting some false auburn curls – she is about the same height. Katherine Grey saw her standing looking out of her window later in the evening and would have been prepared to swear that she was still alive then. Before getting to Lyons, she arranges the body in the bunk, changes ~~Her own~~ into a man's clothing and prepares to leave the train. ~~It must have been then that~~ When Derek Kettering enters his wife's compartment the scene had been set and Ada Mason was in the other compartment waiting for the train to stop so as to leave the train unobserved – it is now drawn into Lyons – the conductor swings himself down – she follows, unobtrusively however, to proceed by slouching inelegantly along as though just taking the air but in reality she crosses over and takes the first train back to Paris where she establishes herself at the Ritz. Her name has been ~~entered~~ registered as booking a room the night before by one of Knighton's female accomplices; she has only to wait for Mr. Van Aldin's arrival. The jewels are in Knighton's possession – not hers – and he disposes of them to Mr Papapolous[21] in Nice as arranged beforehand, entrusting them to her care only at the last minute to deliver to the Greek. All the same she made one little slip . . .'

'When did you first connect Knighton with the Marquis?'
'I had a hint from Mr Papapolous and I collected certain

---

21 Despite the spelling in the published version, this name is spelt Papapolous in Notebook 54.

information from Scotland Yard – I applied it to Knighton
and it fitted. He spoke French like a Frenchman; he had
been in America and France and England at roughly the
same times as the Marquis was operating. He had been last
heard of doing jewel robberies in Switzerland and it was in
Switzerland that you first met Major K. The Marquis was
famous for his charm of manner [which he used] to induce
you to offer him the post of secretary. It was at that time
that rumours were going round about your purchase of the
rubies – the Marquis meant to have these rubies. In seeing
that you had given them to your daughter he installed his
accomplice as her maid. It was a wonderful plan yet like
great men he has his weakness – he fell genuinely in love
with Miss Grey. It was that which made him so desirous
of shifting the crime from Mr Comte de la Roche to Derek
Kettering when the opportunity presented itself. And Miss
Grey suspected the truth. She is not a fanciful woman by
any means but she declares that she distinctly felt your
daughter's presence beside her one day at the Casino; she
says she was convinced that the dead woman was trying
to tell her something. Knighton had just left her – and it
was gradually [borne in on her] what Mrs Kettering had
been trying to convey to her – that Knighton was the man
who had murdered her. The idea seemed so fantastic at the
time that Miss Grey spoke of it to no one. But she acted on
the assumption that it was true – she did not discourage
Knighton's advances, and she pretended to him that she
believed in Derek Kettering's guilt. . . .

'There was one thing that was a shocking blow. Major
Knighton had a distinct limp, the result of a wound – the
Marquis had no such limp – that was a stumbling block.
Then Miss Tamplin mentioned one day that it had been
a great surprise to the doctors that he should limp – that
suggested camouflage. When I was in London I went to

the surgeon who had ~~looked after~~ been in charge at Lady Tamplin's Hospital and I got various technical details from him which confirmed my assumption. Then I met Miss Grey and found that she had been working towards the same end as myself. She had the cuttings to add – one a cutting of a jewel robbery at Lady Tamplin's Hospital, another link in the chain of probability and also that when she was out walking with Major Knighton at St. Mary Mead, he was so much off his guard that he forgot to limp – it was only a momentary lapse but she noted it. She had suspicion that I was on the same track when I wrote to her from the Ritz. I had some trouble in my inquiries there but in the end I got what I wanted – evidence that Ada Mason actually arrived on the morning after the crime.'

UNUSED IDEAS:
ONE

In *Agatha Christie's Secret Notebooks* I discussed some of the ideas that appeared in the Notebooks but were not further developed. Most of those included in the earlier volume were short, single ideas; a few lines scribbled by Christie in a Notebook as the idea came to her. But there are more elaborate ideas that, despite development beyond a few sentences, still did not result in a story. In some cases detailed character descriptions ('young schoolmaster type'), definite backgrounds ('Hellenic cruise setting') or exact plot devices ('real drink poisoned earlier') are listed; even titles ('Mousetrap II') are included. Many of these ideas seem very promising and it is easy to imagine most of them leading to a new 'Christie for Christmas'. Fragments of some of these ideas were used, perhaps slightly adapted, in published works and this was one of the advantages that Christie saw in the chaos of her Notebooks when she wrote in her *Autobiography*, 'What it's all about I can't remember now; but it often stimulates me, if not to write that identical plot, at least to write something else.'

This first selection includes two of the more elaborate sketches.

THE CLUEDO CASE

Book idea

George speaks to Poirot – his sister in law – she 'obliges' – giving evidence – but offered a very good post in Eire [Ireland] – can she take it? (or something [in] France). Or perhaps she is a 'Nannie' who now does a lot of 'cooking' in the house.

What evidence? Murder case but her evidence is quite unimportant

She saw Professor Plum in the library – with the candlestick. Shall the people be

~~General~~ Col. Mustard

Mrs. White – Housekeeper? ~~Or Col. M's sister~~

Miss Scarlet – young woman of doubtful morals – engaged to son? or secretary to Plum

Mrs. Peacock – Colonel's sister

Reverend Green – Former owner – in neighbourhood

Professor Plum – Old friend of Mustard

Result of conversation

'Nannie' or 'Daily Help' dies after cup of tea?

Now – what did she see or know that she didn't know she knew

A Point of Time

The siren goes on a Monday at a certain time. She says it always 'gives her a turn.' The point is siren went off at 11.30 and she has just said Professor Plum down stairs at 11.25 (really 11.35). Electric clock has been stopped and put on again

What a wonderful idea – the ultimate deviser of detective puzzles and the name most associated with the country-house murder mystery adapting the classic country-house murder mystery board game; and what a shame that it was never explored. This sketch appears in Notebook 12 between detailed notes for 1954's *Spider's Web* and the Marple short story 'Sanctuary', so the mid 1950s seems to be the most likely date of composition. This also tallies with the 1950 release date of Cluedo.

In many ways this sketch reads like an elaborate version of the 1924 Mr Quin short story 'The Sign in the Sky'. In that story a housemaid mentions seeing a 'sign' – the Hand of God, in reality the smoke from a passing train – at the time her mistress, Vivien Barnaby, is shot. Although during the investigation the time of the shot is taken from the clocks in the house, in reality the time of the train is accurate and the clocks have been altered by the murderer. Although she does not realise the importance of her evidence, the maid is subsequently offered, and accepts, a lucrative position in distant Canada. The variation in the unused idea above is a siren and an electric clock, but it is essentially the same plot. Unreliable clocks or watches are plot features of *The Murder at the Vicarage*, *Murder on the Orient Express* and *Evil under the Sun*.

The 'Nannie dying' idea featured in *Crooked House*, and the 'post abroad' ploy also appears in other titles. In Chapter 6 of *Why Didn't They Ask Evans?* Bobby is offered an attractive job in Buenos Aires and a similar offer is made to no less a person than Poirot himself in Chapter 1 of *The Big Four*. The concept of a character knowing something (dangerous to the killer) without realising its significance was a regular feature of Christie plots throughout her career. Sir Bartholomew Strange in *Three Act Tragedy*, Miss Sainsbury Seale in *One, Two, Buckle my Shoe*, Agnes Woddell in *The Moving Finger*, Heather Badcock in *The Mirror Crack'd from Side to Side* – all die without knowing why. And the unfortunate Mrs De Rushbridger, also in *Three Act Tragedy*, dies because she knows nothing.

———•◆•———

THE PLASTIC SURGEON

Old man is crook – played market etc. Or surgeon – plastic
Wife was hospital nurse – ill – heart – had to give up her job
– nursed old man – married him –
happy in a quiet way – had had love affair with young
medical student.
Morgan and Eiluned – son and wife – strong feelings
Selina – dau Kathleen – daughter – (Nurse Vernon?)
They have to live together in 'Crooked House' because of
War difficulties.
Old man holds purse strings – two children – Serena and
Edward
Tutor? Young man – wounded in War – a cripple – Miles
Dr. Kirkpatrick – Suggestion is that Gertrude killed him – or
Miles
Money is left to her
Possibly Dr. Kirkpatrick is her old boyfriend – he intends to
marry Kathleen
Triangle
Country House Rich man dead in (1) office (2) study in
suburban house
Crooked Mile (Dr. plastic surgeon – crook)
Old man like gnome – young hospital wife nurse

Crooked House
Crippled soldier with scarred face – old man is treating him
for war wounds – but not war wounds – really a murderer
Combine with Helen idea – man convinced he is a murderer.
Doctor persuades him and says he will remake his face

Crooked Man
Old gnome like man – plastic surgeon – (struck off for
unprofessional conduct – did surgery for crooks) – young

dumb house wife – boisterous son – hard intellectual wife –
grandchildren?
Intelligent boy? girl?
Fantastic persons in the house – young crippled tutor – in
love with wife

Although all of these extracts contain definite elements (and the title) of *Crooked House* – a young tutor, an old gnome-like man holding the purse-strings and a young wife – and all come from Notebook 14, they are included here because they also feature the Plastic Surgeon idea. With three attempts over a dozen pages it would seem that this idea was one that appealed to Christie but ultimately defeated her. It is probable that she abandoned it and subsumed most of these ideas into *Crooked House*. But there are foreshadowings of at least two other novels. The 'rich man dead in office' from the first extract explicitly presages *A Pocket Full of Rye*, and both 'Combine with Helen idea' and 'man convinced he is a murderer' have strong echoes of *Sleeping Murder*.

Favourite Stories and 'The Man Who Knew'

'Looking back over the past, I become increasingly sure of one thing. My tastes have remained fundamentally the same.'

————————◄◊►————————

What were Agatha Christie's own personal favourites among the many stories she wrote? In February 1972, in reply to a Japanese fan, she listed, with brief comments, her favourite books. But she makes an important point when she writes that her list of favourites would 'vary from time to time, as every now and then I re-read an early book . . . and then I alter my opinion, sometimes thinking that it is much better than I thought it was – or nor as good as I had thought'. Although the choices are numbered it is not clear if they are in order of preference; she adds brief comments and reiterates her earlier point when she heads the list:

At the moment my own list would possibly be:
And Then There Were None – 'a difficult technique which was a challenge . . .'
The Murder of Roger Ackroyd – 'a general favourite . . .'
A Murder is Announced – 'all the characters interesting . . .'

Murder on the Orient Express – '. . . it was a new idea for a plot.'

The Thirteen Problems – 'a good series of short stories.'

Towards Zero – '. . . interesting idea of people from different places coming towards a murder instead of starting with the murder and working from that.'

Endless Night – 'my own favourite at present.'

Crooked House – '. . . a study of a certain family interesting to explore.'

Ordeal by Innocence – 'an idea I had for some time before starting to work upon it.'

The Moving Finger – 're-read lately and enjoyed reading it again, very much.'

The list does not contain any great surprises and most fans would probably also select most of the same titles, perhaps replacing *The Thirteen Problems* and *The Moving Finger* with *The Labours of Hercules* and *The A.B.C. Murders* respectively. Despite, or perhaps because of, Christie's lifelong association with Hercule Poirot, there are only two of his cases included, while Miss Marple is represented by three. Each decade of her writing career is represented and no less than five of the list are non-series titles.

A further insight, this time into some of her favourite short stories, came two years later. In March 1974 negotiations began between Collins and the author on the thorny subject of that year's 'Christie for Christmas'. 'Thorny' because the previous year's *Postern of Fate* had been a disappointment and, at the request of Christie's daughter Rosalind, the publisher was not pressing for a new book. The compromise was to be a collection of previously published short stories. Sir William ('Billy') Collins mooted the idea of a collection of Poirot short stories but, in a letter ('Dear Billy'), his creator felt that a book of stories entirely devoted to Hercule

Poirot would be 'terribly monotonous' and 'no fun at all'. She hoped to persuade him that the collection 'could also include what you might describe as Agatha Christie's own favourites among her own early stories'. To this end she sent him a list described as 'my own favourite stories written soon after *The Mysterious Affair at Styles,* some before that'.

Before looking at this list it is important to remember that Dame Agatha was now in her eighty-fourth year, in failing health and a pale shadow of the creative genius of earlier years. She had not written a pure whodunit since *A Caribbean Mystery* in 1964 and the novels of recent years were all journeys into the past (both her own and her characters'), lacking the ingenious plots and coherent writing of her prime. If she had compiled a similar list even ten years earlier is it entirely possible that it would have been significantly different. Even the description of 'early stories' was, as we shall see, misleading.

Christie's 1974 list reads as follows:

The Red Signal
The Lamp
The Gypsy
The Mystery of the Blue Jar
The Case of Sir Andrew Carmichael
The Call of Wings
The Last Séance
S.O.S.
In a Glass Darkly
The Dressmaker's Doll
Sanctuary
Swan Song
The Love Detectives
Death by Drowning

Also included are two full-length novels, *Dumb Witness* and *Death Comes as the End*, although she acknowledges that the former is too long for inclusion. Perhaps significantly, in both these titles, like her recent publications, there are strong elements of 'murder in retrospect'; *Death Comes as the End* deals with murder in ancient Egypt and *Dumb Witness* finds Poirot investigating a death that occurred some months before the book begins. On her list the titles are numbered but there is no indication that the order is significant. I have regrouped them for ease of discussion.

The first eight titles are all from the 1933 UK-only collection *The Hound of Death*. As Christie suspected, many of them had been published prior to this in various magazines, the earliest (so far traced) as far back as June 1924 when 'The Red Signal' appeared in *The Grand*. The supernatural is the common theme linking these stories, with only 'The Mystery of the Blue Jar', published in *The Grand* the following month, offering a rational explanation. This type of story was on Christie's mind as, later in the accompanying letter, she explains that she was planning a 'semi-ghost story', adding poignantly, 'when I am really quite myself again.' Some of these titles are particularly effective – 'The Lamp' has a chilling last line and 'The Red Signal', despite its supernatural overtones, shows Christie at her tricky best. 'The Last Séance' (March 1927) is a very dark and, unusually for Christie, gruesome story, which also exists in a full-length play version among her papers; while 'The Call of Wings' is one of the earliest stories she wrote, described in her *Autobiography* as 'not bad'.

Of the remaining six titles, 'In a Glass Darkly' (December 1934) and 'The Dressmaker's Doll' (December 1958) are also concerned with supernatural events. The former is a very short story involving precognition while the latter is a late story that Christie felt that she 'had to write' while plotting *Ordeal by Innocence*. She passed it to her agent in mid-December 1957 and it was published the following year; in a note she describes it as a 'very favourite' story. 'Sanctuary' is also a late story, written in January 1954 and published in October of that year, for the Fund for the Restoration of Westminster Abbey. Appropriately it features a dying man found on the chancel steps while the sun pours in through the stained-glass window, this picture carrying echoes of similar scenes in the Mr Quin stories. Its setting is Chipping Cleghorn, featured four years earlier in *A Murder is Announced*, and Rev. Harmon and his delightful wife, Bunch, are the main protagonists alongside Miss Marple.

'Swan Song', published in *The Grand* in September 1926, is a surprising inclusion and appears probably due to Christie's lifelong love of music; despite its country house setting of an opera production, it is a lacklustre revenge story with neither a whodunit nor supernatural element. 'The Love Detectives', published in December of the same year, fore-shadows the plot of *The Murder at the Vicarage* and features Mr Satterthwaite, usually the partner of Mr Quin but here making a solo appearance.

The final story, 'Death by Drowning', is the last of *The Thirteen Problems*, although its inclusion jars with the rest of the stories in that collection. Unlike the first 12 problems, 'Death by Drowning', first published in November 1931, the year before its book appearance, does not follow the pat-tern of a group of armchair detectives solving a crime that has hitherto baffled the police. Miss Marple solves this case without her fellow-detectives and makes one of her very rare forays into working-class territory in a story involving a woman who keeps lodgers and takes in washing. As an untyp-ical Miss Marple story, it is another unpredictable inclusion.

Overall, the list is, like much of her fiction, very unex-pected. Though the absence of Poirot can be explained by the fact that this list is an effort to persuade Billy Collins to experiment with characters other than the little Belgian, there is, for instance, only one Mr Quin story, although she describes them in her *Autobiography* as 'her favourite'; and there are only two cases for Miss Marple, neither of which shows her at her best. Why, moreover, no 'Accident', no 'Witness for the Prosecution', no 'Philomel Cottage'? And only three ('Sanctuary', 'The Love Detectives', 'Death by Drowning') can be described as Christie whodunits, albeit not very typical examples. The over-reliance on the supernatural is surprising, although this had been a feature of Christie's fiction from her early days – *The Mysterious Mr Quin, The Hound of Death* – and is a plot feature, although usually in the red herring category, of such novels as *The Sittaford Mystery, Peril at End House, Dumb Witness, The Pale Horse* and *Sleeping Murder.*

In the event, the proposed book never came to fruition and, despite Christie's reservations, *Poirot's Early Cases* was published in November 1974.

Pre-dating both theses lists, in her *Autobiography* Christie names yet another selection of 'favourites'. Here she describes *Crooked House* and *Ordeal by Innocence* as 'the two [books] that satisfy me best', and goes on to state that 'on re-reading them the other day, I find that another one I am really pleased with is *The Moving Finger*'. A *Sunday Times* interview with literary critic Francis Wyndham in February 1966 confirms these three titles as favourites, although the interview may have been contemporaneous with the completion of her *Autobiography* in October 1965 where the mention of the three titles comes in the closing pages. In the specially written Introduction to the Penguin paperback edition of *Crooked House* she wrote: 'This book is one of my own special favourites. I saved it up for years, thinking about, working it out, saying to myself "One day when I've plenty of time, and really want to enjoy myself – I'll begin it."'

127

Whatever her favourites, there seems little doubt about her least favourite title. Not only was *The Mystery of the Blue Train* difficult to compose (See Chapter 2) but in her *Autobiography* she writes 'Each time I read it again, I think it commonplace, full of clichés, with an uninteresting plot.' In the Japanese fan letter referred to above, she calls it 'conventionally written . . . [it] does not seem to me to be a very original plot.' She is even more disparaging in the Wyndham interview when she says, 'Easily the worst book I ever wrote was *The Mystery of the Blue Train*. I hate it.'

THE RED SIGNAL/THE MAN WHO KNEW

In view of the inclusion of 'The Red Signal' on the 1974 list above, it is appropriate that 'The Man Who Knew', a very short short story from the Christie Archive, should appear here in print for the first time; and it is interesting to compare and contrast it with its later incarnation as 'The Red Signal'.

'The Man Who Knew' is very short, less than 2,000 words, and the typescript is undated. The only guidance we have for a possible date of composition is the reference in the first paragraph to No Man's Land, suggesting that the First World War is over. In all probability, its composition pre-dates the publication of *The Mysterious Affair at Styles*; and this makes its very existence surprising. Very few short story manuscripts or typescripts, even from later in Christie's career, have survived, so one from the very start of her writing life is remarkable.

The only handwritten amendments are insignificant ones ('minute service flat' is changed to 'little service flat'), but some minor errors of spelling and punctuation have here been corrected.

The Man Who Knew

Something was wrong . . .

Derek Lawson, halting on the threshold of his flat, peering into the darkness, knew it instinctively. In France, amongst the perils of No Man's Land, he had learned to trust this strange sense that warned him of danger. There was danger now – close to him . . .

Rallying, he told himself the thing was impossible. Withdrawing his latchkey from the door, he switched on the electric light. The hall of the flat, prosaic and commonplace, confronted him. Nothing. What should there be? And still, he knew, insistently and undeniably, that something was wrong . . .

Methodically and systematically, he searched the flat. It was just possible that some intruder was concealed there. Yet all the time he knew that the matter was graver than a mere attempted burglary. The menace was to *him*, not to his property. At last he desisted, convinced that he was alone in the flat.

'Nerves,' he said aloud. 'That's what it is. Nerves!'

By sheer force of will, he strove to drive the obsession of imminent peril from him. And then his eyes fell on the theatre programme that he still held, carelessly clasped in his hand. On the margin of it were three words, scrawled in pencil.

'Don't go home.'

For a moment, he was lost in astonishment – as though the writing partook of the supernatural. Then he pulled himself together. His instinct had been right – there *was* something. Again he searched the little service flat, but this time his eyes, alert and observant, sought carefully some detail, some faint deviation from the normal, which should give him the clue to the affair. And at last he found it. One of the bureau drawers was not shut to, something hanging out prevented it closing, and he remembered, with perfect clearness, closing the drawer himself earlier in the evening. There had been nothing hanging out then.

His lips setting in a determined line, he pulled the drawer open. Underneath the ties and handkerchiefs, he felt the outline of something hard – something that had not been there previously. With amazement on his countenance, he drew out – a revolver!

He examined it attentively, but beyond the fact that it was of somewhat unusual calibre, and that a shot had lately been fired from it, it told him nothing.

He sat down on the bed, the revolver in his hand. Once again he studied the pencilled words on the programme. Who had been at the theatre party? Cyril Dalton, Noel Western and his wife, Agnes Haverfield and young Frensham. Which of them had written that message? Which of them *knew* – knew what? His speculations were brought up with a jerk. He was as far as ever from understanding the meaning of that revolver in his drawer. Was it, perhaps, some practical joke? But instantly his inner self negatived that, and the conviction that he was in danger, in grave immediate peril, heightened. A voice within him seemed to be crying out, insistently and urgently: 'Unless you understand, you are lost.'

And then, in the street below, he heard a newsboy calling.

Acting on impulse, he slipped the revolver into his pocket, and, banging the door of the flat behind him, hurriedly descended the stairs. Outside the block of buildings, he came face to face with the newsvendor.

''Orrible murder of a well known physician. 'Orrible murder of a – paper, sir?'

He shoved a coin into the boy's hand, and seized the flimsy sheet. In staring headlines he found what he wanted.

HARLEY STREET SPECIALIST MURDERED. SIR JAMES
LAWSON FOUND SHOT THROUGH THE HEART.

His uncle: Shot!

He read on. The bullet had been fired from a revolver, but the weapon had not been found, thus disposing of the idea of suicide.

The weapon – *it was in his pocket now.* why he knew this with such certainty, he could not have said. But it was so. He accepted it without doubt, and in a blinding flash the terrible peril of his position became clear to him.

He was his uncle's heir – he was in grave financial difficulties. And only that morning he had quarrelled with the old man. It had been a loud bitter quarrel, doubtless overheard by the servants. He had said more than he meant, of course – used threats – it would all tell against him! And as a culminating proof of his guilt, they would have found the revolver in his drawer . . .

Who had placed it there?

It all hung on that. There might still be time. He thought desperately, his brain, keen and quick, selecting and rejecting the various arguments. And at last he saw . . .

A taxi deposited him at the door of the house he sought.

'Mr Weston still up?'

'Yes, sir. He's in the study.'

'Ah!' Derek arrrested the old butler's progress. 'You needn't announce me. I know the way.'

Walking almost noiselessly upon the thick pile of the carpet, he opened the door at the end of the hall and entered the room. Noel Western was sitting by the table, his back to the door. A fair, florid man; good looking, yet with a something in his eyes that baffled and eluded. Not till Derek's hand touched his shoulder, was he aware of the other's presence. He leaped in his chair.

'My God, you!' He forced a laugh. 'What a start you gave me, old chap. What is it? Did you leave something behind here?'

'No.' Derek advanced a step. 'I came to return you – *this*!'

Taking the revolver from his pocket he threw it on the table. If he had had any doubts, they vanished now before the look on the other's face.

'What-what is it?' stammered Western.

'The revolver with which you shot James Lawson.'

'That's a lie.' The denial came feebly.

'It's the truth. You took my latchkey out of my overcoat pocket this evening. You remember that your wife and I went in the first taxi to the theatre. You followed in another, arriving rather late. You were late because you had been to my rooms to place the revolver in my drawer.'

Derek spoke with absolute certainty and conviction. An almost supernatural fear showed upon Noel Western's face.

'How – how did you know?' he muttered, as it were in spite of himself.

'*I* warned him.'

Both men started and turned. Stella Western, tall and beautiful, stood in the doorway which connected with an adjoining room. Her fairness gleamed white against the sombre green of the window curtains.

'I warned him,' she repeated, her eyes full on her husband. 'Tonight, when Mr Lawson mentioned casually something about returning home, I saw your face. I was just beside you, although you did not notice me, and I heard you mutter between your teeth "There'll be a surprise for you when you do get home!" And the look on your face was – devilish. I was afraid. I had no chance of saying anything to Mr Lawson, but I wrote a few words on the programme and passed it to him. I didn't know what you meant, or what you had planned – but I was afraid.'

'Afraid, were you?' cried Western. 'Afraid for *him*! You still may be! That's why I did it! That's why he'll hang – yes, hang – hang – hang! Because you love him!' His voice had risen almost to a scream, as he thrust his head forward with blazing eyes. 'Yes – I knew! You loved him! That's why you wanted me to see that meddling old fool, Lawson, who called himself a mental specialist. You wanted to make out I was mad. You wanted me put away – shut up – so that you could go to your lover!'

'By God, Western,' said Derek, taking a step forward with blazing eyes. He dared not look at Stella. But behind his anger and indignation, a wild exultation possessed him. She loved him! Only too well he knew that he loved her. From the first moment he had set eyes on her, his doom was sealed. But she was another man's wife – and that man his friend. He had fought down his love valiantly, and never, for one moment, had he suspected there was any feeling on her side. If he had known that – he struggled to be calm. He must defend her from these raving accusations.

'It was a conspiracy – a great conspiracy.' The high unnatural voice took no heed of Derek. 'Old Lawson was in it. He questioned me – he trapped me – found out all about my mother having died in an asylum (Ha ha! Stella, you never knew that, did you?). Then he spoke about a sanitorium – a rest cure – all lies! Lies – so that you could get rid of me and go to your lover here.'

133

'Western, you lie! I've never spoken a word to your wife that the whole world couldn't hear.'

Noel Western laughed, and the laugh frightened them both, for in it was all the low cunning of a maniac.

'You say so, do you? *You* say so!' Carried away by fury, his voice rose higher and higher, drowning the protests of the other, drowning the sound of the opening door. 'But I've been too clever for you! Old Lawson's dead. I shot him. Lord! what fun it was – knowing who'd hang for it! You see, I'd heard of your quarrel, and I knew you were in pretty deep financial water. The whole thing would look ugly. I saw it all clearly before me. Lawson dead, you hung, and Stella – pretty Stella – all to myself! Ha ha!'

For the first time, the woman flinched. She put up her hands to her face with a shivering sob.

'You say you saw it all clearly before you,' said Derek. There was a new note in his voice, a note of solemnity. 'Did you never think that there was something *behind* you?'

Quelled in spite of himself, Noel Western stared fearfully at the man before him.

'What – what do you mean?'

'Justice.' The word cut the air with the sharpness of steel.

A mocking smile came to Western's lips.

'The justice of God, oh?' he laughed.

'And the justice of men. *Look behind you!*'

Western spun round to face a group of three standing in the doorway, whilst the old butler repeated the sentence that his master's words had drowned before.

'Two gentlemen from Scotland Yard to see Mr Lawson, sir.'

An awful change came over Noel Western's face. He flung up his arms and fell. Derek bent over him, then straightened himself.

'The justice of God is more merciful than that of men,' he said. 'You do not wish to detain me, gentlemen? No? Then

I will go.' For a moment his eyes met Stella's, and he added softly: 'But I shall come back . . .'

---◅◦▻---

The expansion of 'The Man Who Knew' into 'The Red Signal' suggests that Christie rewrote this after some experience in plotting a detective story. 'The Red Signal' was first published in June 1924, so we can assume that it was written probably the previous year and, therefore, after the publication of *The Mysterious Affair at Styles* and *The Murder on the Links*, both novels with carefully constructed plots and unsuspected denouements. By the beginning of 1924 she had also published a dozen Poirot short stories. Technically, she was now more adept at laying clues, both true and false, misdirecting the reader and springing a surprise.

Plot-wise both versions of the story are identical, the later one merely longer and more elaborate than the earlier. Some elements remain exactly the same – the description of Stella's husband as 'florid', the ominous words 'Don't go home', the revolver found in the handkerchief drawer. But 'The Red Signal' has a larger cast of characters, a greater emphasis on the supernatural and a more unexpected revelation at the end. Unlike the earlier version the reader is encouraged to trust the character unmasked as the villain; in the earlier version Noel Western is unknown to the reader until his unmasking. The cunning hand of Christie the detective novelist can be seen in some of the plot expansion – the ambiguous conversation between Dermot and his uncle when we are mistakenly confident, after subtle misdirection, that the subject of the conversation about insanity is Clair; the red signal of the title, the warning 'Don't go home', which applies equally to Sir Arlington and to Dermot; and the ruse of Dermot masquerading as his own servant, which would become one of Christie's favourite stratagems for hoodwinking her readers. On a more mundane note however, is it likely that a newsboy would sell newspapers and shout headlines at close to midnight? If the party has just returned from the theatre it cannot be much earlier.

While by no means a typical Christie tale, we can see how, after writing a mere handful of detective stories, Agatha Christie was able to transform a slight short story such as 'The Man Who Knew' into a clever exercise in misdirection.

4

The Second Decade 1930–1939

'The funny thing is that I have little memory of the books I wrote just after my marriage. '

————————◄○►————————

————————◄○►————————

The years 1930 to 1939 were undoubtedly Agatha Christie's Golden Age, in terms of ingenuity, productivity and diversity. In 1930 she published the first Miss Marple novel, *The Murder at the Vicarage*, and the first Mary Westmacott, *Giant's Bread*. By the end of the decade she had produced a further 16 full-length novels and six short story/novella collections (seven if the US-only *The Regatta Mystery* in 1939 is included). Many of her classic titles appeared in this decade. She experimented with the detective story form in *And Then There Were None* (1939), she broke the rules in *Murder on the Orient Express* (1934), she pioneered an early example of the serial

137

killer in *The A.B.C. Murders* (1936) and wrote a light-hearted thriller with *Why Didn't They Ask Evans?* (1934). Reflecting her own love of travel, she sent Poirot abroad in *Murder in Mesopotamia* (1936), *Death on the Nile* (1937) and *Appointment with Death* (1938), for the type of detective experience not shared by most of his literary crime-solving contemporaries.

As well as an impressive output of detective novels, she also published short stories – crime fantasy with *The Mysterious Mr Quin* (1930), the supernatural in *The Hound of Death* (1933), a mixture of crime, romance and light-hearted adventure in *The Listerdale Mystery* and *Parker Pyne Investigates* (both 1934); and mastered the difficult novella form in *Murder in the Mews* (1937). Despite the first appearance of Miss Marple in a full-length book and the publication of some of Poirot's best cases, she also published non-series titles – *The Sittaford Mystery* (1931) and *Murder is Easy* (1939). In addition, she wrote the scripts for *Black Coffee* (1930), her only original Poirot play, and *Akhnaton* (written 1937), a historical drama set in ancient Egypt. She contributed to the round-robin detective stories of the Detection Club, *Behind the Screen* in 1930 and *The Floating Admiral* and *The Scoop* in 1931; and she wrote her first radio play, *Yellow Iris* (1937).

She would never again – perhaps not surprisingly – equal this productivity; the second half of the following decade saw her slow down to a mere one title a year. But the truly astonishing aspect of this output is not just the volume but also the consistency. None of the titles produced in these years fall below the level of excellent. All of them display her talents – ingenuity and readability, intricacy and simplicity – at the height of their powers and many are now recognised classics of the genre, representing a standard which other crime writers strove to match.

Her work was in demand for the lucrative magazine market in the UK and North America and for translation throughout

Europe. She was one of the first writers to be chosen, in 1935, for publication in the new Penguin paperbacks; and her hardback sales for each new title entered the five-figure category. From *Three Act Tragedy* (1935) onwards her first-year sales never fell below 10,000. Film versions of her work – *Alibi* (based on *The Murder of Roger Ackroyd*) and *Black Coffee,* both in 1931, and *Lord Edgware Dies* in 1934 – were released, although all three featured a seriously miscast Austin Trevor, a six foot tall Irishman, in the role of Poirot; and *Love from a Stranger,* adapted from the short story 'Philomel Cottage', appeared in 1937 with Joan Hickson in a small role. *Black Coffee* and *Love from a Stranger* had been produced as stage plays earlier in the decade; and *Chimneys,* her own stage adaptation of her 1925 novel, was scheduled to appear in 1931 but was cancelled for reasons still unknown. The first Christie, and Poirot, on television came in June 1937 with the broadcast of *Wasp's Nest.*

It is entirely possible that Christie's happy personal life was, at least in part, responsible for this productive professional life. In September 1930 she had married Max Mallowan, thus ending the profoundly unhappy period of her life which began with the death of her mother in 1926 and culminated in her divorce from Archie Christie in 1928. Secure in a stable marriage, with a happy and healthy daughter, and spending some months of every year cheerfully working on an archaeological dig with her husband, she produced new books with enviable ease. And to judge from the evidence of the Notebooks, plot ideas for future books were not in short supply. The early 1930s coincide with the most indecipherable pages of the Notebooks, when her handwriting could hardly keep pace with her ingenuity. By the mid 1930s, reading the latest Agatha Christie had become not just a national but an international pastime.

The Murder at the Vicarage
13 October 1930

———————————◄○►———————————

When unpopular churchwarden Colonel Protheroe
is found shot in the vicar's study in St Mary Mead, the
vicar's neighbour identifies seven potential murderers.
Two confessions, an attempted suicide and a robbery
confuse the issue but Miss Marple understands
everything when she realises the significance of the
potted palm.

———————————◄○►———————————

The Murder at the Vicarage was the first Agatha Christie title
issued under the new Crime Club imprint, and the first
book-length investigation for Miss Marple. It appeared in
serial form in the USA three months before its UK publication, leading to the conclusion that the bulk of the novel was
completed during 1929. Disappointingly, Christie writes in
her *Autobiography* that 'I cannot remember where, when or
how I wrote it, why I came to write it or even what suggested
to me that I should select a new character – Miss Marple.'
She goes on to explain that the enjoyment she got from the
creation of the Caroline Sheppard character in *The Murder of
Roger Ackroyd* was a factor in the decision to re-create an 'acidulated spinster, full of curiosity, knowing everything, hearing
everything; the complete detective service in the home'. The
character of Miss Marple in *The Murder at the Vicarage* is considerably different from the Miss Marple of her next case 12
years later, *The Body in the Library*.

Jane Marple made her first appearance in print in a series
of six short stories published between December 1927 and
May 1928 in the *Royal Magazine*, beginning with 'The Tuesday

Night Club'. A further six stories were published between December 1929 and May 1930 in *The Story-Teller* and all 12 were published, with the addition of 'Death by Drowning', as *The Thirteen Problems* in June 1932. In the first story Miss Marple sits in her house in St Mary Mead, dressed completely in black – black brocade dress, black mittens and black lace cap – in the big grandfather chair, knitting and listening and solving crimes that have baffled the police. She is described as 'smiling gently' and having 'benignant and kindly' blue eyes. But the first description we receive of her, from the vicar's wife, Griselda, in *The Murder at the Vicarage* is 'that terrible Miss Marple . . . the worst cat in the village'. The vicar himself, while describing her as 'a white-haired old lady with a gentle, appealing manner', also concedes that 'she is much more dangerous' than her fellow parishioner the gushing Miss Wetherby. He captures the essence of Miss Marple when he states in Chapter 4 that 'There's no detective in England equal to a spinster lady of uncertain age with plenty of time on her hands.' By 1942 and *The Body in the Library*, Miss Marple has cast off, temporarily at least, both St Mary Mead and her black lace mittens to accompany Dolly Bantry to the Majestic Hotel in Danemouth to solve the murder of Ruby Keene. And thereby to join the company of the Great Detectives.

The Murder at the Vicarage has its origins in the Messrs Satterthwaite and Quin short story 'The Love Detectives', published in December 1926 in *The Storyteller* magazine. Here two adulterous lovers commit murder and then confess separately, confident in the knowledge that if they make the 'confessions' incredible enough (they each claim to have used different and incorrect weapons), neither of them will be believed. In both short story and novel the victim is the husband, and the killers are his wife and her lover. Significantly, in each case a stopped clock causes confusion as to the time of death. The novel adapts the motive, the means and the device of false confessions, adds extra suspects and replaces the duo of Satterthwaite and Quin with Miss Marple; but they are, essentially, the same story.

The notes for *The Murder at the Vicarage* are all contained in Notebook 33 and consist of 70 very organised pages that closely follow the progress of the novel. For the early chapters the chapter number is included; thereafter the remainder of the notes follow the novel in chronological order. There is little in the notebook that is not included in the published version. Two maps of St Mary Mead are included and the rest of Notebook 33 contains the draft for *Three Act Tragedy*.

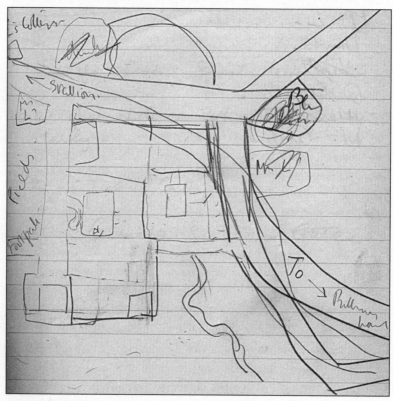

From Notebook 33 Christie's own sketch of St Mary Mead for The Murder at the Vicarage *showing most of the locations that appear in that novel.*

For some reason, the notes for *The Murder at the Vicarage* begin at Chapter 3; there is no record anywhere of the first two chapters. The extracts below have been edited for clarity.

Chapter III
Griselda and Vicar – Vicar meets Mrs L[estrange] at Church – shows her round. Studio – he goes to it to see picture – Anne and Lawrence. Anne comes to him in Study – taps on window
Chapter IV
Dinner that night – Lawrence there – Dennis – afterwards Lawrence with vicar. Dennis comes in after Lawrence has gone – wants to tell things. Says 'What a rotten thing gossip is.' Where does Mrs Lestrange go to at night.
Chapter V
Vicar called away – returns and discovers body.

Although the next extract is labelled 'Chapter VII' in the Notebook, it appears in the published novel as Chapter 6. From here on the Notebook does not specify chapter headings; I have added the actual chapter numbers to preserve the chronology:

Chapter VII [actually Chapter 6]
Inspector shuts up room and window and leaves word no-one is to go in. Learns from Mary next morning Mr Redding has been arrested – Griselda says 'What' – incredulous – couldn't be Lawrence. What earthly motive. Vicar does not want to say about Anne. Entrance of Miss Marple – very terrible business – discusses it with them. Of course one knows who one thinks – one might be wrong. They tell her L arrested. She is suspicious – he has confessed. Oh! Then – I see I was wrong – I must have been wrong. Explain about clock – Griselda says again he knew. Miss M pounces on note – 'Yes that is curious.' Mary says Col. Melchett.

[Chapter 7]
A sad business – young Redding came in to the police station, threw down the pistol, a Mauser 25, and gave himself up. Declined to give motive. One thing I am amazed – the shot not heard. Vicar explains where kitchen is – still, I feel it would have been heard – silencer. They go to Haydock. They tell him Redding has confessed – Haydock looks relieved – that saves us all a lot of anxiety. Say 6.30 not later than that – the body was cold, man. Redding couldn't have shot him then. He looked worried – but if the man says so he's lying. But why on earth should he lie?

[Chapter 8]
The clock – what about the clock – it stopped at 6.22. Oh! I put it back. Note [from Anne] to Vicar. 'Please – please – come up to see me. I have got to tell someone.' Hands it to Col Melchett – they go up – Slack, Col and vicar. They go up. Anne – Want to ask you a few questions – she looks at him. Have you told them? I shook my head. I've been such a coward – such a coward – I shot my husband – I was desperate. Something came over me – I went up behind him and fired. The pistol? It – it was my husband's – I took it out of a drawer. Did you see anyone? No – Oh! yes – Miss Marple.

[Chapter 9]
They go to see Miss Marple. They ask her. Yes – I saw Mrs Protheroe at about a quarter past six. No – not flustered at all. She said she had come to walk home with her husband. Lawrence came from wood path and joined her. They went into the studio – then left and walked off that way. She must have taken the pistol with her. Miss M says no pistol with her. Slack says concealed on her person – Miss M says 'quite impossible.'

144

[Chapter 10]
Vicar goes home – Miss Cram with Griselda – about Guides
– really curious – she goes. Vicar and Mary – about shot.
What time – she is amazed. Griselda says about Archer the
poacher. Colonel and Slack arrive. They go into study.

[Chapter 11]
Miss Marple with Griselda – Miss M says it reminds her of
things etc. etc. – the washerwoman and the other woman –
hate. I wish you would tell me the 7 [suspects]. She shook
her head. The note – the curious point about it.

[Chapter 12]
They go to interview Lawrence. He tells – arrived there to say
I couldn't leave after all – found him dead. Pistol – it was
mine – I picked it up and rushed. I felt demented. You were
sure it was Anne? He bowed his head. I thought that after
we had parted that afternoon she had gone back and shot
him. No, he had never touched the clock. Mrs P, we know
you didn't do it. Now – will you tell me what you did? She
does. If anyone else confesses to the murder, I will go mad.

[Chapter 13]
Miss Hartnell [actually changed to Mrs Price-Ridley]
indignant complaint about being rung up – a degenerate
voice. It threatened me – asked about shot. Yes, I did hear
something down in the wood – just one odd shot – but I
didn't notice it particularly

[Chapter 14]
Haydock says about Hawes – Encephalitis lethargica.
Mention of Dennis age by Haydock.

Although the novel is narrated by the vicar, it is not until
Chapter 15 that 'I', the narrator, appears. Note the fluctua-
tion thereafter between first and third person narrative:

Note from Mrs. Lestrange – I go there. Has hardly greeted her before the Inspector arrives – she asks vicar to stay – questions. She refuses information.

[Chapter 16]
It was after tea time that I put into execution a plan of my own – whoever committed the murder etc. Goes into wood – meets Lawrence with large stone in his hands. He explains – for Miss Marple's rock garden

[Chapter 18]
Inquest that morning [afternoon] – Vicar and doctor and Lawrence give evidence. Anne Protheroe – her husband in usual spirits – Mrs Lestrange – Dr Haydock gave medical certificate. Murder by person or persons unknown.

[Chapter 19]
Then drops into Lawrence's cottage. He describes how he got on at Old Hall – a tweenie overheard something – wasn't going to tell the police.

[Chapter 20]
Vicar goes home – finds Lettice has been there – Mary very angry – has come home and found her searching in study – yellow hat.

[Chapter 21]
After dinner – Raymond West – the crime – Mr Stone. Raymond says it wasn't him. Great excitement – tell the police. Another peculiar thing – I told him about the suit case.

[Chapter 22]
Letter from Anne – Vicar goes up to see her – a very extraordinary occurrence. Takes me to attic – the picture with the slashed face. Who is it? The initials E.P. on trunk.

[Chapter 23]
Vicar on way back knows police are searching barrow –

his sudden brain wave – finds suitcase – takes it to police
station – old silver.

[Chapter 24]
Vicar goes home – Hawes there – says will vicar preach –
reference to headache powder. Notes 3 by hand – one in
box – anonymous one.

[Chapter 25]
Mrs Price Ridley – her maid, standing at gate, saw
something or heard somebody sneeze. Or a tennis racquet
in a hedge – on the way back along footpath.

Near the end of the notes is a draft of the schedule that
appears in Chapter 26. This also tallies in general with the
published version. Minor details – the date of the month and
a difference of minutes in some of the timetable – are, however, changed, as can be seen from a comparison with the
published version.

Occurrences in connection with the death of Colonel
Protheroe
To be explained [and] arranged in chronological order
~~Wednesday~~ Thursday – 20th
11.30 Col. Protheroe alters time of appointment to 6.15 –
easily overheard
12.30 Mrs Archer says pistol was still at Lawrence Redding's
cottage – but has previously said she didn't know
5.30 Fake call put through to me from East Lodge – by whom?
5.30 Col and Mrs P leave Old Hall in car and drive to village
6.14 Col. P arrives at my house Vicarage and is shown into
study by maid Mary
6.20 Anne Protheroe comes to study window – Col P not
visible (writing at desk)
6.23 L and A go into studio

6.30–6.35 The shot
6.30–6.35 Call put through from LR's cottage to Mrs PR
6.45 L.R. visits vicarage finds body
6.50 I find body

The attempted murder of Hawes and the text of the ambiguously worded but apparently incriminating letter of Chapter 29 are sketched in the closing stages of the notes, which end abruptly with the revelation of the guilty names:

[Chapters 27/28]
The call – I – I want to confess. Can't get number. Goes there – finds letter on table.

[Chapter 29]
Dear Clement
It is a peculiarly unpleasant thing I have to say – after all I think I prefer writing it. It concerns the recent peculations.
I am sorry to say that I have satisfied myself beyond any possible doubt of the identity of the culprit. Painful as it is for me to have to accuse an ordained priest of the Church . . .

The Notebook has no mention of Miss Marple's explanation, although her casual mention of the names of the guilty is reflected in the book:

Melchett arrives – Hawes ill – they send for Haydock – overdose of sulphanol.
Miss M says Yes – that's what he wants you to think – the confession of the letter – the overdose – that he took himself. It all fits in – but it's wrong. It's what the murderer wants you to think.
The murderer?
Yes – or perhaps I'd better say Mr Lawrence Redding

[Chapter 30]
They stare at her.
Of course Mr R is quite a clever young man. He would, as
I have said all along, shoot anyone and come away looking
distraught.
But he couldn't have shot Col Protheroe.
No – but she could.
Who?
Mrs Protheroe.

As the first Marple novel, the place of *The Murder at the
Vicarage* in crime fiction history is an important one. Miss
Marple is the most famous, and arguably the most able, of the
elderly female detectives. She was not the first; that honour
goes to Miss Amelia Butterworth, who solved her first case
in *The Affair Next Door* in 1897. Created by Anna Katherine
Green, sometimes called the Mother of the Detective Story,
Amelia's career was predicated on a combination of leisure
and inquisitiveness, as distinct from the professional female
whose motivation was mainly economic. Other well-known
contemporary female sleuths included spinster schoolteacher Hildegarde Withers, the creation of Stuart Palmer;
mystery writer Susan Dare, the creation of M.G. Eberhart;
professional psychologist Mrs Bradley, the creation of Gladys
Mitchell; and private enquiry agent Miss Maud Silver, the
creation of Patricia Wentworth. All these were contemporaries of Miss Marple, although only the heroine of St Mary
Mead can be classified as a complete amateur.

The Murder at the Vicarage is a typical village murder mystery
of the sort forever linked with the name of Agatha Christie;
although, with ten books already published, it was only the
second such novel she had produced, the other being *The
Murder of Roger Ackroyd*. Its central ploy – the seemingly impreg-
nable alibis of a pair of murderous adulterers – was one to

which Christie would return throughout her career. It had already featured in *The Mysterious Affair at Styles; Death on the Nile, Evil under the Sun* and *Endless Night* are other prime examples.

The Sittaford Mystery
7 September 1931

---<o>---

During a séance at Sittaford House the death of Captain
Trevelyan is predicted. The worst fears of his friend
Major Burnaby are realised when he finds the Captain's
body, murdered in his own home, six miles away.
Inspector Narracott investigates with the unsought help
of Emily Trefusis, whose fiancé has been arrested.

---<o>---

Despite the full-length debut of Miss Marple in *The Murder at the Vicarage* the previous year and the absence of Hercule Poirot since *The Mystery of the Blue Train* in 1928, Christie submitted a non-series novel to The Crime Club in 1931. *The Sittaford Mystery* had a six-part serialisation in the USA, as *Murder at Hazelmoor*, six months prior to its UK release.

The small bungalows, each with a quarter-acre of ground, described in Chapter 1 of *The Sittaford Mystery* owe their inspiration, according to an early draft of Christie's *Autobiography*, to the granite bungalow in Throwleigh, Dartmoor purchased for £800 by Christie and her sister Madge for their brother Monty on his return from Africa in 1923. The background of Dartmoor, and the sub-plot of the escaped convict, inevitably recalls Arthur Conan Doyle and his Sherlock Holmes novel *The Hound of the Baskervilles* (1896), which uses the same evocative and atmospheric setting as well as a similar sub-plot. Conan Doyle himself is referenced in Chapter 11 when Charles Enderby plans to write to him for an opinion on séances; this is a reference to Conan Doyle's enthusiasm for spiritualism, an interest that dominated the last years of his life. Despite the passing reference in Chapter 7 to Trevelyan's will, dated 13 August 1926, having been written 'five or six years ago', the mention of Conan Doyle indicates that *The Sittaford Mystery* was written, at the latest, in early 1930, as Conan Doyle died in July of that year.

As a plot device, the supernatural appeared spasmodically throughout the works of Agatha Christie. Two years after *The Sittaford Mystery* Christie published *The Hound of Death*, a collection of short stories, most of them published years earlier in various magazines, whose overall theme is the supernatural. It includes stories about a psychic in 'The Hound of Death', second sight in 'The Gipsy', a ghost in 'The Lamp', possession in 'The Strange Case of Sir Arthur [sometimes Andrew] Carmichael'; and in 'The Last Séance' and 'The Red Signal' a séance, also the main plot device of *The Sittaford Mystery*. In the later novels *Dumb Witness* and *The Pale Horse*, the supernatural plays a part; and in *Taken at the Flood* it is her psychic 'gift' that directs Katherine Cloade to approach Hercule Poirot. However, in the case of the novels, the paranormal is merely a smokescreen used by the author (and a character) to conceal a clever plot. And so it is with *The Sittaford Mystery*. The table-turning is not merely atmospheric but a vital part of the plot concocted by the murderer (i.e. the author) to camouflage his intentions and, essentially, provide him with an alibi.

All of the notes for *The Sittaford Mystery* are contained in 40 pages of Notebook 59. Also in this Notebook are the notes for *Lord Edgware Dies* and brief notes for some of the Mr Quin stories. The *Sittaford* notes are very organised and there

151

is little in the way of extraneous material. Most of the chapters are sketched accurately and even some of the chapter headings are included, although the chapter numbers in the Notebook do not correspond exactly with those of the published novel. Unusually, most of the characters' names, with the exception of the Inspector, are also as published. The notes for the two novels sketched in this Notebook follow each other in an orderly fashion and there are no shopping lists, no breaking off to plan a stage play, no digressions to a different novel. The year 1931 was also the last of the decade in which Christie had only one title published. From 1932 onwards, starting with *Peril at End House* and *The Thirteen Problems*, Collins Crime Club published more than one Christie title per year. This increased rate of production is probably one of the reasons that the subsequent Notebooks become more chaotic.

Following in the footsteps of Tuppence Beresford in *The Secret Adversary* and more recently, *Partners in Crime*, Anne Beddingfeld from *The Man in the Brown Suit* and 'Bundle' Brent from *The Secret of Chimneys*, Emily Trefusis in *The Sittaford Mystery* is another young Christie heroine with an independent mind and a yearning for adventure. She also foreshadows Lady Frances (Frankie) Derwent in *Why Didn't They Ask Evans?* and, 20 years later, Victoria Jones in *They Came to Baghdad*.

The first four chapters of the novel are accurately reflected in the early notes, although the time of death in the novel is amended to 5.25. Oddly, the secret of the novel upon which the alibi is based, is not mentioned at this stage and the brief summary below, while the truth, is not the whole truth.

The séance
Burnaby insists on going off to see his friend. Starts in the snow, goes up to house, rings and then goes in. Finds

body, rings up doctor. Hit by sand bag (put under door for draughts). Dead two hours; could he have died at 6.15? Yes – very probably.
Inquest – Scotland Yard
Inspector – he questions Major Burnaby: Why did you say 6.15? Hums and haws – at last explains. Goes to see friend who is scientific.

Following this, Christie rather chaotically considers possible suspects before returning to the beginning of the novel. She confidently heads page 26 . . .

Chapter I At Mrs Willet's
Major Burnaby put on his gum boots, took his hurricane lantern. Goes through snow to Mrs. Willets. Arrive at house – description. Captain Trevelyan – his qualities – 6 bungalows – first for his old friend and crony and lets the others.
Major B – Ronnie Garfield – young ass staying with invalid Aunt for Xmas
Mr Rycroft – entomologist dried up little man
Mr Duke – big square man
The conversation – the glasses – mention of it being the first Friday for two years he hasn't gone down to Midhampton to Capt. Trevelyan. 'I walk. What's twelve miles – keep yourself fit.' Looks at Violet . . . they said curves were coming in again – all for curves

Young man (journalist) arrives at hotel, accosts Major Burnaby. I'm on the staff of the Daily Wire. Overheard – young man explains – presents with cheque – No 1 The Cottages. Then gets into cottage conversation – goes out and wires to his paper. Comes back and talks loudly. Tells Burnaby he wants to photograph his cottage. Mr Enderby then goes out and finds Batman. So then things <u>are</u> square after all. Explains how the late captain used his name.

Each person at séance must have connection
Violet Wilton and a ne'er do well
Captain Trevelyan
Mary Trevelyan married a man called Archer – 3 sons?
Bill [Brian Pearson] the ne'er-do-well – nothing much known of him, supposed to be in Australia, really in Newton [Abbot] seeing Violet.
John, the good stay-at-home, in Town for a literary dinner. He is married – really having an intrigue with an actress. [Martin Dering?]
Another was at the theatre with a girl (Story changes – girl agrees) they give wrong theatre – play has moved there – or different actor in it yes, better – Gielgud instead of Noel Coward.
Ronald Payne, in love with Mary Archer, has come down here to persuade old uncle to do something.
Batman has married – living with wife 2 cottages away – comes in to do for him. A prize of new books has arrived for him at Batman's.

Brief sketches of potential chapters cover eight pages and while some of the descriptions below match the published chapters, as the list progresses the matches become less faithful. It is entirely possible, of course, that the original manuscript followed this pattern and that subsequent editing resulted in the book we now know. I have added chapter numbers where the descriptions seem to tally but in some cases this is not feasible.

I Afternoon at Sittaford [Chapter 1]
II Round the Table [Chapter 2]
III Discovery at Midhampton [Chapter 3]

IV Inspector Pollock [Narracott] takes over [Chapter 4]

V At Mr and Mrs Evans [Chapter 5]

VI Inspector P and B visit lawyer – the will [Chapter 7]

VII The journalist bit [Chapter 8]

VIII Exeter and Jennifer Gardiner, Nurse – husband – names of nephews and nieces [Chapter 9]

IX James Pearson – facts about detained during his Majesty's pleasure [Chapter 10]

X She decides on taking counsel of Mr Belling. You poor dear girl – the young gentleman – the attraction between [Chapter 11 and 12]

XI Sittaford – photograph of Major Burnaby's cottage – Sittaford House – Mrs and Miss Willett [Chapter 13/14]

XII The Professor on Psychical Research consents to be interviewed [Chapter 16]

XIII Prolonged interview at Exeter – alibis examined

XIV Mrs Grant – her husband, Ambrose Grant – author – literary dinner

XV Looking up AG's alibi [Chapter 24]

XVI The four – Major B out of it – the three others

XVII The Willets – nothing to be got out of them [Chapter 18]

XVIII Duke and Pollock – Duke indicates doubt of what has happened

XIX His story – engaged to Violet on way home

At the very end of the notes Christie reverts to her alphabetical method of cut and paste – assigning letters to a series of short scenes and then rearranging these letters to suit the purposes of her plot. I list the alphabetical sequence first and then her rearrangement, with comments:

A. Mrs C[urtis] full of ~~death~~ convict [Chapter 15]

B. Enderby and his interview with Emily – eye of God etc. [Chapter 25]

C. Young Ronald comes along – wants Emily to come and see his aunt [Chapter 17]

D. Miss Percehouse – acid spinster – Emily feels some kinship with her etc. Emily arranges with her to get a message . . . . to talk to Willetts – or Ronald goes with her. Label business. [Chapter 17]

E. She sees Violet Willett – evidently very nervous. Emily goes back for umbrella – creeps up stairs – the door. My God, will the night never come [Chapter 18]

F. Captain Wyatt and bulldog – eyes her up and down [Chapter 18]

G. Duke's house – Inspector Pollock comes out of door [Chapter 19]

H. Emily's interview with him [Chapter 19 and 27]

I. Enderby's theory – before [Chapter 19]

J. Emily's interview with Dr. Warren [Chapter 20]

K. The trunk label [Chapter 17]

L. The watch by night – Brian Pearson [Chapter 22]

M. Pollock at Exeter – Brian's movements checked up to Thursday [Chapter 24]

N. Since then? Since then – I don't know [This cryptic reference remains a mystery]

O. Enderby says Martin Dering not at dinner. Says he knows because Harris [Carruthers] was there – had one empty place – one side of him [Chapter 19]

P. Pollock clears up Martin Dering – the wire – answer comes all right [Chapter 27]

Q. Jennifer – either Emily or Inspector [Chapter 20]

R. Investigates her alibi – possible [Chapter 20]

S. Rycroft – name in book [Chapter 24]

T. Letter from Thomas Cronin about boots [Chapter 28]

U. Interview with Dacre the solicitor [Chapter 20]

Z. Emily interviews Mr Duke [Chapter 29]

Below are the regroupings as they appear in Notebook 59, with the relevant chapters added. The rearrangement does not follow the novel exactly but the broad outline is accurate, although for some reason the letters H, K, N and R do not appear at all. The scene F obviously gave trouble as it appears twice, each time with a question mark.

A   B   C   F?   D   E [Chapters 15/17/18, apart from B
   which is Chapter 25]
I   O   G   O   F? [Chapters 18/19]
J   Q   U   L [Chapters 20/22]
M   S   P   T   Z [Chapters 22/24/27/28]

A very interesting question in connection with the three novels published between 1931 and 1934 arises from a brief note in Notebook 59. As discussed in *Agatha Christie's Secret Notebooks*, certain motifs – the legless man, the chambermaid, a pair of artistic and criminal friends – seemed to preoccupy Christie for several years. Similarly, she toyed on a number of occasions with the possibilities of the question 'Why didn't they ask Evans?' As she approached the end of her career, in the lengthy Introduction to her 1970 novel *Passenger to Frankfurt*, she explained that sometimes a title was settled even before any story was in mind. She gave as an example the time that she visited a friend whose brother was just finishing the book he was reading; he tossed it aside and said 'Not bad, but why on earth didn't they ask Evans?' She immediately decided that this would be the title for an as yet unwritten novel but, she wrote, she did not worry about the plot or the question of who Evans might be. That, she was sure, would come to her; as, indeed, it did – but when? She gives no date for the event and it is not mentioned in her *Autobiography*.

There are however a few possibilities. During the plotting of *The Sittaford Mystery*, page 24 of Notebook 59 reads: 'The

Inspector killed – concussion confirmed Why Didn't they ask Evans? Ada Evans – also name of gardener.' During the plotting of *Lord Edgware Dies*, page 53 of Notebook 41 reads: 'Chapter XXVI Why didn't they ask Evans.' And earlier in Notebook 41 she also wrote a note to herself: 'Can we work in Why Didn't they ask Evans.'

When plotting *The Sittaford Mystery*, could Christie have possibly toyed with the idea of killing the Inspector? I think she may have intended that the Inspector be attacked and knocked unconscious, uttering the significant words as he collapsed. This theory gains some support from the fact that up to this point in the plotting the Inspector is the only investigator. Emily is not mentioned in the notes until 20 pages later, when Christie had gone back to the beginning of the novel and begun to draft individual chapters. *The Sittaford Mystery* has a character called Ada, and the gardeners are both involved in witnessing the will of Captain Trevelyan. Calling any of these characters Evans would have solved her dilemma. It is clear from the notes that she speculated about this possibility, as all three are questioned in the course of the investigation. And Captain Trevelyan's batman is named Evans. He is 'asked' more than once and it is Emily's final questioning of him that is responsible for drawing her attention to the fact of the missing boots – and thereby to the solution of the murder. When Christie did eventually incorporate Evans into a novel called, not surprisingly, *Why Didn't They Ask Evans?*, the witnessing of a will was the very event that caused Evans not to be asked, because she is a bright girl who might realise that there is subterfuge afoot. For further speculation upon this intriguing enigma see the discussion on *Lord Edgware Dies*.

'The Second Gong'
July 1932

————————◄○►————————

Hubert Lytcham Roche is found shot dead in his locked study, but luckily one of his dinner guests is Hercule Poirot.

————————◄○►————————

The short story 'The Second Gong' was first published in the UK in July 1932 in *The Strand* magazine but it was not until the posthumous 1998 UK collection *Problem at Pollensa Bay* that it appeared between hard covers. The reason for this is that Christie expanded and rewrote the story as 'Dead Man's Mirror', one of the four novellas comprising *Murder in the Mews*.

Notes for it appear in three Notebooks, 30, 41 and 61, although the reference in Notebook 30 is only to the possibility of expanding it. Notebook 41 has, unusually for a short story, ten pages of notes neatly summarising the main plot at the outset, the only difference being the smashing of a window rather than a mirror. The notes reflect accurately the progress of the story with the usual changes of names and minor plot details (I have inserted the actual names used in the story against the names given in the notes):

> Bullet passed through him and out to gong. Then door was locked on inside and body turned so that shot would have gone through window.
> Second Gong
> Girl coming down stairs late – meets boy – they ask butler – No, Miss – first gong. Secretary joins them (or girl anyway) – murderer – the shot fired from library just when he joins them

Dinner 8.15 – First gong 8.5. At 8.12 Joan comes down with
Dick – butler says 1st gong (shot!). ~~Geor~~ Jervis joins them.
Exeunt
At 7 Diana picks flowers – stain on dress. At 8.10 Diana
hurries out – gets rose – tries window – is going away when
shot is heard from road
Murderer shoots [victim] at 8.6 – shuts and locks door,
goes out through window – bangs it and it shuts, smoothes
over footprints – is in library when shot is fired.

Mrs Mulberry [No equivalent in story]
Diana Cream [Cleves] clever (adopted daughter)
Calshott – the agent – a one-armed man – ex-soldier
[Marshall]
Geoffrey Keene (secretary)
John Behring – old friend – rich man [Gregory Barling]
They go in to drawing room. Diana joins them – Mrs
Lytcham Roche – vague – spectral – John Behring – 2nd
gong – M. Poirot. No L[ytcham] R[oche] – an extraordinary
thing. Butler says still in his study. Diana mentions that he's
been very queer all day – yes, he may do something dreadful.
P watches her – they go to study – locked.
Break down door – dead man – mirror – window locked –
(reopened by John Behring) pistol by hand – 'Gong' – key in
his pocket. Inspection of window – he opens it – ground –
no footprints. Police sent for – questions.
John Behring
Mrs LR [Lytcham Roche]
Miss Cleves
[Geoffrey] Keene (pick[s] up from hall)
Butler [Digby]
Police satisfied – doctor a little uncertain as to mirror.
Poirot goes out with torchlight – comes back – asks Joan
for shoes – comes out – J with him (and Dick) Diana –

Michaelmas daisies. Come, mes enfants, Shows them
window (gong then?). Asks butler about Michaelmas daisy
– Yes – then a few words with him.

As can be seen, the notes, telegrammatic in style, are very
close to the finished story, which includes even the details of
the Michaelmas daisies and the stain on Diana's dress. The
novels immediately preceding 'The Second Gong' – *The
Murder at the Vicarage, The Sittaford Mystery, Peril at End House*
– all appear in the Notebooks more or less as they eventually
appeared in print. Rough work, if any, may have been done
elsewhere and the Notebooks represented an outline as distinct from the working out of details of the plot.

The plot of 'The Second Gong' features one of the few
experiments that Christie made with that classic situation
of detective fiction – the locked room problem, where the
victim is found in a room with all the doors and windows
locked from the inside, making escape for the killer seemingly impossible. *Why Didn't They Ask Evans?*, *Murder in
Mesopotamia* and *Hercule Poirot's Christmas* also have similar
situations. But fascinating though these situations can be,
Christie does not make them a major aspect of any of these
titles. And nor does she with 'The Second Gong', where the
solution is disappointingly mundane.

But there is another connection with one of these titles.
Both 'The Second Gong' and *Hercule Poirot's Christmas* feature a killer faking the time of the murder in order to provide himself with an alibi. And more importantly, in both
titles a character picks something off the floor, obviously
an important clue as it gets a note of its own above, 'Picks
up from hall'; when confronted with this fact, the killer in
each case offers a different object in the hope of avoiding
detection. And there is a thematic connection with the only
Poirot stage play written directly for the stage, *Black Coffee,*

premiered the year before the short story. In each case the killer proves to be the male secretary of a wealthy man.

There are no notes for the elaboration of 'The Second Gong' into 'Dead Man's Mirror', apart from the appearance of the names Miss Lingard and Hugo Trent on a single page of Notebook 61. The plot is almost identical and although a different killer is unmasked, their position in the household is essentially the same as in the original.

Lord Edgware Dies
4 September 1933

When Lord Edgware is found stabbed in his study it would seem that his wife, actress Jane Wilkinson, has carried out her threat. But her impeccable alibi forces Poirot to look elsewhere for the culprit. Two more deaths follow before a letter from the dead provides the final clue.

Lord Edgware Dies, set amongst the glitterati of London's West End, began life in Rhodes in the autumn of 1931 and was completed on an archaeological dig at Nineveh on a table bought for £10 at a bazaar in Mosul. It was dedicated to Dr and Mrs Campbell Thompson, who led the archaeological expedition at Nineveh, and a skeleton found in a grave mound on site was christened Lord Edgware in honour of the book.

The inspiration for the book and for the character of Carlotta Adams came from the American actress Ruth Draper, who was famed for her ability to transform herself from a Hungarian peasant to a Park Lane heiress in a matter of minutes and with a minimum of props. In her *Autobiography* Christie says, 'I thought how clever she was and how good her impersonations were . . . thinking about her led me to the book *Lord Edgware Dies*.'

Although never mentioned in the same reverent breath as *The Murder of Roger Ackroyd* or *Murder on the Orient Express*, *Lord Edgware Dies*, despite its lack of a stunning surprise solution, is a model of detective fiction. The plot is audaciously simple and simply audacious and, like many of the best plots, seems complicated until one simple and, in retrospect, obvious, fact is grasped; then everything clicks neatly into place. Every chapter pushes the story forward and almost every conversation contains information to enable Poirot to answer the question, 'Did Lady Edgware carry out her threat to take a taxi to her husband's house and stab him in the base of the skull?'

Lord Edgware himself is in the same class as the victims from both 1938 novels, Mrs Boynton from *Appointment with Death* and Simeon Lee from *Hercule Poirot's Christmas*; he is a thoroughly nasty individual whose family despises him and whose passing few mourn. There are also unspoken suggestions of a relationship between himself and his Greek god-like butler, Alton.

The progress of *Lord Edgware Dies* was mentioned sporadically by Christie to her new husband, Max Mallowan, in letters written to him from Grand Hotel des Roses, Rhodes in 1931.

Tuesday Oct. 13th [1931]
I've got on well with book – Lord Edgware is dead all right – and a second tragedy has now occurred – the Ruth Draper having taken an overdose of veronal. Poirot is being most mysterious and Hastings unbelievably asinine.
. . . breakfast at 8 . . . meditation till 9. Violent hitting of the typewriter till 11.30 (or the end of the chapter – sometimes if it is a lovely day I cheat to make it a short one!)

163

Presumably there were 'lovely days' at the time of writing Chapters 8 and 16!

> Oct. 16th
> Lord Edgware is getting on nicely. He's dead – Carlotta Adams (Ruth Draper) is dead – and the nephew who succeeds to the property is just talking to Poirot about his beautiful alibi! There is also a film actor with a face like a 'Greek God' – but he is looking a bit haggard at present. In fact a very popular mixture I think. Just a little bit cheap perhaps . . .

> Oct. 23rd
> True, I have got to Chapter XXI of Lord Edgware which is all to the good . . . I should never have done that if you had been there . . . I must keep my mind on what the wicked nephew does next . . .

All of the notes for this novel are spread over almost 50 pages of a pocket-diary sized Notebook 41. They outline most of the novel very closely and there is little in the way of deletions or variations. Unless there were earlier discarded notes it would seem that the writing of this novel went smoothly and that the plot was well established before Christie began writing. The first page of this notebook is headed 'Ideas – 1931' and the first ten pages, prior to the notes for *Lord Edgware Dies*, contain brief notes for 'The Mystery of the Baghdad Chest' (1932) and an even briefer note for *Why Didn't They Ask Evans?*, as well as a one-sentence outline of the crucial idea behind *Three Act Tragedy*.

There are also two references to *Thirteen at Dinner*, the title under which *Lord Edgware Dies* appeared in the USA, but it is not clear if these two references are coincidental or if the idea of 13 guests at a dinner (as mentioned in Chapter 15) was an earlier idea that Christie subsumed into *Lord Edgware Dies*. The first reference lists 13 members of the Detection Club in connection with this plot (as discussed in *Agatha Christie's Secret Notebooks*), and five pages later the idea of 'Thirteen at Dinner as a short story?' is considered though not pursued.

Two jottings, a dozen pages apart, accurately reflect the first two chapters of the book; and in between these, in the last extract below, Christie summarises the murder plot. As can be seen, the only details to change are minor ones – the name Mountcarlin changes to Edgware, the secretary Miss Gerard becomes Miss Carroll and Martin Squire becomes Bryan Martin, although at this stage he is merely an admirer rather than a fellow actor. The Piccadilly Palace Hotel, the door ajar, the waiter and the corn knife all appear in the book.

An actress Jane W comes to see Poirot – engaged to Duke of Merton – her husband – not very bright – best way would be to kill him she drawls – Hastings a little shocked. But I shouldn't like to be hanged. Door is then seen to be a little ajar. Martin Squire [Bryan Martin] – pleasant hearty young fellow – an admirer of Miss Wilkinson's. He is seen next evening having supper with Carlotta

Sequence
At theatre – CA's performance – H's reflections – Is JW really such a good actress? Looks round – JW – her eyes sparkling with enthusiasm. Supper at Savoy – Jane at next table – CA there also (with Ronnie Marsh) – rapprochement – JW and Poirot – her sitting room – her troubles. I'll have to kill him (just as waiter is going out) Enter Bryan (and CA). JW has gone into bedroom. B asks what did she say – means it – amoral – would kill anyone quite simply

Plot
Jane speaks to Carlotta – bribes her – a thousand pounds

– to go to Mr? Jefferson's dinner. Rendezvous at Piccadilly
Palace at 7.30. They change clothes – C goes to dinner.
At 9.15 J. rings her up. C. says quite alright. J goes to
Montcarlin House – rings – tells butler (new) that she is
Lady Mountcarlin goes in – Hullo John. Secretary (Miss
Gerard) sees her from above. Shoot? Or stab? Ten minutes
later she leaves. At 10.30 butler goes to room – dead.
Informs police – they come. Go to Savoy – Lady M came in
at half an hour ago or following morning. J kills him with
corn knife belonging to her maid Eloise

Christie then considers her suspects, although this list is
much shorter than the eventual cast of characters:

People
Lord Mountcarlin [Edgware]
Other man Duke? Millionaire?
Bryan Martin – actor in films with her
Lord Mountcarlin's nephew Ronnie West – debonair Peter
Wimseyish
Miss Carroll – Margaret Carroll – Middle-aged woman – a
Miss Clifford

The reference to 'debonair Peter Wimsey' is to Lord Peter
Wimsey, the detective creation of Christie's crime-writing
contemporary Dorothy L. Sayers and the hero of (at that
stage) a half-dozen novels and a volume of short stories. The
Clifford reference is, in all likelihood, to a member of the
Clifford family at whose home the young Agatha attended
social evenings.

The vital letter written by Carlotta and forwarded from
her sister in Canada (Chapters 20 and 23) is sketched, but
only the crucial section, containing the giveaway clue:

Arrival of a letter
he said 'I believe it would take in Lord Mountcarlin himself.
Now will you take something on for a bet. Big stakes, mind.'
I laughed and said 'How much' but the answer fairly took
my breath away. 10,000 dollars, no more no less. Oh, little
sister – think of it. Why, I said, I'd play a hoax on the King
in Buckingham Palace and risk lese majeste for that. Well,
then we got down to details.

And the Five Questions of Chapter 14 are listed in cryptic
form:

Then Points?
A. Sudden change of mind
B. Who intercepted letter
C. Meaning of his glare
D. The pince-nez – nobody owns them – except Miss
Carroll?
E. The telephone call (they will go to Hampstead)

The Notebook does include one intriguing sequence, not
reflected in the book:

. . . or says I have been used as a tool – I feel ill. I didn't
know what I ought to do – letter to Superintendent of police
(rang up) – letter to Bryan Martin. A telephone number
Victoria 7852 . . . No, no, I forgot – he wouldn't be there.
Tomorrow will do.
A letter she writes but does not post? Or a friend comes to
see her?

These would seem to be the actions of Carlotta Adams as
described by her maid in Chapter 10; perhaps the original
intention was to report the abandoned phone call directly.

167

And the second reference is to the vital letter to her sister, the facsimile of which, in Chapter 23, gives Poirot the clue that eventually solves the case.

Page 53 of Notebook 41 throws a further intriguing sidelight on *Why Didn't They Ask Evans?*. The following note appears under a heading:

Chapter XXVI
Why didn't they ask Evans
Ah! I can see it all now – Evans comes. Questions about BM [Bryan Martin]. She answers – pince-nez left behind

This refers to Chapter 28 of *Lord Edgware Dies* and the questioning of Carlotta's maid, Ellis. At the end of the previous chapter Poirot has a revelation when, passing a cinema-goer in the street, he overhears the observation, 'If they'd just had the sense to ask Ellis . . .'; or, in other words, 'Why didn't they (have the sense to) ask Ellis.' It is entirely possible that the writing of *Why Didn't They Ask Evans?* followed closely on the completion of *Lord Edgware Dies*. Although there are no notes for the later novel its serialisation began the same month, September 1933, in which *Lord Edgware Dies* was published. Christie possibly felt that the questioning of Evans/Ellis, and the intriguing reason for the lack of questioning, deserved a more elaborate construction than the one given in *Lord Edgware Dies*. And so she wrote *Why Didn't They Ask Evans?*, where the identification and questioning of Evans is the entire raison d'être of the book. Is it entirely coincidental that the Evans of the later novel is also a maid? For further discussion of the Ellis/Evans enigma see the notes on *The Sittaford Mystery*.

Three Act Tragedy
7 January 1935

―――――――――◄○►――――――――――

Who poisoned Reverend Babbington at Sir Charles's
cocktail party? And, more bafflingly, why? What became
of Sir Bartholomew's mysterious butler Ellis? What secret
did Mrs de Rushbridger hide? In the last act Poirot
links these three events to expose a totally unexpected
murderer – and an even more unexpected motive.

――――――――――◄○►――――――――――

Three Act Tragedy is based on one of the most original ideas
in the entire Christie output. A single sentence in the
Notebooks shows the inspiration for the novel and from it
Christie produced a perfectly paced and baffling whodunit.
In fact the book is full of clever and original ideas. Apart
from the brilliant central concept we also meet a victim murdered not because of what she knows but on account of what
she *doesn't* know; a new conjuring trick in a clever poisoning gambit; a witty yet chilling closing line; and, unwittingly,
a foreshadowing, in the final chapter title, of a famous case
to come. Mr Satterthwaite, normally the partner in crime of
the mysterious Mr Quin, here makes one of two appearances
alongside Hercule Poirot, the other being the novelette
'Dead Man's Mirror' from *Murder in the Mews*.

    Three Act Tragedy has ideas in common with *Lord Edgware
Dies* from two years earlier. Both are set firmly among the
glittering classes; both feature a murderous member of the
acting profession involved in a deadly masquerade; both
feature a clothes designer and an observant playwright
among the suspects; and both feature Hercule Poirot.
Oliver Manders' motorcycle 'accident' on the night of Sir

Bartholomew's death is the same as that engineered by Bobby and Frankie in the previous year's *Why Didn't They Ask Evans?*. A variation on the impersonation at the centre of the plot was also to appear in the following year's book, *Death in the Clouds*, with a murderer disguised as a plane steward; and, in more light-hearted vein, the same ruse was the basis for the short story 'The Listerdale Mystery', first published in 1925. This ploy, and its reverse – a servant masquerading as an employer – is used in many Christie titles, for example *The Mystery of the Blue Train, Appointment with Death, One, Two, Buckle my Shoe, Sparkling Cyanide, Taken at the Flood* and *After the Funeral*, as well as the long short story 'Greenshaw's Folly'.

It is also possible that this novel is Christie's adaptation, tongue somewhat in cheek, of that well-known cliché of classic detective fiction, the guilty butler. With *Three Act Tragedy* she managed a solution in which The Butler Did It – and at the same time, The Butler Didn't Do It. And the other old chestnut, the secret passage, also gets an airing, although almost as an aside.

The notes for *Three Act Tragedy* are the last to outline the course of a novel accurately with little extraneous material or ideas not included in the published version. From *Death in the Clouds* onwards notes contain speculation and changes of mind, but the notes for titles up to, and including, *Three Act Tragedy* are relatively organised and straightforward.

Notebooks 33 and 66 contain the bulk of the plotting, 40 pages, but the brilliantly original basis for the book was sketched, four years before publication, in Notebook 41. This is the Notebook whose first page is headed 'Ideas – 1931', the first half-dozen pages of which include outlines for 'The Mystery of the Baghdad/Spanish Chest', 'The Second Gong/Dead Man's Mirror' and a brief allusion to *Why Didn't They Ask Evans?*, before the detailed draft for *Lord Edgware Dies*. In the middle of these we find the following:

Idea for book
Murder utterly motiveless because dead man and murderer
unacquainted. Reason – a rehearsal

This unique idea was left to percolate for two years before
the bulk of the novel was written during 1933. Almost inevitably, the background would have to be somewhat theatrical. And from the first page of the book Sir Charles
Cartwright's ability to assume a role onstage is emphasised.
Mr Satterthwaite watches Sir Charles walk up the path from
the sea and observes 'something indefinable that did not
ring true' about his portrayal of 'the Retired Naval man'; and
this is, in effect, the foundation on which the novel is built.

Notebook 33 sketches, in cryptic notes, the opening scene of the book – Sir Charles, observed by Mr
Satterthwaite, climbing the hill towards his house. This is
followed by a list of the characters and, apart from the mysterious Richard Cromwell, who may be the forerunner of
Oliver Manders, the names listed are close to those in the
published book.

The Manor House Mystery
Ronald [Sir Charles] Cartwright walks up – shiplike rolling
gait – clean shaven face – not have been sure [if he actually
was a sailor]. Mr Satterthwaite smiling to himself
Egg/Ray Lytton Gore
Lady Mary Lytton Gore
Richard Cromwell
Mr and Mrs Babbington
Sir Bartholomew Frere [Strange]
Capt. and Mrs Dakers
Angela Sutcliffe
Satterthwaite
Captain Dacres – bad lot – little man like jockey

Mrs Cynthia Dacres runs dress shops (Ambrosine)
Anthony McCrane [Astor] – playwright
Miss Hester [Milray] – secretary – dour ugly woman of
forty-three

The title at the top of the page – 'The Manor House Mystery' – is a generic and inadequate one and does not appear again. *Three Act Tragedy* is more dramatic and is in keeping with the theatrical theme – an actor, a playwright, a dress designer, a masquerade and the motive of a rehearsal.

The all-important discussion of Ellis, the butler, and his mysterious disappearance is sketched, as is the possible connection between the two fatal dinner-parties:

Bit about butler
Chapter II
Interview with Johnson – mellow atmosphere. Then it
must be this fellow, Ellis; tells all about butler – not there a
fortnight – questioned by police – not seen to leave house
but be left – looks fishy. Says Miss Lytton Gore told him
about other death. Must be some connection but was likely
to be the butler. Why did the fellow disappear if he hadn't
got a guilty conscience?
Port analysed – found correct. Inspector comes in – talks
about nicotine poisoning. [Second Act, Chapter 2]

London – Egg arrives over to dine with them – pale,
wounded looking. The position – the three of us –
questions. Are the deaths of Sir B[artholomew] and
B[abbington connected?]
Yes
If so, what people were at one and which at the other
Miss Sutcliffe, Captain and Mrs Dacres, Miss Wills and Mr
Manders

> You can wash out Angela and Mr Manders
> Egg says can't wash out Miss Sutcliffe. I don't know her
> Mr S says can't wash out anybody
> She has washed out Mr Manders
> Egg agrees [Second Act, Chapter 7]

Notebook 66 opens when the investigation is well under way and the interviews with the suspects are divided between the self-styled detectives. The first page is headed:

> Division of work
> P suggests Egg should tackle Mrs Dacres; C[harles Cartwright] Freddie D[acres] and A[ngela] S[utcliffe]; S[atterthwaite] Miss Wills and O[liver] M[anders]. Says Miss Wills will have seen something. C. says S. do AS – will do the Wills woman. P suggests S. should do OM [Third Act, Chapter 5]

> Miss W[ills]
> Sir C. – birthmark on butler's arm. She gets him to hand her the dish. As he goes out looks back – her smile was disquieting in the extreme. She writes in a little book.
> [Third Act, Chapter 9]

> An experiment – I will give the party. Charles stays behind – the glasses etc. Miss Will's face – P appeals for anyone to tell anything they know [Third Act, Chapter 11]

The third death, that of Mrs de Rushbridger, and the revelatory discussion of the play rehearsal are also sketched briefly.

> Mr Satterthwaite and Poirot go to Yorkshire. Mrs R dead – a small boy got it from a man who said he got it from a

loony lady – 'Bit loony she was.' She cannot speak now, says Poirot. This must be stopped – then is someone else in danger [Third Act, Chapter 13]

Happy families – I ask for a pack of cards – I get them. Mrs Mugg – the Milkman's wife – Egg explains. P says he hopes she will be very happy. She goes off to dress rehearsal of Angela Sutcliffe's play by Miss Wills – Little Dog Laughed. Tiens – I have been blind – the motive for the murder of Mr Babbington [Third Act, Chapter 14]

There are two interesting points to consider about this novel. The first is a further variation on the Evans/Ellis issue. As discussed in the notes for *The Sittaford Mystery* and *Lord Edgware Dies*, the cryptic note in Notebook 41 – 'Can we work in Why Didn't They Ask Evans?' – could conceivably also apply to *Three Act Tragedy*. Ellis/Evans in *Lord Edgware Dies* and Evans in *The Sittaford Mystery* both provide vital clues that lead to the solution of the mystery. And if Poirot had been able to question the missing Ellis of *Three Act Tragedy*, he would almost certainly have prevented the death of Mrs De Rushbridger. But because he doesn't, in reality, exist, it is obvious Why They Didn't Ask Ellis.

The second, and little remarked upon, enigma is The Mystery of the Altered Motive. As discussed in *Agatha Christie's Secret Notebooks*, the US and UK texts of *The Moving Finger* and *Murder is Easy/Easy to Kill* are considerably different. In *Three Act Tragedy* we find the same situation but the disparity is even more dramatic. In the UK edition of the book, during Poirot's explanations in the final chapter, the motive attributed to Sir Charles, the supposed bachelor, is that, unknown to most people, he is actually married: 'And there is the fact that in the Haverton Lunatic Asylum there is a woman, Gladys Mary Mugg, the wife of Charles Mugg' (Sir

Charles' real name). And, Poirot explains, Sir Bartholomew Strange as 'an honourable, upright physician . . . would not stand by silent and see you enter into a bigamous marriage with an unsuspecting young girl' (Egg). During Chapter 12 of the Third Act, Sir Charles tells Egg about his real name but otherwise the reader has no reason to suspect that he already has a wife, albeit one confined to an asylum.

In the US edition, however, it is Sir Charles, and not his wife, who is insane and as Poirot clarifies, 'In Sir Bartholomew he saw a menace to his freedom. He was convinced that Sir Bartholomew was planning to put him under restraint. And so he planned a careful and extremely cunning murder.' And, as he is being led away, Sir Charles breaks down – 'His face . . . was now a leering mask of impotent fury. His voice rang shrill and cracked . . . *Those three people had to be killed . . . for my safety.*' Melodramatic descriptions aside, it must be admitted that of the two potential motives, this one is by far the more compelling.

The reason for this change is more difficult to explain. And it inevitably leads to the question 'Which is the original version?'

The amended denouement means that certain passages in the book which foreshadow the altered motive are significantly different. The most crucial changes occur in Chapters 7 and 26 of the US edition. In Chapter 7 Sir Charles and Mr Satterthwaite interview the Chief Constable, Colonel Johnson. In the course of this conversation Sir Charles says, 'I've retired from the stage now, as you know. *Worked too hard and had a breakdown two years ago*'; and extracts from Sir Bartholomew's diary are quoted, including one significant one: '*Am worried about M . . . don't like the look of things*' (my emphasis). Chapter 26 includes a lengthy conversation between Poirot and Oliver Manders. None of these passages appear in the equivalent chapters (Second Act, Chapter

2 and Third Act, Chapter 14) of the UK edition. The first two changes provide the clues to Sir Charles' breakdown, the M referring to his real name, Mugg, and showing Sir Bartholomew's concern over Cartwright's mental health. The third prepares the way for Manders to replace Sir Charles in Egg's affections, although this new romantic scenario applies in either case.

However, as the book was published (both as a magazine serial and in book form) in the USA in advance of its UK publication it is likely that it was the latter edition that was altered. But the question remains: why?

In a letter (undated, as usual, but from internal evidence probably late 1972/early 1973) to her agent, Christie herself briefly refers to the problem and states, 'I am studying the problem of *Three Act Tragedy* . . . in the Dodd Mead [the US edition] Sir Charles goes mad . . . I have a feeling that was what I originally wrote.' But this is by no means conclusive; and the Notebooks throw no light on this intriguing mystery.

UNUSED IDEAS: TWO

UNUSED IDEAS:
TWO

This second batch of Unused Ideas feature foreign settings, both inspired by holidays taken by Christie.

THE HELLENIC CRUISE

There are two lengthy sketches in the Notebooks of a murder plot during a Hellenic cruise, possibly inspired by Christie's own cruise to Greece in the late summer of 1958. Chronologically this makes sense: the first extract below is sandwiched between the pages of notes for *Cat among the Pigeons*, published in 1959; the second extract, from Notebook 15, appears alongside notes for 1961's *The Pale Horse*.

Book with Hellenic cruise setting
A murderer
Possible scene of actual murder Ephesus or could be
electrocuted during lecture on deck
People
Lecturers – little man with beard his wife calls him Daddee –
a professor

177

Young schoolmaster type of man – uncouth and rather dirty
– superior in manner
Miss Courtland – a Barbara type – two schoolmistresses
travelling together – one has had a nervous breakdown
Mrs. Oliver??
The 2 spinsters idea could be combined with this. The
'friend' schoolmistress came on deliberately – have planned
to kill someone going on cruise – camouflaging it by going
with a friend, really sending money to friend anonymously
to pay expenses. Alibis helped by the two of them being
places – but M[iss Courtland or, possibly, Murderer?]
makes friend believe that she occasionally has short lapses
of memory – appear to be very devoted.
Motive?

Although a possible plot involving two female friends is a
recurring motif in the Notebooks, the sketch here is different;
here one friend is the dupe, rather than the partner-in-crime,
of the other. The reference to 'Barbara' is probably to Barbara
Parker, Max Mallowan's long-time assistant and, after the
death of Dame Agatha, his wife for the last year of his life. The
idea of convincing someone that they suffer from memory
loss had earlier appeared in 'The Cretan Bull', the seventh
Labour of Hercules, and would reappear a few years later in
A Caribbean Mystery when Molly Kendall is drugged into forget-
fulness and hallucination. It would seem from the ambiguous
phrase 'appear to be devoted' that the friend with the nervous
breakdown in her background is set to be the dupe of Miss
Courtland, the putative murderer. And the reference to elec-
trocution 'during lecture on deck', not a very obvious murder
method, would suggest that Christie had something definite
in mind, although what it was remains a mystery.

The second outline, while retaining essentially the same
characters, adds some new scenarios to the first:

Hellenic cruise – murder – where? Ephesus? During lecture
in the evening on deck?
By whom committed – and why
A Miss Marple?
Wife decides to kill husband? Or she and her lover? Say she
has had lovers – one, a foreigner? an American? Dismisses
him abruptly because she knows he will react – actually
he is framed by her and another lover whom she pretends
she hardly knows? Possibly Cornish Mystery type of story?
Academic background – woman like J.P.? or like M.C.
Anyway 2 people in it – and a fall guy!
Or a Macbeth type of story – ambitious woman – urges on
husband – husband turns out to have a taste for murder.
Perhaps murder is done when someone is sleeping on
deck – or Murder is Easy idea – monomaniac who believes
everyone who opposes him dies – this is really suggested to
him by woman who hates him.
One of lecturers little man with beard – his wife calls him
Dadee – encounters young schoolmistress – rather dirty –
Miss Cortland (a Barbara type! Good Company).
Mrs Oliver ?!!
Two Schoolmistresses travelling together (one has had
nervous breakdown). One of them is murderer – she sent
money anonymously to ill friend to enable her to come too
– impresses on friend that she has 'black outs' short lapses
if memory so that friend and she have alibis together

If Christie had used either of the inspirations from her own
earlier titles – *Murder is Easy* and 'The Cornish Mystery' – we
can be sure that she would have rendered them unrecognisable, as she did with *Death on the Nile/Endless Night* and *Dead
Man's Folly/Hallowe'en Party*.

Elements from each extract can be found elsewhere in
Christie – the stage-managed dismissal has echoes of *Death on*

the Nile and 'two people and a fall guy' is similar to 'Triangle at Rhodes'. And there are some compelling new variations: the husband who 'turns out to have a taste for murder' after his initial reluctance and the anonymous gift of money to set up an alibi. The references to 'J.P.' and 'M.C.' have proved elusive but may simply refer to two of Christie's fellow passengers on the cruise.

Miss Marple, a few years before her only foreign case, *A Caribbean Mystery*, makes a brief appearance. Interestingly, Mrs Oliver was intended to appear, whichever scenario was chosen. Ariadne Oliver, Agatha Christie's alter ego, is a prolific detective novelist with a foreign detective, the Finnish Sven Hjerson, one of whose cases is *The Body in the Library*. Doubtless she would, like her creator, have been using the trip as a background for her next masterwork. In the event she did feature in *The Pale Horse*, published shortly afterwards. Both of these outlines could be a revisitation, 20 years later, of *Death on the Nile* – a group of people with emotional entanglements cut off from the world aboard a ship in a foreign country. The two female friends, here schoolmistresses, appear in each sketch, each time with more background detail.

――――•◆•――――

THE GIRL-IN-THE-BAHAMAS

These examples, all from different Notebooks, show Christie experimenting with an intriguing idea before eventually deciding to send Miss Marple, who is not mentioned here, to essentially the same place, St Honore, and have her solve Major Palgrave's murder in *A Caribbean Mystery*:

> Girl gets job – sent out to Bahamas – plane brought back.
> She goes back to flat – another girl there acting as her

West Indies Book
Begins girl secretary – told by Company to go to Barbados
(Tobago) on business – meet certain executives there –
passage paid etc. Goes off from London Airport – Shannon
etc. – then back again following evening – her flat occupied
by someone else – she and boy friend decide to investigate

How about girl gets job – a flat is given her – after a month
she is sent to Barbados – return of plane she goes to flat
– finds dead body or finds she is supposed to have died –
young man she telephones him – they discuss it – what is
the point? Person to die first – a lawyer – head of solicitor's
firm? New member of a country solicitors? A Q.C.?

The common denominator of the West Indies was the *idée
fixe* of these jottings, probably inspired by her holiday there
in the early 1960s.

5

'How I Created Hercule Poirot'

'Why not make my detective a Belgian?'

◄○►

SOLUTIONS REVEALED
Death on the Nile

◄○►

Agatha Christie wrote the article that follows to herald the *Daily Mail*'s serialisation of *Appointment with Death* (or, as they renamed it, *A Date with Death*) on 19 January 1938, prior to the publication of the novel by Collins Crime Club in May of that year.

The appearance of the 'latest Agatha Christie' in a newspaper or magazine was mutually advantageous. Both author and periodical enjoyed a boost in sales and publicity. Although not every novel had a pre-publication appearance, as early in her career as *The Mysterious Affair at Styles* and as late as *Sleeping Murder* Christie was regularly serialised on both sides of the Atlantic. Changes to the title and often to the text were tolerated, as the financial rewards were significant. The *Saturday Evening Post* in America paid $14,000 for *Cards on the Table* and $16,000 for *Dumb Witness*. But the enterprise was not without its pitfalls. A competition to accompany the serialisation of *The A.B.C. Murders*, in which readers were invited to send in their solutions, was won by a reader who got every detail of the plot correct.

Christie's account of the genesis of Hercule Poirot has appeared in print only once since, in the *Agatha Christie Centenary Celebration* book, edited by Lynn Underwood and published in September 1990. The version below is reproduced from the pages of Notebook 21 and I have left intact many of the original deletions, made by Christie herself. This will help to show how fluently she could produce 1,400 words with a minimum of cutting and rearrangement. Unusually, the text in Notebook 21 is continuous and, apart from the slightly amended drafts of the final paragraphs, would seem to have been completed at one sitting. It is impossible at this stage to be absolutely certain that this was the case, but it is all written with the same ink and, until the final stages, in the same handwriting on 12 consecutive pages. The earlier 1990 publication is shorter and slightly different; some paragraphs were there rearranged to create a more coherent structure – for example the discussions of Poirot's earlier cases were brought together – but I include here the entire text exactly as it was first written.

How did the character of Hercule Poirot come into being?

Difficult to say – ~~he came perhaps about accidentally that is~~ I realise that he came into being not at all as he himself would have wished ~~it~~. 'Hercule Poirot first,' he would have said. 'And then a plot to display his remarkable talent to the best advantage.' But it was not so. The ~~idea often~~ plot of the story, *The Mysterious Affair at Styles*, was roughed out and then came the dilemma: a detective story – now what kind of detective? It was ~~wartime~~ in the early autumn ~~days~~

of 1914 – Belgian refugees were in most country places.[22] Why not have a Belgian refugee, ~~for a detective,~~ a former shining light of the Belgian Police force.

What kind of man ~~he~~ should he be? A little man perhaps, with a somewhat grandiloquent name. Hercule – something – Hercule Poirot – yes, that would do. What else about him? He should be very neat – very orderly (Is that because I was a wildly untidy person myself?)[23]

Such was the first rough outline – mostly, you will note, externals – but certain ~~fad~~ traits followed almost automatically. Like many small dandified men, he would be conceited and he would, of course, (why 'of course?') have a ~~luxuriant~~ handsome moustache. That was the beginning. Hercule Poirot emerged from the mists and took concrete shape and form. ~~but he was a particularly~~ Once ~~he was~~ that had happened he took charge, as it were, of his own personality – there were all sorts of things about him that I did not know, but which he proceeded to ~~develop~~ show me. There was more in this little man than I had ever suspected. There was, for instance, his intense interest in the psychology of every case. As early as *The Murder on the Links*

---

22 Germany invaded Belgium in early August 1914, so the arrival of refugees would probably have been nearer to late than early autumn 1914. This chronology is at variance with her own *Autobiography*, where she writes that she first conceived of writing a detective story while working at the hospital dispensary (1915–16). And a key point in the plot of *The Mysterious Affair at Styles* is dependent on knowledge of the properties of poisons, gained through her experience there.

23 As if to emphasise this point, the page immediately preceding this essay has a heading 'Ideas 1940', obviously written at least two years afterwards; one of the ideas listed would become, later again, *The Moving Finger*. Presumably, the 12 pages needed for this essay were, conveniently, blank at the back of Notebook 21 when Christie went in search of a suitable gap.

he was showing his appreciation of the mental processes of
~~the~~ a murderer – and insisting that ~~planning of a~~ every crime
had a definite signature.[24]

Method and order still meant much to him – but not
nearly so much as before. In *The Murder of Roger Ackroyd*
he was at his best investigating a crime in a quiet country
village and using his knowledge of human nature to get at
the truth. For the terrible death on the Blue Train ~~he was~~
I have always suspected ~~not I have always thought he was~~
~~not, I think, quite~~ he was not at his best but the solution
of Lord Edgware's death was, I consider, a good piece of
work on his part, though he gives some of the credit to
Hastings.[25] *Three Act Tragedy* he considers one of his failures
though most people do not agree with him – his final
remark at the end of the case has amused many people
[but] Hercule Poirot cannot see why![26] He considers that he
merely stated an obvious truth.

And now, what of the relation between us – between
the creator and the created? Well – let me confess it –
there has been at times a coolness between us. There are
moments when I have felt 'Why, why, did I ever invent this
detestable, bombastic tiresome little creature? Eternally

---

24 In Chapter 9 of *The Murder on the Links* Poirot lectures the
examining magistrate Hautet, and the policeman Giraud, on the
psychology of the criminal.
25 This is a reference to the chance remark that Hastings makes in
Chapter 27, and which is acknowledged by Poirot at the end of
Chapter 29, concerning the ill-fated Donald Ross. It is immediately
followed by the equally vital and chance remark made by a cinema-
goer and overheard by Poirot as they cross the Euston Road.
26 Why Poirot should consider *Three Act Tragedy* one of his failures is
not clear, unless it is the fact that two further people die before he
spots the vital point that motivated the first murder. His remark in
the very last line of the book – 'It might have been ME!' – would
not surprise anyone who knew him well.

straightening things, forever boasting, always twirling his moustaches and tilting his 'egg-shaped head.' Anyway, what is an egg-shaped head? Have I ever seen an egg-shaped head? When people say to me, 'Which way up is the egg? – do I really know[?] I don't, because I never do see pictorial things clearly. But nevertheless, I know that he has an egg-shaped head covered with black, suspiciously black, hair[27] and I know that his eyes occasionally shine ~~and some~~ with a green light. And ~~once or~~ twice in my life I have actually seen him – once on a boat going to the Canary Islands[28] and once having lunch at the Savoy. I have said to myself, 'Now if you had only had the nerve you ~~would~~ could have snap-shotted the man in the boat and then when people have said "Yes, but what is he like? I could have produced that snap shot and said 'This is what he is like.' And in the Savoy perhaps I would have gone and explained the matter but life is full of lost opportunities. If you are doubly burdened – first by acute shyness and secondly by only seeing the right thing to do or say twenty-four hours late – what can you do? ~~Except~~ only write about quick-witted men and resourceful girls whose reactions are like greased lightning!

Yes, there have been moments when I have disliked M. Hercule Poirot very much indeed –when I have rebelled bitterly against being yoked to him for life (usually at one of these moments that I receive a fan letter saying 'I know you must love your little detective by the way you

---

27 In the first chapter of *The A.B.C. Murders* Poirot extols the virtues of Revivit, a hair dye.

28 The mention of 'seeing' Hercule Poirot while in the Canary Islands is most probably a reference to the holiday Christie spent there with Rosalind and Carlo in 1927 after the trauma of 1926. It was here that she worked on *The Mystery of the Blue Train*.

write about him.)[29] But now, I must confess it, Hercule
Poirot has won. A reluctant affection has sprung up
for him. He has become more human, less irritating.
I admire certain things about him – his passion for
the truth, his understanding of human frailty and his
kindliness. ~~I did not understand suspect before that he
felt so strongly so strictly not for the punishment of the
guilty but for the vindication of the innocent.~~ And he
has taught me something – to take more interest in my
own characters; to see them more as real people and
less as pawns in a game. In spite of his vanity he often
chooses deliberately to stand aside and let the main
drama develop. He says in effect, 'It is their story – let
them show you why and how this happened.' He knows,
of course, that the star part is going to be his all right
later. He may make his appearance at the end of the first
act but he will take the centre of the stage in the second
act and his big scene at the end of the third act is a
mathematical certainty.

He has his favourite cases. *Cards on the Table* was the
murder which won his complete technical approval;[30] the

---

29 The arrival of a fan letter extolling the virtues of her detective
rouses the same reaction in Agatha Christie as it does some years
later in Ariadne Oliver in Chapter 14 of *Mrs McGinty's Dead.* 'Why
all the idiotic mannerisms he's got? These things just happen. You
try something – and people seem to like it – and then you go on –
and before you know where you are, you've got someone like that
maddening Sven Hjerson tied to you for life. And people even write
to you and say how fond you must be of him. Fond of him? If I met
that bony, gangling, vegetable-eating Finn in real life, I'd do a better
murder than any I've ever invented.'
30 In the 'Foreword by the Author' to *Cards on the Table* Christie
confirms that 'it was one of Hercule Poirot's favourite cases'; and in
the final chapter Poirot calls it 'one of the most interesting cases I
have ever come across'.

Death on the Nile saddened him.[31] Since *Appointment with
Death* is *sub judice* he must not comment on it here; let me
only say that three points in it appealed to him strongly.
Firstly the fact that desire for truth on the part of another
man coincided with his own strong feelings on that point.
[Secondly] the limitations of his investigation also appealed
to him – the necessity of getting at the truth in twenty four
hours with no technical evidence, post-mortems or the
usual facilities of his background resources And thirdly he
was fascinated by the peculiar psychological interest of the
case and ~~particularly~~ by the strong malign personality of the
dead woman.[32]

   Well, I have told you all I can of Hercule Poirot –
it is possible he has not finished with me yet – there may
be more of him – facts to know which I have not
fathomed.

Having drawn a line, literally, under the essay at this point
Christie then decides to redraft the last paragraph and
expand it slightly, although she omits the third reason for
including *Appointment with Death* among Poirot's favourite
cases:

---

31 At the end of *Death on the Nile* Jacqueline de Bellefort asks Poirot,
    'About me, I mean. You do mind, don't you?' And he answers, 'Yes,
    Mademoiselle.'
32 Oddly, both books of 1938, *Appointment with Death* and *Hercule
    Poirot's Christmas*, feature two of the most detestable characters
    in the entire Christie output: Mrs Boynton in *Appointment with
    Death* and Simeon Lee in *Hercule Poirot's Christmas*. A monstrous
    character automatically provides motive, although in neither case
    is their sheer detestability the reason for their murder. But it seems
    unlikely that this, and not the stunning and unique Petra setting,
    should be one of the characteristics of the case that appealed to
    Poirot.

Firstly that he undertook the case at the express desire of a man whose passion for truth was equal to his own.[33] Secondly the technical difficulty of the investigation ~~put him on his mettle~~ made a special appeal to him and the necessity of reaching the truth in twenty four hours without the help of expert ~~brilliance~~ evidence of any kind

Well, I have given you some of my impressions of Hercule Poirot – they are based on an acquaintance of many years standing. We are friends and partners. I must admit that I am considerably beholden to him financially. Poirot considers that I could not get along without him <u>but</u> on the other hand I consider that but for me Hercule Poirot would not exist.

There are times when I, too, have been tempted to commit murder.[34] I am beholden to him financially. On the other hand, he owes his very existence to me. In moments of irritation I point out that by a few strokes of the pen (or taps on the typewriter) – I could destroy him utterly. He replies grandiloquently 'Impossible to get rid of Hercule Poirot like that – he is much too clever! ~~To permit such a thing to happen~~ And so, as usual, the little man has the last word!

---

33 This is a reference to Colonel Carbury, the man who asks Poirot to investigate the death of Mrs Boynton. In Part II, Chapter 15 Poirot says, 'The truth, I have always thought, is curious and beautiful.'
34 This telling phrase, 'tempted to commit murder', may have been the musing that led, eventually, to *Curtain: Poirot's Last Case*. The chronology fits. This article would have been written, in all likelihood, at the end of 1937 or the very beginning of 1938 and page 7 of Notebook 21, the source of this essay, is headed 'Poirot's Last Case'; and there are a further four pages in the same Notebook with more detailed notes.

The Third Decade 1940–1949

'I never found any difficulty in writing during the war . . . '

───────◄○►───────

SOLUTIONS REVEALED

And Then There Were None • *The Body in the Library* •
Curtain • *Murder on the Orient Express* • *N or M?*

───────◄○►───────

During the Blitz of the Second World War Agatha Christie
lived in London and worked in University College Hospital
by day; and, as she explains in her *Autobiography*, she wrote
books in the evening because 'I had no other things to do.'
She worked on *N or M?* and *The Body in the Library* simultaneously and found that the writing of two totally different books
kept each of them fresh. During this period she also wrote the
final adventure of Hercule Poirot, *Curtain: Poirot's Last Case*,
although it was always asserted that Miss Marple's last case,
Sleeping Murder, was written at around the same time, I showed
in *Agatha Christie's Secret Notebooks* that the date of composition
of that novel is much later. And it was at this time too that she
worked on *Come, Tell Me How You Live* (1946), her 'meander-
ing chronicle' of life on an archaeological dig.

Production slowed down during the 1940s, but only slightly.
Thirteen novels, all but one, *N or M?* (1941), detective stories,

were published; and a collection of short stories appeared towards the end of the decade. But if the quantity decreased, the quality of the writing increased. While still adhering to the strict whodunit formula Christie began, from *Sad Cypress* (1940) onwards, to take a deeper interest in the creation of her characters. For some of her 1940s titles, the characters take centre stage and the detective plot moves further backstage than heretofore. The central triangle of *Sad Cypress* is more carefully portrayed, and the emotional element is stronger, than most of the novels of the 1930s, with the possible exception of *Death on the Nile.* Similarly *Five Little Pigs* (1943), *Towards Zero* (1944), *Sparkling Cyanide* (1945) and especially *The Hollow* (1946) all contain more carefully realised characters than many previous novels.

In 1946 Christie wrote an essay, 'Detective Writers in England', for the Ministry of Information. In it she discusses her fellow writers in the Detection Club – Dorothy L. Sayers, Margery Allingham, Ngaio Marsh,[35] John Dickson Carr, Freeman Wills Crofts, R. Austin Freeman, H.C. Bailey, Anthony Berkeley. She then adds a few modest words about herself, including this interesting remark: 'I have become more interested as the years go on in the preliminaries of crime. The interplay of character upon character, the deep smouldering resentments and dissatisfactions that do not always come to the surface but which may suddenly explode into violence.' *Towards Zero* is an account of the inexorable events leading to a vicious murder at the zero hour of the title; *Five Little Pigs,* her greatest achievement, is a portrait of five people caught in a maelstrom of conflicting emotions culminating in murder; *Sparkling Cyanide,* adopting a similar

---

35 Ngaio Marsh did not become a member of the Detection Club until 1974. This was solely for reasons of geography; because she lived in New Zealand it was impossible for her to attend regular meetings.

technique to *Five Little Pigs*, is a whodunit told through the individual accounts of the suspects, many of them caught in the fatal consequences of an adulterous triangle. And the 'deep smouldering resentments' of her essay are more evident than ever in the prelude to the sudden explosion of violence at a country-house weekend in *The Hollow*. This novel, which could almost be a Westmacott title, features Poirot, although when Christie dramatised it some years later, she wisely dropped him. For once, his presence is unconvincing and the detective element almost a distraction, although the denouement is still a surprise. Through all of this, she managed the whodunit factor though with less emphasis on footprints and fingerprints, diagram and floor plans, and initialled handkerchiefs and red kimonos.

And still she experimented with the detective novel form – *Death Comes as the End* (1945), set in Ancient Egypt in 2,000 BC, is a very early example of the crime novel set in the past; *N or M?* is a wartime thriller; *The Body in the Library* (1942) takes the ultimate cliché of detective fiction and dusts it off; and for *Crooked House* (1949) she wrote an ending so daring that her publishers asked her to change it.

Her only short story collection of this decade, *The Labours of Hercules* (1947), is also her greatest (its genesis and history is discussed in detail in *Agatha Christie's Secret Notebooks*). Apart from her detective output she also published two Westmacott novels. One of them, *Absent in the Spring* (1944), was written in 'a white-heat' over a weekend; this was followed three years later by *The Rose and the Yew Tree*. As further proof of her popularity, she made publishing history in 1948 when she became the first crime writer to have a million Penguin paperbacks issued on the same day, 100,000 each of ten titles.

After a lacklustre stage adaptation, by other hands, of *Peril at End House* in 1940, she wrote her own stage adaptation of *Ten Little Niggers* in 1943, thoroughly enjoying the experience; and dramatisations of two of her 'foreign' novels, *Appointment with Death* and *Death on the Nile*, followed onstage in 1945 and 1946 respectively. And the last play of the decade was Miss Marple's stage debut, *Murder at the Vicarage*, not adapted by Christie herself, appeared in 1949. One of the best screen versions of a Christie work, René Clair's wonderful film *And Then There Were None*, appeared in 1945 and was followed two years later by an inferior second version of *Love from a Stranger*, the inaptly titled film of the excellent short story 'Philomel Cottage'.

Her most enduring monument, *The Mousetrap*, began life in May 1947 as the radio play *Three Blind Mice*, written as a royal commission for Queen Mary's eightieth birthday. In October of that year it also received a one-off television broadcast. The following year another play written directly for radio, *Butter in a Lordly Dish*, was broadcast.

During her third decade of writing Agatha Christie consolidated her national and international career, attracted the attentions of royalty and Hollywood, and experimented with radio. In continuing to extend the boundaries of detective fiction she graduated from a writer of detective stories to a detective novelist.

⮑✕⮐

N or M?
24 November 1941

————————◄○►————————

Which of the guests staying at the guest house Sans Souci is really a German agent? A middle-aged Tommy is asked to investigate and although Tuppence's presence is not officially requested, she is determined not to be left out. Which is just as well, because Tommy disappears . . .

————————◄○►————————

N or M? marked the return of Tommy and Tuppence. We last met them in 1929 in *Partners in Crime*, although the individual stories that make up that volume had appeared up to five years earlier. So this was the first time Christie had written about them for 15 years. By now they are the parents of twins Derek and Deborah, although the chronology of their lives does not bear much scrutiny. At the end of *Partners in Crime* Tuppence announces that she is pregnant, which would make her eldest child a teenager, at most; and yet both children are involved in the war effort. Like Miss Marple's age and the timescale of *Curtain*, the chronology should not interfere with our enjoyment.

N or M? was serialised six months ahead of book publication in UK and two months earlier again in the USA. This tallies with a November 1940 letter from Christie to her agent, Edmund Cork, wondering if she should rewrite the last chapter. It was her intention to set it in a bomb shelter where Tommy and Tuppence find themselves after their flat has been bombed. As she explains in her *Autobiography*, she worked on this book in parallel with *The Body in the Library*, alternating between the two totally different books, thereby ensuring that each one remained fresh. This combination is mirrored in the brief mention – very formally as 'Mr and Mrs Beresford' – below, from Notebook 35.

As a couple, Tommy and Tuppence have not lost their sparkle and the subterfuge undertaken by Tuppence in the early chapters, which enables her to overcome the reluctance of Tommy and his superiors to involve her in events, is very much in keeping with earlier manoeuvres in both *The Secret Adversary* and *Partners in Crime*. In the novel Christie manages to combine successfully the spy adventure and the domestic murder mystery. There is the overriding question of the fifth-column spy but also the more personal mystery of the kidnapped child. With customary ingenuity Christie brings them both together.

Notebook 35 considers the as-yet-unnamed novel:

3 Books

Remembered death [published in the UK as *Sparkling Cyanide*]
The Body in the Library
Mr and Mrs Beresford

And six pages later she sketches in the opening of the book. It would seem from the notes that the fundamentals of the plot were clear before she began it. Most of the notes in Notebooks 35 and 62 are in keeping with the completed novel, although there are the usual minor name changes. Many of the notes for *N or M?* are telegrammatic in style, consisting mainly of combinations of names. These short scenes are often jumbled together in the final draft, the whole not needing as much detailed planning as a formal whodunit with its timetables, clues and alibis.

In the middle of the notes there are some pages of 'real' spy detail culled, presumably, from a book. It is a fascinating glimpse into a relatively unknown area of the Second World War, and somewhat surprising that Christie was able to access this information while the war was still in progress:

Holy figures of Santa containing Tetra (explosive)
Man in telephone booth – are numbers rearranged
Cables on bottom of Atlantic – submarines can lay wires
and copy messages
Mention of 'illness' means spying is under observation.
Recovery is at risk

And Christie experiments with creating a code herself. In Notebook 35 she sketches the notes of the musical scale and the lines and spaces of the musical stave. She adds words – CAFE, BABE, FACE – all composed from the notes of the scale, ABCDEFG. And she outlines a possible character who combines a musical background and a workplace with musical-scale initials: 'A pianist at the BBC'.

Christie next considers potential characters, most of them very cryptically.

T and T
T (for Two)

Tommy approached by MI – Tuppence on phone – really listens – when T turns up at Leahampton – first person he sees is Tuppence – knitting!

Possible people
Young German, Carl – mother a German?
Col Ponsonby – old dug out [Major Bletchley]
Mrs Leacock (who keeps guest house) [Mrs Perenna]
Mr Varney [Mr Cayley]
Mrs Varney [Mrs Cayley]
Daughter with baby comes down to stay [Mrs Sprot]

Later in the same Notebook, she unequivocally states the 'main idea' of the book, though this description is only partly reflected in the novel itself:

Main idea of T and T
Woman head of espionage in England?

In fact, in the opening chapter we read of the 'accidental' death of the agent Farquhar who, with his dying breath, managed to say 'N or M,' confirming the suspicion that two spies, a male, N and a female, M, are at work in England. The concealment of this dangerous female is as clever as anything in Christie's detective fiction and few readers will spot her; in particular, the psychology of the concealment is ingenious.

Notebook 13 has a concise and accurate outline of the book. Details were to change but this is the essence of the plot and would seem to be the first jottings. Not all of these details were to be included and others, not listed here, were to appear, but as a rough initial sketch it is possible to see that Christie had a good idea of where the book was going. The alternative title indicates that Christie possibly considered the book as a 'second innings' for Tommy and Tuppence:

N or M

2nd innings

Possible course of plot
T and T walk – meet – plan of campaign – T's sons
[Chapter 2]
Following incidents
Sheila and Carl together [Chapter 2]
Tuppence and Carl [Chapter 2]
Golf with Major Quincy (Bletchley) 'too many omen' –
Commander Harvey [Haydock] has house on cliff – a coast
watcher [Chapter 3 ii]
Mrs. O'Rourke [Chapter 4]
Mildred Skeffington – 'Betty' [Chapter 2]
Mr. and Mrs. Caley – (Varleys?)
Miss Keyes [Minton] [Chapter 3]
Mrs. Lambert and son

The foreign woman – speaks to Carl in German [Chapter 5
iii]

Kidnapping of child [Chapter 7 ii]
Carl tries to gas himself
Does T hide in Commander's house?
Is he kidnapped on golflinks? Or go to Commander's house
– and be drugged there – the sailing boat [Chapter 9 ii]
A reference to 'Little Bo Peep' – 'Mary has a little lamb' Jack
Warner Horner [Chapter 14 i]
Mrs. O'Rourke – her voice loud and fruity – really drugged
teas with Mrs Skeffington

Notebook 35 has more about Carl and the foreign woman as well as the first mention of the death of the child's mother, although nothing more about the subterfuge around that aspect of the plot. And it is in this Notebook that Christie gives her solution; unlike other books she does not seem to have considered any other names for the two killer spies.

Possible plots

T and T established – Carl immediate object of suspicion
– unhappy – nervy – he and Margaret Parotta – Mrs P –
sinister. Tommy and Col Lessing – play golf together – Col
tells him something suspicious about someone (Mrs P?)
also very much against German boy.

Tup meets foreign looking woman hanging round

Tup has letters – from her 'sons' – leaves them in drawers –
they have been tampered with.
Child kidnapped – found alive – woman dead – documents
planted on her

Information thus sent is true to inspire confidence – Col. L
[Haydock] and Mrs Milly ~~Turnbull~~ Saunders [Sprott] are N
and M

Notebook 62 lists a few more scenes. Scene B appears in the book despite its deletion in the notes:

A. Tommy – supper Haydock – discovery – hit on head – imprisoned [9 ii]
B. ~~Deb and young man – about mothers Leamouth~~ [10 iv]
C. Tup finds Tommy disappeared. Mrs B says never came back last night. Rung up a day later – young man says all right – not to worry. Penny plain and Tuppence coloured – Deborah – Derek [10 iii and 11 iii]

And this short final extract from the same Notebook encapsulates quite an amount of plot, although in such cryptic style that it would be impossible to make sense of it – especially the final phrase – as it stands:

The kidnapping of Betty – Mrs Sprott shoots Polish woman – with revolver taken from Mrs Keefe's drawer – arrest of Karl – incriminating papers – initials ink on bootlaces

An accusation often levelled against Christie's writing is that it never mirrors reality and is set in 'Christie-time'. This adventure of the Beresfords is very much rooted in reality and features the war as part of the plot more than any other title. It is also sobering to remember that when she wrote this book the war still had five years to run. *N or M?* has a lot of clever touches and the interplay between Tommy and Tuppence remains as entertaining as it was on their two previous appearances. Sadly, it was the last we were to read of Tommy and Tuppence until *By the Pricking of my Thumbs,* over 25 years later.

The Body in the Library
11 May 1942

―――――――――――◄O►―――――――――――

When the body of a glamorous blonde is found on Mrs
Bantry's library rug in Gossington Hall, she decides to call
in the local expert in murder – Miss Marple. Together
they go to the Majestic Hotel where Ruby Keene was last
seen alive. And then a second body is found . . .

―――――――――――◄O►―――――――――――

As explained above, the writing of *The Body in the Library* was
done in parallel with that of *N or M?*. Thus the two very dissimilar novels, one a classical whodunit, the other a wartime
thriller, would remain fresh. If indeed they were both written
together, it was during 1940, as *N or M?*, the first to see print,
appeared as a serial in the USA in March 1941. *The Body in the
Library* was serialised in the USA in May/June 1941 and published as a novel there in February 1942. It is probable that
N or M? was completed before *The Body in the Library* as the
timescale for Basil Blake's injuries (mentioned in Chapter 16
ii) in the Blitz, which began in September 1940, would seem
to place the completion of the Marple title well into 1941.

There are references to Miss Marple's previous successes.
In Chapter 1 iv she mentions that her 'little successes have
been mostly theoretical', an allusion to *The Thirteen Problems*,
the last time she had featured in a Christie title. A few pages
later Inspector Slack ruefully recalls his earlier encounter
with the elderly sleuth in *The Murder at the Vicarage*, and Mrs
Bantry reminds Miss Marple (as if she needed it) that the
earlier murder had occurred next door to her. Sir Henry
Clithering recalls her perspicuity in 'Death by Drowning',
the last of *The Thirteen Problems*, in Chapter 8.

Unusually for Christie, the social reaction to the discovery of a body in Colonel Bantry's library is remarked upon. Playful at first, with exaggerated reports circulating in St Mary Mead in Chapter 4, more serious discussion ensues in Chapter 8 ii when Miss Marple considers the potential long-term effect of social ostracism. Some years earlier in *Death in the Clouds* Poirot had questioned Jane Grey and Norman Gale about the practical effects on their lives, and businesses, of involvement in a murder, but he was considering motive and not social reaction.

The main plot device of this novel – the interchangeability of bodies – is very similar to that of the previous year's *Evil under the Sun*. In that novel, in order to establish an alibi a live body masquerades as a dead one; in *The Body in the Library* one dead body is intentionally misidentified as another, again in order to establish an alibi. This sort of ploy was available to detective fiction only in the days before DNA evidence and the enormous strides in forensic medicine. Despite its light-hearted beginning there is a genuinely dark heart to *The Body in the Library*, with its use of a totally innocent schoolgirl as a 'decoy' body, chosen solely on the basis of her similarity to the 'real' corpse, Ruby Keene. This is the earliest example in Christie's oeuvre of the murder of a child (apart from the almost incidental murder of Tommy Pierce in *Murder is Easy*) and unlike later examples – *Dead Man's Folly* and *Hallowe'en Party* – the victim is cold-bloodedly selected and murdered solely to provide a corpse.

Notes for this novel are contained in six Notebooks, the bulk of them in Notebook 62. The plot variations are minimal, leading to the conclusion that Christie had sketched the book mentally before she began serious work on it. And in her *Autobiography*, she admits that she had been thinking about the plot for 'some time'. One note, in Notebook 35, is however at strange variance with the finished novel; the 'disabled' reference could have inspired Conway Jefferson, but otherwise the only similarity is 'Killed somewhere else?'

> Body in Library
> Man? Disabled? Sign of power? No name on clothes
> Inhaling Prussic acid vapour (glucose) Manager of a
> disinfecting process. Killed somewhere else?

An earlier draft, from Notebook 13, outlines the basic plot device – the switch of the bodies and the misidentification – but many of the surrounding details are different. Oddly, one of the conspirators in this first draft is Ruby Keene, the victim in the published novel. At this stage in the planning there is no mention of Conway Jefferson, who provides the motive, and his extended family, which provides most of the suspects. The Girl Guide, the buttons, the bleached blonde – all these plot elements are in place, though as yet the background is not filled in:

> Body in Library
> Mrs. B – awaiting housemaid etc. – telephone to Miss
> Marple. Peroxide blonde connected with young Paul Emery
> [Basil Blake] – rude young man who has fallen out with
> Bantry and who had a platinum blonde down to stay
> (scandal). Paul is member of set in London – real murderer
> has it in for him – dumped body on him – Paul takes it up
> to Bantry's house or real blonde girl knew Paul's blonde
> girl and about cottage – so decoyed Winnie there (with key
> from friend). Body is really Girl Guide decoyed by Mavis
> who pretends she has film face. She and man make her up
> after she is dead. Paul proves he was in London at party at
> 11 pm. Really arrives home about 3 – finds dead girl – is a
> bit tight – thinks we'll push her onto old Bantry.
> Now – <u>why</u>?

Idea is that Mavis de Winter, night club dancer, is dead.
Say: Ruby Keene, Mavis de Winters, were friendly in Paris
– come over here – live separately or share flat. Ruby Keen
goes to the police – her friend disappeared – went off with
man. She identifies body as Mavis – Mavis was fond of Mr
Saunders. Mr. S has alibi because he was seen with Mavis
after certain time. Later ~~Body of~~ Mavis is killed and burnt in
car – girl guides uniform found.
Why variants
Idea being to kill Ruby Treves

This is followed by a bizarre variation, presumably taking the
name Ruby as inspiration:

A. Is Ruby Rajah's friend?
He gave her superb jewels – young man – Ivor Rudd –
attractive – bad lot – takes her to England – tells her there's
been an accident – girl guide dead – fakes body – drives
it down to Paul Seton's. Later identifies it as Ruby's body
– later takes Ruby out in car and sets fire to it – girl guide
buttons and badge found

Notebook 31 is headed confidently on the first page and followed by a list of characters to which I have added the probable
names from the book. Then the main timetable is sketched,
with a further paragraph filling in some of the details:

The Body in the Library
People
Mavis Carr [Ruby Keene]
Laurette King [Josie Turner]
Mark Tanderly [Mark Gaskell]
Hugo Carmody – legs taken off in last War – very rich
[Conway Jefferson]

Step children   Jessica Clunes
                Stephen Clunes
                Edward

Man (Mark or Steve) takes her [Mavis] to Paul's cottage.
Leaves her there – carefully asks way or draws attention to
car? Body left there at (say) 9.30 – Mavis seen alive last at
9.15 in hotel. Both girls had drink. W[innie] doped at 6.30
or 7. Pansied up after being killed at 9 pm – driven ½ hours
drive by Mark 9.~~30~~ to 10 – Mavis in hotel 9 to 10 – goes
upstairs at 10 (killed). Mark dancing 10–12. Body in empty
bedroom – [body] taken out and put in car between 12 and
1 – covered with rug. Driven off early morning – set on fire
(time fuse) in wood. Mavis last seen 10 pm – did not come
on and dance – car found missing, later found abandoned
in St. Loo.

One of the dangers inherent in writing two books at the
same time is shown in the extract below from Notebook
35, which has another possible sketch of the plot. The plot
summary includes a Milly Sprott, who is actually one of the
characters from *N or M?*. Presumably she was to be the Girl
Guide character, as the list of characters that follows includes
a Winnie Sprott. This extract may be the very first musings
on the book.

Body in the Library   Suggestions
Body immature – yellow bleached hair – extravagant
make-up – (really girl guide – lost – ~~or a VAD~~ – adenoidy).
Suggestion is <u>actress</u> – handbag with clippings of theatrical
news – revue – chorus – foreign artist. Body planted on
young artist who has had row with Col B – (in war – military
service etc.) and who has had blonde girl friend down. He
plants her on Col B with help of real blonde friend. She can
turn up later alive and well. Does girl in London come down

and identify dead girl as Queenie Race. Really QR is alive –
later Queenie killed and body dressed in Guide's clothes.
Why was Milly Sprott killed – she saw too much – or
overheard it? She is identified by Ruby – Ruby is accomplice
of villain

Body L[ibrary]
Calling the Bantry etc.
Platinum blonde – everything points to young Jordan
Body
Blonde girl
Young Jordan's friend
Winnie Sprott – girl guide
Mrs Clements – Brunette
Ruby Quinton – actress
Identified by best fr sister or friend or gentleman friend
Why?
Real Ruby engineers whole story – she – young man – life
insurance?

Notebook 62 lists individual chapters and although the chapter headings do not tally, the material covered is as it appears
in the novel. The names too are mostly retained, although
Col. Melrose becomes Melchett, and Michael Revere and
Janetta transform into Basil Blake and Dinah Lee:

The Body in the Library
Chapter I
Mrs B housemaid etc. Miss Marple comes up and sees body
Chapter II
Col Melrose – his attitude to Col B – Michael Revere and
his blonde. Col M goes down there – M[ichael] in very
bad temper – got down after party. Arrival of Janetta ['his
blonde']

Chapter III
Melrose in his office – Inspector Slack – missing people.
Who came down by train the night before? Lot of people
at station. Bantrys – Mrs B went to bed early – Col B out at
meeting of local Conservative Association
Chapter IV
Arrival of Josie – she is taken to the hall – sees body – Oh
Ruby all right. Story begins to come out – Conway Jefferson
– Mrs Bantry knows him
Chapter V
At hotel – Jefferson – Adelaide – Mark – Raymond (the pro)
– evidence about girl
Chapter VI
Mrs B finds Jefferson – old friend – Miss M with her
Chapter VII
Adelaide and Miss M and Mrs B – Josie and Raymond

In the middle of these listings Christie sketches what she
refers to as the 'real sequence', the mechanics of the murder
plot, as well as a list of the characters. The deletions suggest that she amended this afterwards to reflect the eventual
choices:

Real sequence – Winnie King leaves rally 6.30 – goes with
Josie to hotel – drugged in tea – put in empty bedroom.
After dinner 9.30 Mark takes girl to car and drives her to
bungalow (Friday night). Strangles her 10 and puts her in –
drives back – Ruby is on view 10 to 10.30 – then killed with
veronal or chloral – put in room by Josie's. 5 am – Mark
and Josie take her down to car – (pinched from small house
in street . . . young man's car) ~~Josie~~ Mark drives her out to
wood – leaving trail of petrol – gets away – walks back –
arrives in time for breakfast or his bathe?

People
(Josie!) Josephine Turner
Ruby Keene
Raymond Clegg [Starr]
Conway Jefferson
Adelaide Jefferson – Rosamund?
Peter Carmody
Mark Gaskell
Then
Bob Perry (car trader)
~~Michael Revere~~ Basil Blake
Diane Lee Dinah Lee
Mrs ~~Revere~~ Blake
Hugo ~~Trent~~ Curtis McClean (Marcus)
Pam Rivers [Reeves]
~~Basil Penton~~
George Bartlett

Reason why Miss Marple knows
Bitten nails
Teeth go down throat (mentioned by Mark). 'Murderers always give themselves away by talking too much'
[Chapter 18]

Abandoning her list of chapters, Christie briefly sketches some scenes all of which appear in the second half of the novel, although the combination of characters sometimes varies:

A. Interviewing girls – Miss M present [14 ii]
B. Col Clithering interviews Edwards [14 i]
C. Col C and Ramon [13 iii but with Sir Henry]
D. Addie and Miss M [12 ii but with Mrs. B]
E. Mark and Mrs B or Miss M [12 iv but with Sir Henry]

F. Mrs B and Miss M [13 iv]

G. Doctor and Police [13 i]

In her specially written Foreword for the 1953 Penguin edition of *The Body in the Library*, Christie explains that when she tackled one of the clichés of detective fiction – the body in the library – she wanted to experiment with the convention. So she used Gossington Hall in St Mary Mead and Colonel Bantry's very staid, very English library but made her corpse a very startling one – young and blonde, with cheap finery and bitten fingernails. But, as so often happens in a Christie novel, what may seem to be mere dramatics is actually a vital part of the plot. *Three Act Tragedy, Death on the Nile, Sparkling Cyanide, A Murder is Announced* – all feature a dramatic death, but in each case the scene in question is part of an artfully constructed plot; and so it is with *The Body in the Library*. Christie also considered the opening of this novel – Mrs Bantry's dream of winning the Flower Show is interrupted by an hysterical maid with the early morning tea – the best she had written; and it is difficult not to agree.

Curtain: Poirot's Last Case
22 September 1975

A frail Poirot summons Hastings to Styles, the scene of their first investigation and now a guest house. Poirot explains that a fellow-guest is a murderer. Convinced that another killing is imminent he asks Hastings to help prevent it. But who is the killer and, more importantly, who is the victim?

'Do you know, Poirot, I almost wish sometimes that you would commit a murder.'

'Mon cher!'

'Yes, I'd like to see how you set about it.'

'My dear chap, if I committed a murder you would not have the slightest chance of seeing – how I set about it! You would not even be aware, probably, that a murder had been committed.'

'Murder in the Mews'

'I shouldn't wonder if you ended up by detecting your own death,' said Japp, laughing heartily. 'That's an idea, that is. Ought to be put in a book.'

'It will be Hastings who will have to do that,' said Poirot, twinkling at me.

The A.B.C. Murders, Chapter 3

These telling and prophetic exchanges, both between Poirot and Inspector Japp, may have sowed the seeds of an idea in Christie's fertile brain. *The A.B.C. Murders* was begun in 1934 and 'Murder in the Mews' was completed in early 1936, so both pre-dated *Curtain*. But, as will be seen, she had been considering a plot very like it for some years.

Curtain: Poirot's Last Case is the most dazzling example of legerdemain in the entire Christie output. It is not only a nostalgic swan song, but also a virtuoso demonstration of plotting ingenuity culminating in the ultimate shock ending from a writer whose career was built on her ability both to deceive and delight her readers. It plays with our emotional reaction to the decline, and eventual demise, of one of the world's great detective creations, and it also recalls the heady days of the first case that Poirot and Hastings shared, also in the unhappy setting of the ill-fated country house Styles.

The return to Styles was inspired; it encompasses the idea of a life come full circle, as Poirot revisits the scene both of his momentous reacquaintance with Hastings, and of his first great success in his adopted homeland. Like Poirot himself, Styles has deteriorated from its glory days and, instead of having a family gathered under its roof, is now host to a group of strangers; and one of them (at least) has, as in yesteryear, murder in mind. And the claustrophobic atmosphere of the novel is accentuated by having only two short scenes – those depicting Mrs Franklin's inquest and funeral and the visit to Boyd Carrington's house – set elsewhere. The novel also toys with the vexed question of natural versus legal justice. This is not the first time that a classic Christie has explored this theme. *And Then There Were None* and *Murder on the Orient Express* are both based on this difficult concept; and *Ordeal by Innocence, Five Little Pigs, Mrs McGinty's Dead* and 'Witness for the Prosecution', in both short story and stage versions, further explore this theme.

But as usual with Christie, and certainly the Christie of the era in which she wrote *Curtain,* almost everything is subservient to plot; as it was throughout her career, the theme of justice – natural versus legal, justice in retrospect, posthumous free pardons – is merely the starting point for a clever plot. Two of her best and most famous titles – *And Then There Were None* and *Murder on the Orient Express* – are predicated on this theme but in each case the moral dilemma is secondary to the machinations of a brilliant plot. In each case, in order to make her plot workable and credible she needed a compelling reason to motivate her characters. Lawrence Wargrave in the former novel, despite his status as a retired judge, needs to be provided with a convincing reason for his ingenious plan for mass murder; the murderous conspirators on board the famous train need an even more persuasive one. In each case miscarriage of justice fitted the bill as a motivating force better than any other; *Murder on the Orient Express* carries an added emotional factor – the killing of a kidnapped child despite the ransom being paid. In 1934 few more heinous crimes could be imagined, or at least written about. Discussion of justice is perfunctory in each title; plot mechanics override any philosophical consideration.

When was *Curtain* written? In *Agatha Christie's Secret Notebooks* I showed that the writing of Miss Marple's last case, *Sleeping Murder*, took place much later than was formerly believed, and certainly not during the Blitz of the Second World War. Because there are no dated pages among the notes for *Curtain*, the case here is less clear. *Sad Cypress*, mentioned in Chapter 3 ('the case of Evelyn [Elinor] Carlisle'), was published in March 1940 with a US serialisation beginning in November 1939. The address on the manuscript of *Curtain* is 'Greenway House', which Christie left in October 1942 on its requisition by the US navy. These are the two parameters on the writing of *Curtain*.

But from the evidence of the Notebooks it would seem that it was written earlier, rather than later, than previously supposed. The clearest evidence for this is in Notebook 62. The early pages of this Notebook contain the notes for the stories that make up *The Labours of Hercules*, beginning with 'The Horses of Diomedes' on page 3 and 'The Apples of the Hesperides' on page 5. The first page contains a short list of 'Books read and liked' and the latest publication date involved is 1940. (The list includes *Overture to Death*, the 1939 Ngaio Marsh title and her first to be published by Collins Crime Club.) Sandwiched between this list and the first page of notes for 'The Horses of Diomedes' is a page headed unequivocally 'Corrections Curtain'; page 4 continues with the corrections and the final revisions appear below the half-page of notes for 'The Apples of the Hesperides'; these stories were published in *The Strand* in June and September

1940 respectively. Combined with the reference on the first page of the novel to 'a second and a more desperate war', this would seem to place the writing of this novel in the early days of the Second World War.

For the reader, the main difficulty with *Curtain* is one of fitting the case into the Poirot casebook, containing as it does inevitable chronological inconsistencies for a book written 35 years before its 1975 publication. It is impossible to state with any certainty when the book is set. Although he has been married for over 50 years, Hastings has a 21-year-old daughter. Poirot has declined dramatically since his previous appearance three years earlier in *Elephants Can Remember*, and even the most generous estimate must place his age at around 120. In Chapter 3 there are references to cases that were all written, and published, during the late 1930s or early 1940s – 'Triangle at Rhodes', *The A.B.C. Murders, Death on the Nile, Sad Cypress*; the main character in the last of these is, oddly, referred to as Evelyn, instead of Elinor, Carlisle. Countess Vera Rosakoff (*The Big Four*, 'The Capture of Cerberus', 'The Double Clue') is also mentioned in the same chapter and the bloodstained butcher, also from *The Big Four*, is mentioned in passing in Chapter 5. There is a reference in Chapter 15 to the original Styles case as happening '20 years ago and more'; the earlier case could not have been simply ignored and this reference is vague enough to have little chronological significance.

The question that has to be asked, but unfortunately cannot be answered, is: Did Christie write *Curtain* intending that it would appear long after many 'future' cases of Poirot had been published, or did she write it *as if* she was writing it after many such cases had been published? Are references to 'long ago' (Chapter 7) *actually* to long ago or to the 'long ago' Christie imagined would have elapsed by the time the book was published? There is no indication on any of the

the original typescripts of any major deletions or updating, putting paid to the theory that the resurrected manuscript received major surgery to remove obvious chronological anomalies. One of the surviving typescripts contains minor corrections, and these correspond to the list of corrections in Notebook 62, which seems to date from the early 1940s, possibly 1940 itself.

But if you accept that the book was written many years prior to publication and treat it as a 'lost' case, then these problems disappear and it is possible to enjoy this master-work of plotting for what it is – the ultimate Christie con-juring trick. Technically it is a master class in plotting a detective story. Arguably there is no murder, although there are three deaths. The breakdown is as follows: Colonel Luttrell attempts to murder his wife, while Mrs Franklin attempts to murder her husband; Hastings proposes to murder Allerton and is responsible for the unintentional murder (i.e. manslaughter) of Mrs Franklin; and Poirot's 'execution' of Norton is followed by his own death.

Hastings' intended murder of Allerton is foiled by Poirot, who realises what he means to do. Mrs Franklin, thanks to an innocent action on the part of Hastings, is hoist with her own petard when she unintentionally drinks the poison she intended for her husband. Colonel Luttrell's shooting of his wife is a failure because, as Poirot puts it, 'he wanted to miss.' And Poirot, in effect, executes Norton. In this regard, it should be remembered that Poirot was not above taking the law into his own hands and had done so, to a greater or lesser degree, throughout his career. In *The Murder of Roger Ackroyd, Peril at End House, Dumb Witness, Death on the Nile, Appointment with Death* and *The Hollow,* he 'facilitated' (at least) the suicide of the culprit. And in *Murder on the Orient Express* and 'The Chocolate Box' he allowed the killers to evade (legal) justice.

The references to *Curtain* are scattered over nine Notebooks. Notebooks 30, 44 and 61 each have a one-page reference, while half a dozen other Notebooks have a few pages each, but the bulk of the plotting is contained in Notebooks 62 and 65 (ten pages each) and Notebook 60 with over 40 pages. It is difficult to be sure if this was because Christie mulled it over for a long time, jotting down a note whenever she got an idea, or because the plotting of it presented a challenge to her creativity. I would incline towards the latter theory, as many of the jottings are a reiteration of the same situation with changes of name, character, profession or other minor detail. This would seem to indicate that the basic idea (Styles as a guest house and Poirot as an invalid inhabitant) remains the same and that, as she intended this to be Poirot's swan song (and the notes would back this up), she wanted it to be stunning; as indeed it is.

In *Curtain* Agatha Christie played her last great trick on her public. Throughout her career she fooled readers into believing the innocent guilty and, more importantly, the guilty innocent. Her first novel made the most obvious parties the guilty ones; a few years later she made the narrator the murderer. Throughout the 1930s and 1940s she rang the changes on the least likely character – the investigating policeman, the child, the likeable hero, the supposed victim; she had everyone guilty and everyone victim. She repeated the Ackroyd trick in her last decade but made it unrecognisable until the last chapter. By the time of *Curtain* her only remaining least likely character was the one she chose – Poirot, her little Belgian hero. And in so doing, her title was also the only possible one – *Curtain*.

The idea of a 'last case' for Poirot was one that Christie toyed with intermittently while plotting earlier titles. The following references are scattered through seven Notebooks and all refer to such a case, often with the name *Curtain* included:

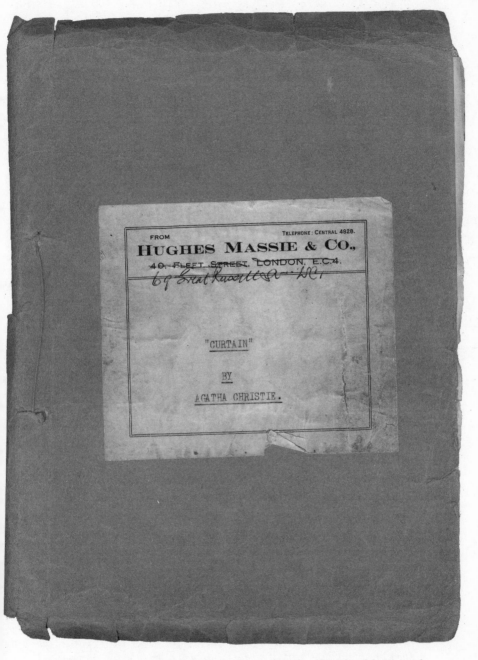

FROM

TELEPHONE: CENTRAL 4828.

HUGHES MASSIE & CO.,

40, FLEET STREET, LONDON, E.C.4.

"CURTAIN"

BY

AGATHA CHRISTIE.

The cover of a typescript of Curtain. *Edmund Cork of Hughes Massie and Co. was Christie's agent* from The Murder of Roger Ackroyd *onwards.*

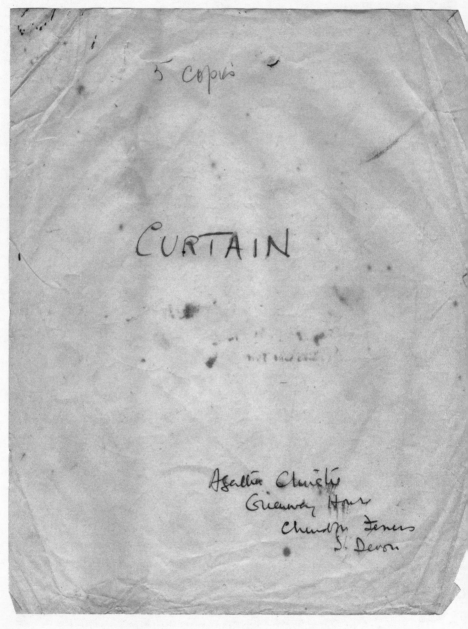

The title page of the Curtain *typescript, showing the title and name-and-address in Christie's own handwriting.*

Curtain
Poirot investigates story of death believed caused by ricin

B. Poirot's Last Case
Styles – turned into convalescent home or Super Hotel

A. Poirot's Last Case
History repeats itself – Styles now a guest house

Double murder – that is to say: A poisons B [and] B stabs A
but really owing to plan by C (perhaps P's last case?)

Curtain
Letter received by Hastings on boat. His daughter with him
– Rose? Pat? At Styles

The Unsolved Murder – Poirot's Last Case?

~~The~~ Curtain
H[astings] comes to Styles – has heard about P[oirot]

Short Stories
Scene of one – Road up to Bassae? (Hercule's last case)

That last, very short and cryptic example from Notebook
60 refers to the Temple of Bassae in Greece, one of the
places that Christie visited on her honeymoon. Both her
Autobiography and Max Mallowan's *Memoirs* mention it,
mainly because it involved a ten-hour mule ride. At first
glance it seems that she was considering it as a possible setting for *Curtain* but it is far more likely that it is the last of
The Labours of Hercules she had in mind, although in the end
it came to nothing. This would have been totally in keeping

with the international flavour of many of those cases (see *Agatha Christie's Secret Notebooks*).

Possible characters are considered in six Notebooks, with Hastings and/or his daughter appearing in many of the lists:

The people
Sherman is the man who likes power – attractive personality. Victim is Caroline

Curtain Characters
Judith – H's daughter
Mrs Merrit – tiresome invalid
Her husband – tropical researcher medicine
Girl – B.Sc. has done work for him – very devoted
Or
Judith
Miss Clarendon – nurse companion – fine woman – experienced – mentions a 'case' of murder – 'I once had to give evidence in a murder case'
Sir C. Squire – fine English type – wants to fight – H. terrifically taken by him –

2nd set of people?
Betty Rice (old friend of Landor) – A difficult life – her husband takes drugs
Dr. Amberly – clever man tropical medicine
Mrs Amberly tiresome invalid but with charm
Sir Roger Clymer – old school tie – fine fellow – has known Mrs A[llerton] as girl
Miss Clarendon – a nurse companion
A girl, Betty, and her friend come down together – she is an archaeologist or B.Sc. or something in love with Dr. Amberley
Or

Judith H's daughter
Superior and unpleasant young man? (Mrs A's son by
former marriage?)

At Styles
Dr Amory – keen man of forty-five – wants to go to Africa,
study tropical medicine
His wife, Kitty – invalid imaginaire – a blight but attractive
Governess Bella Chapstowe
Nurse companion Miss Olroyd
Martin Wright – cave man – naturalist

People
John Franklin
Adela Franklin
Langton
Nurse Barrett
? Mrs. L[angton] (Emilia?)
Roger Boyd
Old Colonel Luxmoore
Mrs Luxmoore

People there
The Darwins – Fred – patient, quiet – his wife querulous
He wants to go off to Africa – his wife won't let him
Betty Rousdon – a girl staying there – very keen on his work
Wife's companion – Miss Collard – principal false clue
John Selby – cave man – fond of birds – a naturalist –
becomes great friends with Joan Hastings
Girl and mother (latter impossible)
Young man who wants to marry her
Has Selby a wife?

Col. Westmacott and wife – (like Luards?) some secondary
resentment between them
Langdon – lame man – keen on birds – has alibi <u>genuine</u> for
some previous case
P[oirot] – invalid – thinks Egypt etc. not George another
valet – (not totally helpless)
Triangle drama
(Hastings daughter?) sec. to scientific man – nagging invalid
wife who won't let him go to S. America

Some of the characters seem to have been decided early on
and, apart from name changes, remained constant until the
finished novel. They include a doctor interested in tropical medicine and his invalid wife, under various names (the
Amberleys/Merrits/Darwins/Amorys/Franklins); a young
professional woman (Betty Rousdon/'a Girl'/Judith) in love
with him and his work; a nurse companion (Miss Collard/
Oldroyd/Clarendon/Nurse Barrett); an 'old school tie'
(Roger Boyd/Sir C. Squire/Sir Roger Clymer); a naturalist
(Sherman/Martin Wright/Selby); and the owners of Styles
(the Westmacotts/Luxmoores). These remain, in one form
or another, through most of the notes. The young professional woman was not always Hastings' daughter, Judith;
this amendment was introduced possibly in order to give
Hastings the necessary motive for murder.

Note the one-time proposal to use the name Westmacott
for the owners of Styles. Although it is now well known that
Mary Westmacott is a pseudonym for Agatha Christie, at the
time these notes were written it was a carefully preserved
secret. The reference to the Luards in the final extract is to
a once-famous real life murder case in 1908 involving a love
triangle.

Eventually, in Notebook 60, we get the listing that is
nearest to the novel. At this point, as in some of the earlier

listings, there was to be a Mrs Langton. However, Langton as a 'loner' makes more sense, psychologically as well as practically.

People
Judith Hastings
John Franklin
Barbara Franklin
Nurse Campbell [Craven]
Sir Boyd Carrington
Major ~~Neville~~ Nugent [Allerton] (seducer) really after Nurse
Col and Mrs Luttrell own the place
Miss Cole – handsome woman of 35
Langtons [Norton]

Chapter 2 of the novel lists the cases on which Poirot bases his assertion that a death will take place at Styles in the near future. Some of the scenarios sketched below, from Notebooks 60 and 65, tally closely with that chapter though, in general, details have been selected and amalgamated:

The Cases
On a yacht – a row – man pitched another overboard – a quarrel – wife had had nervous breakdown
Girl killed an overbearing aunt – nagged at her – young man in offing – forbidden to see or write to him
Husband – elderly invalid – young wife – gave him arsenic – confessed
Sister-in-law – walked into police station and admitted she'd killed her brother's wife. Old mother (of wife) lived with them bedridden [elements of the Litchfield Case]

Curtain The Cases
Man who drinks – young wife – man she is fond of – she kills

husband – arsenic? [the Etherington Case] (Langton's her
cousin – or friend?)
Man in village – his wife and a lodger – he shoots them both
– or her and the kid (It comes out L[angton] lived in that
village) [elements of the Riggs Case]
Old lady – the daughter or granddaughter – elder polishes
off old lady to give young sister a chance [elements of the
Litchfield Case]

The only scenario not to appear in any way is the first one.
In many ways these recapitulations are reminiscent of a
similar set-up in *Mrs McGinty's Dead,* where four earlier and
notorious murder cases affect the lives of the inhabitants of
Broadhinny.

The following extract, from Notebook 61, appears as Idea
F in a list that includes the germs of *Sad Cypress* ('illegitimate daughter – district nurse') and 'Dead Man's Mirror'
('The Second Gong – Miss Lingard efficient secretary') and
is immediately followed by detailed notes for *Appointment
with Death,* published in 1938. As this jotting was probably
written around late 1936 ('Dead Man's Mirror' was first published in March 1937 in *Murder in the Mews*) this would put
the early plotting of *Curtain* years ahead of its (supposed)
writing. The theory that Christie wrote *Curtain* and *Sleeping
Murder* in case she was killed in the Blitz begins to look questionable, as the 1940 Blitz was an unimagined horror four
years earlier. Nor can it have been a book held in reserve
in case of a 'dry' season when she didn't feel like writing.
Curtain could only be published at the end of Poirot's (and
Christie's) career, so it can in no way be considered a nest
egg. Ironically, despite the fact that this is a very precise and
concise summation of *Curtain,* this Notebook contains no
further reference to it.

The Unsolved Mystery   Poirot's Last Case?
P very decayed – H and Bella [Hastings' wife, whom he
met in *The Murder on the Links*] come home. P shows H
newspaper cuttings – all referring to deaths – about 7 – <u>4</u>
people have been hanged or surprise that no evidence. At
all 7 deaths <u>one person</u> has been present – the name is cut
out. P says that person X is present in house. There will be
another murder. There is – a man is killed – that man is
really X himself – executed

And this extract, from Notebook 62, mentions another
important point – the absence of George and his replacement with another 'valet':

Hastings arriving at the station for Styles – Poirot – black
hair but crippled – Georges away – the other man – a big
one – quite dumb
After dinner (various people noted) P in his room gives H
cases to read – X

Notebook 65 recaps this with some added detail – Poirot and
Egypt, the sadism angle – but the note about warning the
victim is puzzling. As he says in Chapter 3, Poirot knows from
his experiences in *Death on the Nile* and 'Triangle at Rhodes'
how fruitless warning a potential murderer can be. And he
makes the point in the same chapter that warning the victim
in this case is impossible as he does not know who the victim
is to be. So why is the 'Warn the victim?' question answered
with 'I have done that'?

~~The~~ Curtain
H comes to Styles – has heard about P from Egypt – has
arthritis – Georges is back with him – Master much worse
since he went to Egypt.

I am here because a crime is going to be committed. You
are going to prevent it
No – I can't do that
Warn the victim?
I have done that
It is certain to happen because the person who has made
up his mind will not relent
Listen –
The story of 5 crimes – H stupefied – no motive in ordinary
sense? No – spoilt – sadistic

The first 'murder', that of Mrs Luttrell by her husband,
is considered in Notebook 60. The finished novel follows
these notes accurately, even down to the quotation from
Julius Caesar.

Col L shoots Mrs L – rifle not shot gun as he thinks –
prepared by 'brother' batman story – then good shot –
quick etc. Accident. He is terribly upset that night – cares
for her – remembers her as 'girl in a blue dress' [Chapter 9]

P goes down – finds Colonel and Langton – former has been
shooting rabbits – Langton flattering him. Talk of accident
– he talks of shot beater etc. BC [Boyd Carrington] comes
along – tells story of batman – goes off. Langton says he'll
never be bullied or henpecked – Langton quotes 'Not in our
Stars, dear Brutus but in ourselves.' Col. shoots at rabbit
– shoots Mrs – bending over flowers. Franklin and Nurse
attend to her. ~~Colonel~~ latter comes later to Colonel – says
it's all right, ~~Colonel~~ all broken up – talks of her and old
days – where he met her [Chapter 9]

H[astings] has conversation with Nurse. She asks about
Styles – was in murder case once. Talks about Mrs Franklin.

Boyd Carrington comes up 'Good looking girl' – come and
see house. H goes with him – the house – his uncle – a very
rich man – has everything – lonely. About Col L – fine shot
[Chapter 7 iii]

There are three sketches of Hastings' proposed murder and
two of his unintentional murder, all from Notebook 60.

H decides (goaded by Langton) to kill 'seducer' of Judith –
J. very secretive – plants Boyd as decoy – really when with
Franklin. Boyd a boaster – fond of travel – carrying on with
pretty hospital nurse. P. drugs H so that he wakes up next
morning and has not killed B – his relief

Hastings plans a murder. Gets tablets from Poirot's room or
from Boyd's own room – P drugs him

Conversation between BC, Langton, Judith and H. BC – his
magnetic personality – goes off. Langton tries to persuade
Judith she wouldn't have the courage etc. He comes to
reassure Hastings she wouldn't really do anything. Then
tries to warn him – is it wise to let her see so much of
Atherton – married etc. He looks through glasses – shows
his bird – then snatches them away – changes subject – he
can see the figures. Goes in very unhappy – very worried.
Personal problem ousts all others. Judith comes out of
his room – H upset – speaks to her – she flares out – nasty
mind – spends a night of increasing anxiety – the following
day Langton tells him – rather unlovely story (quote him)
– Atherton and a girl – she committed suicide. He goes to
Judith – real row – H. is miserable. Hangs about – I could
kill the fellow – Langton says not really – one hasn't the
guts when it comes to it. H goes upstairs to see P (with L) –
passes A's room – he is talking to someone – (nurse) that's

fine, my dear – you run up to town – I go so and so – send a wire you can't get back – will go to other D – etc. Finds L – pulling him away. I'll go to her – No, you'll make things worse. L goads him – one feels responsible. H makes up his mind – it's his duty to save her. Gets drug – waits up – P makes him drugged chocolate. He sleeps. Next morning – his relief – tells P – P reassures him – you can't lead other people's lives for them – points out just how he would have been found out [Chapters 11 and 12]

More points
It is <u>Hastings</u> who kills Mrs F. He changes glasses or cups so that she gets it, not husband

Everyone asked up afterwards. She is lying on divan – coffee – makes it herself. Crossword – everyone there – at least ~~Nurse~~ F. J. BC. Coles and H. Col and Mrs L L. Miss Cole. The stars – they go out to look – H puzzling over crossword. BC comes back – picks up Mrs [Franklin] in his arms – carries her out laughing and protesting. H's eyes fill remembering Bella. J comes in – he disguises his feeling by pretending to look in bookcase – swings it round – muddle about 'Death.' J gives him correct word – he replaces book. Goes out with her – they come back – take their places. J by request brings medicine – F goes off to work. Dead the next day [Chapter 13]

There is an irony in the fact that having 'saved' Hastings from an intentional murder, Poirot is unable to save him from committing an accidental murder. And, arguably, the explanation of Mrs Franklin's death is as big a surprise to the reader as the explanation in Poirot's letter at the end of the book.

There are also a few versions of the death of Langton/ Norton, all of them in Notebook 60, but none of them include a shooting:

Langton tells H he has an idea about murder. P stops him
'Dangerous' – he goes to P's room that evening. Chocolate
put in trintium. He dies at once. H woken by striking against
his door – looks out – Sees L – go into own room – limp,
dressing gown etc. Next day – found dead – key of his room
in own pocket – locked. P says gave him trintium tablets
1/10 – by mistake in 1/100 box. P says his fault – H knows
better – says to P same method – always a mistake – P
agrees

P has had door key stolen – had new one made – (old
room!) (a mention of P coming after Langton) P has
trintium tablets for high blood pressure – takes them –
induces tolerance. Shares chocolate with L – L dies. P
wheels him to room – returns and plays part of L in dressing
gown – hair – his own is wig – fake moustache – deliberately
for Hastings. Goes in and locks door

Mrs Langton – Emilia – realises truth – tells Hastings
so – kills herself – cuts throat. Langton arrested – P's
machination – limp – razor blade dropped – blood on it etc.
fingerprint – L and Hast. only – L put in invalid chair and
pushed to room

Emilia realises L is insane. First writes letter saying she is
afraid of him, then ~~cuts her~~ shows herself in his dressing
gown and limping, hides razor (wiped) with blood on it –
then cuts her throat. P's point is to lie – say L left him at
12.10. Or guillotine idea – L to put his head down – steel
shutter

P sends for L – confronts him with story. L admits it all,
shows himself in his true colours –Emilia hears it all. P gives
him narcotic – goes to Emilia's room. She has killed herself

with razor. P takes L along, lets him hold razor – blood on
it, on him. Then leaves room waking up H – shows himself
in L's dressing gown hiding razor in pot. H finds it

It is difficult to think of any advantage to the method, in
which Mrs Langton (Emilia) plays a large and blood-soaked
part, over the shooting Christie eventually settled on.
Especially as the bullet-wound has the added symbolic reso-
nance of the Mark of Cain; this was also a significant clue in
And Then There Were None, making one wonder which came
first. The 'guillotine' idea is one of the most bizarre in the
entire Christie opus.

The notes for *Curtain*, in both volume and invention, show
a professional working at the height of her considerable
powers. The manipulation of plot variations, the exploration
of character possibilities, the evocation of earlier crimes, all
culminating in an elegiac letter from the dead, combine to
display the unique gifts of the Queen of Crime.

UNUSED IDEAS: THREE

UNUSED IDEAS:
THREE

SOLUTIONS REVEALED
*Death in the Clouds • The Mirror Crack'd from Side to Side •
A Murder is Announced • One, Two, Buckle my Shoe • Peril
at End House • Sparkling Cyanide • Three Act Tragedy*

Batch three of Unused Ideas includes a number of
sketches for possible plays.

THE MOUSETRAP II

Mousetrap II?
A reunion dinner – the survivors of revolution? war (Airman
and passengers lost in desert)
Man gate crashes – a lawyer? elderly? Mannered? Felix
Aylmer type or a [Sir Ralph] Richardson.
A murder – here – one of group is a murderer – one of group
is a victim. Doesn't know victim
End of Scene – I'm the prospective victim amn't I? (Really
murderer)

Possibility of house in street Soho hired for party – waiters
hired for joke! One man is waiter – brings drink to guest –
later enters as guest – with moustache.
Death at the Dinner – man drinks – dies – a doctor present
says this glass must be kept. It is then he puts poison in it –
real drink was poisoned earlier – before dinner
(A mixture of 3 Act Tragedy (Sir Charles) and Sparkling
Cyanide?) Is wrong person killed?

The biggest mystery about this sketch is the reason for calling it
'Mousetrap II', as it has nothing in common with that famous
play. Perhaps it was so called in the hope of another stage success that might rival the record-breaking title? It is also difficult to date this extract as most of the contents of Notebook 4,
from which these notes are excerpted, remain unpublished.
Much of it is taken up with notes for the relatively unknown
play *Fiddlers Five* (later *Fiddlers Three*), first staged in 1971, so
it seems reasonable to assume this extract dates from the late
1960s. Strength is also lent to this argument by the fact that by
then *The Mousetrap* was a record-breaker.

As Christie herself states, there are strong similarities with
Three Act Tragedy – the subterfuge with glasses, the cryptic
note 'Doesn't know victim', the guest disguised as a waiter/
butler – and *Sparkling Cyanide* – the unexpected death at the
dinner table and a similar waiter/guest ploy. This ruse is
also a variation on that adopted by the killer in *Death in the
Clouds*. The oddly specific reason outlined for the reunion
– survivors of a revolution – has echoes of the revolution in
Ramat that culminated in murder at Meadowbank School
in *Cat among the Pigeons*. And the prospective victim as murderer was a favourite throughout Christie's career – *Peril at
End House, One, Two, Buckle my Shoe, A Murder is Announced,
The Mirror Crack'd from Side to Side*. Despite these echoes of
earlier novels, this late in her career Christie was still coming

up with original ideas: the trick with the glass did not feature in any of her earlier poisonings.

The actor Felix Aylmer played Sir Rowland Delahaye in the first production of *Spider's Web* in 1954; and Sir Ralph Richardson would play, many years later, one of Christie's most famous creations, Sir Wilfrid Robards, in a 1983 TV remake of *Witness for the Prosecution.*

———◆———

THE REUNION DINNER

Reunion Dinner 3 Act Play
Collinaris Restaurant
Waiter – old man like a tortoise
Waiter – young Italian type (conversation between them about this dinner)
Victor Durel – business type (approves menu etc. – wines)
Valentine Band (Clydesdale? Harborough?) – rich furs and so on
Major Allsop – sharp practice type company partner
Isadore Cowan – old Jew
Janet Spence – Middle aged, forthright (missionary? UNESCO?!)
Captain Harley ex pilot – now rich
Lowther – Company lawyer
Canon Semple (not a Canon – an actor pretending)

The Dinner
Before it begins Durel makes speech – object of dinner
The plane came down – our miraculous preservation –
~~two~~ three of our number left us – to the memory of our missing friends – Joan Arlington – Gervase Cape – Richard Dymchurch. Canon says grace – For what we are about to receive may the Lord
Conversation?

The old man waits about watching – pours wine

Possibilities
1. Wine – a truth drug?
2. Wine – poison for somebody
3. Canon is shown to be not a canon – but CID? Or oil surveyor
4. Victor Durel points out – item out paper tonight – two skeletons have been found on an oil survey –
Joan A[rlington]? R[ichard Dymchurch]? G[ervase Cape]?
5. Isadore asks Harley about circumstances – dismissed for error of judgement – but very well off?
Suggests: was it an error of judgement? Or were you paid to put down jet there

These very detailed notes from Notebook 52 may be connected to the previous entry, from Notebook 4, although the two Notebooks seem to date from different years. The idea of survivors of an air crash is common to both and there are indications that, in each case, poison is the murder method. The full names (even of the missing characters) and backgrounds included would seem to indicate that considerable thought went into this idea. But there is no script, not even a rough draft – nothing but these intriguing notes. This Notebook also contains the notes for *The Mirror Crack'd from Side to Side* and *The Clocks*, both published in the early 1960s, and is directly ahead of the notes for the screen adaptation of Dickens's *Bleak House*, on which Christie worked in 1962. Puzzlingly, therefore, it would seem that this more detailed sketch preceded the first sketch, discussed above. UNESCO had recently designated Christie the most translated writer, apart from the Bible, so the exclamation mark after their name may be a private joke.

In many ways this is uncharted and untypical Christie territory – survivors of a plane crash, someone paid to 'put a jet down', skeletons found during an oil survey, a truth drug. During the 1950s she published two 'foreign travel' titles – *They Came to Baghdad* and *Destination Unknown* – and the latter does contain much air travel as well as a crashed plane. But while the background to the plot outlined above may contain adventurous concepts, the murder plot is Christie on home ground: a poisoning during dinner at a restaurant ('Yellow Iris', *Sparkling Cyanide*); a clergyman who is not a clergyman (*Murder in Mesopotamia*); a middle-aged missionary (*Murder on the Orient Express*); a detective in disguise (*The Mousetrap, And Then There Were None*). The description of the elderly waiter as 'like a tortoise' has distinct echoes of Lawrence Wargrave from Chapter 13 of *And Then There Were None*; this possibility is further strengthened when we read the 'old man waits about watching'. And is it pure coincidence that there are ten characters listed – eight guests and two servants?

Miss Marple and 'The Case of the Caretaker's Wife'

'Miss Marple insinuated herself so quickly into my life that
I hardly noticed her arrival.'

————————◄o►————————

SOLUTIONS REVEALED
Endless Night • 'The Sign in the Sky' • 'The Case of the
Caretaker's Wife'

————————◄o►————————

The Miss Marple short story 'The Case of the Caretaker' was
first published in the UK in *The Strand* in January 1942, followed by 'Tape Measure Murder' in February and 'The Case
of the Perfect Maid' in April. These short stories can be seen
as preludes to Miss Marple's looming investigation of *The
Body in the Library* in May 1942. Between *The Thirteen Problems*
in 1932 and the publication, in quick succession, of these
three short stories UK readers had seen the elderly detective in action only in the slight 'Miss Marple Tells a Story' in
1935. In the USA the *Chicago Sunday Tribune* published 'The
Case of the Caretaker' in July 1942.

Apart from being a very typical Marple murder-in-a-village
case – the 'big house', the local doctor, gossiping neighbours,

the post office – this short story is important in the Christie output as it is the precursor of the last great novel that she was to write over a quarter-century later, *Endless Night*. The similarities are remarkable – wealthy heiress marries ne'er-do-well charmer, builds a house in the country and is menaced by a peculiar old woman. Her death, following a horse-riding 'accident', is shown to have been orchestrated by her husband and his lover. What distinguishes the plot in the novel is the manner of its telling, the characterisation of the main protagonists and the shock ending.

In common with many short stories, there is little Notebook material relating to 'The Case of the Caretaker'. The first brief note below, reflecting the theme and the final poignant words of the story, appears in Notebook 60 and its accompanying page contains notes for the companion story, 'The Case of the Perfect Maid'. The surrounding pages of this Notebook contain early notes for what would become *The Moving Finger* (1943) and *Curtain*, so a composition date of 1940/41 is confirmed.

> Poor little rich girl
> Old Mr Murgatroyd turned out – shakes fist etc. – really is
> paid by husband – accident at home – she is called in. Miss
> M tells Haydock what to look for

The second, slightly elaborated note below is from Notebook 62. There, the inspiration is one of a list of one-sentence short story ideas, many of which remained undeveloped. The list is followed by the detailed notes for *N or M?* (1941) and then a page headed 'Books 1941', so it is reasonable to assume that the following was also written during 1940.

> A. Poison Pen
> B. A Cricket story
> C. Committee crime

D. Infra Red photograph
E. 'Facing up' story
F. District Nurse
G. Charwoman comes to Miss M.
H. Arty spinster friends
I. Poor little rich girl
J. Lady's maid and parlour maid
K. Stamp story
L. Dangerous drugs stolen
M. Legless man
N. Extra gong at dinner

Idea A became *The Moving Finger*, K became 'Strange Jest', G and J were combined in 'The Case of the Perfect Maid', and I became 'The Case of the Caretaker'. Idea N remains a mystery; both versions of this idea – 'The Second Gong' in 1932 and the more elaborate adaptation 'Dead Man's Mirror', in 1937's *Murder in the Mews* – had previously appeared by this time, as cases for Hercule Poirot. At a later date, to judge from the different pen and less sprawling handwriting, Christie begins to expand ideas I, G, C and J and then added ideas K, L, M and N. This expansion is an accurate sketch of 'The Case of the Caretaker/Caretaker's Wife':

I.
Esme Harley, rich heiress, married to self serving man (politician? younger son ne'er-do-well?) unused to country life – old woman (or man) curses her when she is out riding – horse swerves. Horse shot with air gun – bolts – Esme is thrown. Clare Wright (doctor's daughter?) comes up to her – injects digitalin? Heart gives out as she is taken home.
Or
Husband does it – the clock tower gives time. Yes, but he winds it or butler winds it (like 'Sign in the Sky')

As can be seen, this draft is very similar to the published version – an heiress, a ne'er-do-well son, a bolting horse and an injection – but there also differences. As frequently happens, the names change, but there is also uncertainty about the sex of the caretaker, and the doctor's daughter is sketched in as the villain of the piece. The second possibility, the clock tower, contains an explicit reference to the Mr Quin story 'The Sign in the Sky'; there the murderer alters the time of the clocks in his house in order to give himself an alibi. But altering the domestic clocks is far removed from changing the tower clock and thereby attempting to fool an entire population, which seems a very impractical and unconvincing idea. Wisely, Christie abandoned it.

The 'doctor's daughter' as murderer idea is more complicated. In the published version it is the chemist's wife, a former lover of the husband, who conspires with him by supplying the poison, although she does not actually administer the injection. In the Notebook at this stage the husband is not the first choice for murderer, but trying to arrange for the innocent-seeming presence of the doctor's daughter in order for her to administer an injection is perhaps one of the reasons for her replacement with Esme's husband.

Dr Haydock's niece – not daughter – Clarice is one of the main characters in the story; and she also, unsuspectingly, provides a subsidiary motive for the murder. But as Dr Haydock appears throughout Miss Marple's detective career, starting with *The Murder at the Vicarage* and making his final appearance in *Sleeping Murder*, it would hardly be fitting for her to alight on his daughter as the killer. Hence the name 'Clare Wright' and the question mark in the Notebook.

Both the UK and US versions of the short story are identical. But among Christie's papers is a second, significantly different version, and this version is published here for the first time.

Why this second version should exist is open to speculation. Most Christie short stories were originally published in
magazines and many of her novels appeared, prior to book
publication, in newspapers and periodicals. Editors were
notorious for their predilection for changing stories and cutting novel serialisations, often for reasons of space. Christie
complained about this when asked to change *Dumb Witness*
(see *Agatha Christie's Secret Notebooks*) and a 1944 letter from
her agent talks about the 'serial version' of *Towards Zero* that
Christie had prepared 'in accordance with their [*Colliers
Magazine*] instructions'. In Chapter 4 I discuss the different
versions of *Three Act Tragedy*, also accounted for, in all likelihood, by an editor. So the different versions of 'The Case of
the Caretaker/Caretaker's Wife' may well be explained away
that simply. But if that is the explanation, it means that the
edited version was the one also submitted to the US for its
subsequent appearance; and as the newly discovered version
remains the more straightforward and logical one, it would
seem an odd decision.

One of the main differences between the known version
(Version A) and the new version (Version B) is the method
of narration. In Version A the story is told in the form of a
manuscript prepared, for reasons never made clear, by Dr
Haydock and given to Miss Marple to read while recovering
from flu; Version B tells a similar story directly, without the
device of the manuscript, and this certainly makes for a more
convincing narration. But the differences are not merely in
the manner of telling.

The setting of St Mary Mead is firmly established by the
second sentence of Version B, but in Version A we have to
wait until four pages from the end for confirmation of this,
despite the fact that 'the village' is mentioned but unnamed
on the second page. Version B features Miss Marple's neighbours, familiar to readers from their appearances in *The*

Murder at the Vicarage and the soon-to-be-published *The Body in the Library* – Mrs Price Ridley, Miss Hartnell and Miss Wetherby; Version A has the vaguely analogous Mrs Price, Miss Harmon and Miss Brent. These changes are not only completely inexplicable in themselves but it is very difficult to see how they were explained or justified to Christie and/or her agent. To confuse the issue still further, 'Harmon' is the name of the vicar's wife in another Marple book, *A Murder is Announced*, as well as the later Marple short story 'Sanctuary'.

Version B finds Miss Marple playing a much more central role; she talks to Mrs Murgatroyd, and Clarice and the doctor, and generally acts as the observant old lady that she is. While the circumstances of reading the doctor's manuscript and then propounding her solution is adequate, and similar to the plan of the short stories in *The Thirteen Problems*, it seems cumbersome and unnecessary in view of the now-published alternative.

The title of Version B also makes more sense than its predecessor. Mrs Murgatroyd's husband was the caretaker and he has been dead for two years in both versions; so why call the story 'The Case of the Caretaker'? And Notebook 62, as we have seen, vacillates about this anyway. The title of version B is more logical and accurate.

In this first-ever publication, some minor errors of spelling and punctuation have been corrected.

The Case of the Caretaker's Wife

'And where is the bride?' asked old Miss Hartnell genially.

The village of St Mary Mead was all agog to see the rich and beautiful young wife that Harry Laxton had brought back from abroad. There was a general indulgent feeling that Harry, wicked young scapegrace, had all the luck! Everyone had always felt indulgent towards Harry. Even the owners of windows that had suffered from his indiscriminate use of a catapult had found their just indignation dissipated by young Harry's abject expressions of regret. He had broken windows, robbed orchards, poached rabbits, and later ran into debt, got entangled with the local tobacconist's daughter, been disentangled, and sent off to Africa – and the village as represented by various ageing spinsters had murmured indulgently:

'Ah well. Wild oats! He'll settle down.'

And now, sure enough, the prodigal had returned – not in affliction, but in triumph. Harry Laxton had 'made good' as the saying goes. He had pulled himself together, worked hard, and had finally met and successfully wooed a young Anglo-French girl who was the possessor of a considerable fortune.

Harry might have lived in London, or purchased an estate in some fashionable hunting county – but at least he was a faithful soul. He came back to the part of the world that was home to him. And there, in the most romantic way, he purchased the derelict estate in the Dower House of which he had passed his childhood.

Kingsdean House had been unoccupied for nearly seventy years. No repairs were ever done to it and it had gradually fallen into decay and abandon. It was a vast unprepossessing grandiose mansion, the gardens overgrown with rank vegetation, and as the trees grew up higher around it, it seemed more and more like some gloomy enchanter's den. An elderly caretaker and his wife lived in the habitable corner of it.

The Dower House was a pleasant unpretentious house and had been let for a long term of years to Major Laxton, Harry's father. As a boy, Harry had roamed over the Kingsdean estate and knew every inch of the tangled woods, and the old house itself had always fascinated him.

Major Laxton had died some years ago, so it might be thought that Harry would have had no ties to bring him back. But on his marriage, it was to St Mary Mead that he brought his bride. The ruined old Kingsdean House was pulled down. An army of builders and contractors swooped down upon the place and in an almost miraculously short space of time, (so marvellously does wealth tell!) the new house rose white and gleaming amongst the trees.

Next came a posse of gardeners and after them a procession of furniture vans. The house was ready. Servants arrived. Lastly a Rolls Royce deposited Harry and Mrs Harry at the front door.

St Mary Mead rushed to call, and Mrs Price Ridley who owned the large house near the Vicarage and who considered herself to lead society in the place sent out cards of invitation for a party to 'meet the bride.'

It was a great event in St Mary Mead. Several ladies had new frocks for the occasion. Everyone was excited, curious, anxious to see this fabulous creature. It was all so like a fairy story.

him. And there, in the most romantic way, he purchased the derelict
estate in the ~~D~~ower ~~H~~ouse of which he had passed his ~~childish~~ life. [childhood.]

Kingsdean House had been ~~un~~occupied for nearly seventy years.
~~The property of a ruined owner,~~ (it had gradually fallen into
~~decay and abandon.~~ [and decayed abandon] No repairs wer~~e~~ ever done to it, ~~An elderly~~
~~caretaker and wife lived in the one habitable corner of it.~~ It
was [a] vast unprepossessing gra~~d~~iose mansion ~~and of~~ the gardens ~~left~~
~~so~~ overgrow~~n~~ ~~and~~ [while] rank vegeta~~t~~ion [as] and the trees grew up higher ~~round~~
around it, it seemed more and more like some gloomy enchanter's den.
An elderly caretaker & his wife lived in the one habitable corner of it'
~~The D~~ower ~~H~~ouse, ~~near its western boundary, had been kept in~~
~~repair.~~ ~~It~~ was a pleasant unpretentious house and had been let
for a long term of years to Major Laxton, Harry's father. As a
boy, Harry had roamed over the ~~abandoned~~ [Kingsdean] estate and knew every inch
of the tangled woods, and the [old] house itself had always fascinated him.

Major Laxton had died l~~eaving a bare pittance to his son.~~ *some years ago, so it might be thought*
that Harry would have had no ties to bring him back
But on his marriage, it was to St Mary Mead that ~~Harry~~ [he] brought
his bride~~, and it was soon learned that the whole estate had been~~
~~bought by them and that~~ The ruined old ~~building~~ [Kingsdean House] was to ~~be~~ pulled
down ~~and a new house erected on the site.~~ ~~And almost at once~~
an army of b~~ri~~lde s [builders] and cont~~r~~actors swooped down upon the place
and in an almost miraculously short space of time, (so marvellously
does wealth tell,) the new house rose white and gleaming amongst
the trees.
~~Then~~ [Next] came a ~~p~~osse of gardners and ~~finally~~ [after them] a procession of
furniture vans. The house was ready. Servants arrived. Lastly

Miss Hartnell, weather beaten hearty spinster, threw out her question as she squeezed her way through the crowded drawing room door. Miss Wetherby, a thin acidulated spinster, fluttered out information.

'Oh my dear, *quite* charming. Such pretty manners. And quite young. Really, you know, it makes one feel quite *envious* to see someone who has *everything* like that. Good looks and money, and breeding – (*most* distinguished, nothing in the least *common* about her) and dear Harry *so* devoted.'

'Ah,' said Miss Hartnell, 'It's early days yet.'

Miss Wetherby's thin nose quivered appreciatively.

'Oh my dear, do you really think—?'

'We all know what Harry is,' said Miss Hartnell.

'We know what he *was*. But I expect *now*—'

'Ah,' said Miss Hartnell. 'Men are always the same. Once a gay deceiver, always a gay deceiver. *I* know them.'

'Dear, dear. Poor young things!' Miss Wetherby looked much happier. 'Yes, I expect she'll have trouble with him. Someone ought really to *warn* her. I wonder if she's heard anything of the old story?'

The eyes of the two ladies met significantly.

'It seems so very unfair,' said Miss Wetherby, 'that she should know *nothing*. So awkward. Especially with only the one chemist's shop in the village.'

For the erstwhile tobacconist's daughter was now married to Mr Edge, the chemist.

'It would be so much nicer,' said Miss Wetherby, 'if Mrs Laxton were to deal with Boots in Much Benham.'

'I daresay,' said Miss Hartnell, 'that Harry Laxton will suggest that *himself*.'

Again a significant look passed between them.

'But I certainly think,' said Miss Hartnell, 'that she ought to *know*.'

ii

'Beasts!' said Clarice Vane to old Miss Marple. 'Absolute beasts some people are!'

Miss Marple looked at her curiously.

Clarice Vane had recently come to live with her Uncle, Dr Haydock. She was a tall dark girl, handsome, warm hearted and impulsive. Her big brown eyes were alight now with indignation.

She said:

'All these *cats* – *saying* things – *hinting* things!'

Miss Marple asked:

'About Harry Laxton?'

'Yes, about his old affair with the tobacconist's daughter.'

'Oh *that*!' Miss Marple was indulgent. 'A great many young men have affairs of that kind, I imagine.'

'Of course they do. And it's all over. So why harp on and bring it up years after? It's like ghouls feasting on dead bodies.'

'I daresay, my dear, it does seem like that to you. You are young, of course, and intolerant, but you see we have very little to talk about down here and so, I'm afraid, we do tend to dwell on the past. But I'm curious to know why it upsets you so much?'

Clarice Vane bit her lip and flushed. She said in a curious muffled voice: 'They look so *happy*. The Laxtons, I mean. They're young, and in love, and it's all lovely for them – I hate to think of it being spoilt – by whispers and hints and innuendoes and general beastliness!'

Miss Marple looked at her and said: 'I see.'

Clarice went on:

'He was talking to me just now – he's so happy and eager and excited and – yes, *thrilled* – at having got his heart's desire and rebuilt Kingsdean. He's like a child about it all.

244

And she – well, I don't suppose anything has ever gone wrong in her whole life – she's always had everything. You've seen her, don't you think—'

Miss Marple interrupted. She said:

'As a matter of fact I haven't seen her yet. I've only just arrived. So *tiresome*. I was delayed by the District Nurse. Her feelings, you know, have been hurt by what—'

But Clarice was unable to take an interest in the village drama which Miss Marple was embarking upon with so much zest. With a muttered apology she left.

Miss Marple pressed onwards, full of the same curiosity that had animated everyone in St Mary Mead, to see what the bride was like.

She hardly knew what she expected, but it was not what she saw. For other people Louise Laxton might be an object of envy, a spoilt darling of fortune, but to the shrewd old lady who had seen so much of human nature in her village there came the refrain of a popular song heard many years ago.

'*Poor little rich girl . . .*'

A small delicate figure, with flaxen hair curled rather stiffly round her face and big wistful blue eyes, Louise was drooping a little. The long stream of congratulations had tired her. She was hoping it might soon be time to go . . . Perhaps, even now, Harry might say—? She looked at him sideways. So tall and broad shouldered with his eager pleasure in this horrible dull party.

Oh dear, here was another of them! A tall grey haired fussily dressed old lady bleating like all the rest.

'This is Miss Marple, Louise.'

She didn't understand the look in the old lady's eyes. She would have been quite astonished if she had known what it was:

'*Poor little rich girl . . .*'

iii

'Ooph!' It was a sigh of relief.

Harry turned to look at his wife amusedly. They were driving away from the party. She said:

'Darling, what a frightful party!'

Harry laughed.

'Yes, pretty terrible. Never mind, my sweet. It had to be done, you know. All these old pussies knew me when I lived here as a boy. They'd have been terribly disappointed not to have got a good look at you close up.'

Louise made a grimace. She said:

'Shall we have to see a lot of them?'

'What? Oh no – they'll come and make ceremonious calls with cardcases and you'll return the calls and then you needn't bother any more. You can have your own friends down or whatever you like.'

Louise said after a minute or two:

'Isn't there anyone *amusing* living down here?'

'Oh yes. There's the country set, you know. Though you may find them a bit dull too. Mostly interested in bulbs and dogs and horses. You'll ride, of course. You'll enjoy that. There's a horse over at Eglinton I'd like you to see. A beautiful animal perfectly trained, no vice in him, but plenty of spirit.'

The car slowed down to take the turn into the gates of Kingsmead. Harry wrenched the wheel and swore as a grotesque figure sprang up in the middle of the road and he only just managed to avoid it. It stood there, shaking a fist and shouting after them.

Louise clutched his arm.

'Who's that – that horrible old woman?'

Harry's brow was black.

'That's old Murgatroyd – she and her husband were caretakers in the old house – they were there for thirty years.'

'Why did she shake her fist at you?'

Harry's face got red.

'She – well, she resented the house being pulled down. And she got the sack, of course. Her husband's been dead two years. They say she got a bit queer after he died.'

'Is she – she isn't – starving?'

Louise's ideas were vague and somewhat melodramatic. Riches prevented you coming into contact with reality.

Harry was outraged.

'Good Lord, Louise, what an idea! I pensioned her off, of course – and handsomely, too. Found her a new cottage and everything.'

Louise asked bewildered:

'Then *why* does she mind?'

Harry was frowning, his brows drawn together.

'Oh how should I know? Craziness! She loved the house.'

'But it was a ruin, wasn't it?'

'Of course it was – crumbling to pieces, roof leaking, more or less unsafe. All the same I suppose it – *meant* something to her. She'd been there a long time. Oh! I don't know! The old devil's cracked I think.'

Louise said uneasily:

'She – I think she cursed us . . . Oh Harry, I wish she hadn't.'

iv

It seemed to Louise that her new home was tainted and poisoned by the malevolent figure of one old crazy woman. When she went out in the car, when she rode, when she walked out with the dogs there was always the same figure waiting. Crouched down on herself, a battered hat over wisps of iron grey hair, and the slow muttering of imprecations.

Louise came to believe that Harry was right, the old woman *was* mad. Nevertheless that did not make things easier. Mrs Murgatroyd never actually came to the house, nor did she use definite threats, nor offer violence.

Her squatting figure remained always just outside the gates. To appeal to the police would have been useless and in any case Harry Laxton was averse to that course of action. It would, he said, arouse local sympathy for the old brute. He took the matter more easily than Louise did.

'Don't worry yourself about it, darling. She'll get tired of this silly cursing business. Probably she's only trying it on.'

'She isn't, Harry. She – she *hates* us! I can *feel* it. She – she's ill wishing us.'

'She's not a witch, darling, although she may look like one! Don't be morbid about it all.'

Louise was silent. Now that the first excitement of settling in was over, she felt curiously lonely and at a loose end. She had been used to life in London and the Riviera. She had no knowledge of, or taste for, English country life. She was ignorant of gardening, except for the final act of 'doing the flowers.' She did not really care for dogs. She was bored by such neighbours as she met. She enjoyed riding best. Sometimes with Harry, sometimes, when he was busy about the estate, by herself, she hacked through the woods and lanes, enjoying the easy paces of the beautiful horse Harry had bought for her.

Yet even Prince Hal, most sensitive of chestnut steeds, was wont to shy and snort as he carried his mistress past that huddled figure of a malevolent old woman . . .

One day Louise took her courage in both hands. She was out walking. She had passed Mrs Murgatroyd, pretending not to notice her, but suddenly she swerved back and went right up to her. She said a little breathlessly,

'What is it? What's the matter? What do you want?'

The old woman blinked at her. She had a cunning dark gypsy face, with wisps of iron grey hair, and bleared suspicious eyes. Louise wondered if she drank.

She spoke in a whining and yet threatening voice.

'What do I want, you ask? What indeed? That which has been took away from me. Who turned me out of Kingsdean House? I'd lived there girl and woman for near on forty years. It was a black deed to turn me out and it's black bad luck it'll bring to you and him.'

Louise said:

'You've got a very nice cottage and—' she broke off.

The old woman's arms flew up. She screamed!

'What's the good of that to me? It's my own place I want, and my own fire as I sat beside all them years. And as for you and him I'm telling you there will be no happiness for you in your new fine house! It's the black sorrow will be upon you – sorrow and death and my curse! May your fair face rot . . .'

Louise turned away and broke into a little stumbling run.

She thought:

'*I must get away from here.* We must sell the house. We must go away . . .'

At the moment such a solution seemed easy to her. But Harry's utter incomprehension took her aback. He exclaimed:

'Leave here? Sell the house? Because of a crazy old woman's threats? You must be mad!'

'No, I'm not. But she – she frightens me . . . I know something will happen.'

v

A friendship had sprung up between Clarice Vane and young Mrs Laxton. The two girls were much of an age, though dissimilar both in character and in tastes. In Clarice's company

Louise found reassurance. Clarice was so self reliant, so sure of herself. Louise mentioned the matter of Mrs Murgatroyd and her threats but Clarice seemed to regard the matter as more annoying than frightening.

'It's so stupid, that sort of thing,' she said. 'But really very annoying for *you*!'

'You know, Clarice, I – I feel quite frightened sometimes. My heart gives the most awful jumps.'

'Nonsense, you mustn't let a silly thing like that get you down. She'll soon get tired of it.'

'You think so?'

'I expect so. Anyway don't let her see you're frightened.'

'No. No, I won't.'

She was silent for a minute or two. Clarice said:

'What's the matter?'

Louise paused for a moment, then her answer came with a rush.

'I hate this place! I hate being here! The woods, and this house, and the awful silence at night, and the queer noise owls make. Oh and the *people* and everything!'

'The people? What people?'

'The people in the village. Those prying gossiping old maids.'

Clarice said sharply:

'What have they been saying?'

'I don't know. Nothing particular. But they've got nasty minds . . . when you've talked to them you feel you wouldn't trust anybody . . . not *anybody* at *all*!'

Clarice said:

'Forget them. They've nothing to do but gossip. And most of the muck they talk they just invent.'

Louise said:

'I wish we'd never come here . . . but Harry adores it so – Harry.'

Her voice softened. Clarice thought, 'How she adores him!'
She said abruptly:

'I must go now.'

'I'll send you back in the car. Come again soon.'

Clarice nodded. Louise felt comforted by her new friend's
visit. Harry was pleased to find her more cheerful and from
then on urged her to have Clarice often to the house.

Then one day he said:

'Good news for you, darling.'

'Oh, what?'

'I've fixed the Murgatroyd! She's got a son in America,
you know. Well, I've arranged for her to go out and join him.
I'll pay her passage.'

'Oh Harry, how wonderful! I believe I might get to like
Kingsdean after all.'

'*Get* to like it? Why, it's the most wonderful place in the
world!'

'To *you* darling, not to me!'

'You wait!' said Harry confidently.

Louise gave a little shiver. She could not rid herself of her
superstitious fears so easily.

vi

If the ladies of St Mary Mead had hoped for the pleasure of
imparting information about her husband's past into the
ears of the bride, they were disappointed by Harry Laxton's
own prompt action.

Miss Hartnell and Clarice Vane were both in Mr Edge's
shop, the one buying mothballs and the other a packet of indi-
gestion lozenges, when Harry Laxton and his wife came in.

After greeting the two ladies, Harry turned to the counter
and was just demanding a toothbrush when he stopped in
mid speech and exclaimed heartily:

251

'Well, *well*, just see who's here! Bella, I do declare!'

Mrs Edge, who had hurried out from the back parlour to attend to the congestion of ladies, beamed back cheerfully at him showing her big white teeth. She had been a dark handsome girl and was still a reasonably handsome woman, though she had put on weight and the lines on her face had coarsened, but her large brown eyes were full of warmth as she replied:

'Bella it is, Mr Harry, and pleased to see you after all these years.'

Harry turned to his wife.

'Bella's an old flame of mine, Louise,' he said. 'Head over ears in love with her, wasn't I, Bella?'

'That's what *you* say,' said Mrs Edge.

Louise laughed. She said:

'My husband's very happy seeing all his old friends again.'

'Ah,' said Mrs Edge, '*we* haven't forgotten you, Mr Harry. Seems like a fairy tale to think of you married and building up a new house instead of that ruined old Kingsdean House.'

'You look very well and blooming,' Harry said, and Mrs Edge laughed and said there was nothing wrong with her and what about that toothbrush?

Clarice, watching the baffled look on Miss Hartnell's face, said to herself exultantly:

'Oh well *done*, Harry! You've spiked their guns!'

Indeed, though Miss Hartnell did her best, with mysterious hints of having seen Harry Laxton and Mrs Edge talking together on the outskirts of the village, to revive a bygone scandal, she met with no success, and had to fall back upon vague hints as to the general depravity of men.

vii

It was Dr Haydock who said abruptly to Miss Marple:

'What's all this Clarice tells me about old Mrs Murgatroyd?'

'Mrs Murgatroyd?'

'Yes. Hanging about Kingsdean and shaking her fist and cursing the new regime.'

Miss Marple looked astonished.

'How extraordinary. Of course Murgatroyd and his wife were always a queer couple, but I always thought the woman was devoted to Harry – and he's found her such a nice new cottage and everything.'

'Just so,' said the doctor drily. 'And by way of gratitude she goes up and makes a nuisance of herself and frightens his wife to death.'

'Dear dear,' said Miss Marple. 'How peculiar. I must have a word with her.'

Mrs Murgatroyd was at home this afternoon and was smoking a pipe. She received Miss Marple without undue deference.

'I thought,' said Miss Marple reproachfully, 'that you were fond of Mr Laxton.'

Mrs Murgatroyd said:

'And who told you that?'

'You used to be when he was a boy.'

'That's a long time since. He hadn't pulled down house then.'

'Do you mean you'd rather be living there in that lonely ruined place than here in this nice cottage?'

'What I feel's my own business.'

'Do you mean that it's really true that you go up there and frighten young Mrs Laxton with curses?'

A strange film came over the dirty old woman's eyes. She said, and there was dignity and menace in her voice:

253

'I know how to curse, I do. I can do it proper. You'll see.'

Miss Marple said:

'What you are doing is cruel and uncivilised and – and I don't understand it. What harm has Harry Laxton ever done you?'

'That's for me to say.' She leaned forward nodding her head triumphantly. 'I can hold my tongue, I can. You won't get anything out of me.'

Miss Marple came away looking puzzled and worried. She met the doctor just outside his own gate.

He said, 'Well?'

'Oh dear, I am very much upset. There is – I am convinced there is – something very dangerous going on. Something that I don't understand.'

'Get anything out of the old woman?'

'Nothing at all. She – I can't understand her.'

Haydock said thoughtfully:

'She's not crazy, you know. She's got *some* idea at the back of her mind. However, I'm glad to say Laxton is shipping her off to America next week.'

'She's consented to go?'

'Oh yes, jumped at it. I wondered – well, she's an artful old devil. I wondered if she had been playing for just this to happen? What do *you* think?'

Miss Marple said, 'I don't know what to think. But I wish – I wish she were gone . . .'

The next morning Louise Laxton was thrown from her horse and killed.

viii

Two men in a baker's van had witnessed the accident. They saw Louise come out of the big gate, saw the old woman spring up and stand in the way waving her arms and shouting, saw the horse start, swerve and then bolt madly down the road throwing Louise Laxton over his head . . .

One of them stood over the unconscious figure, not knowing what to do next, while the other rushed to the house to get help. Harry Laxton came running out, his face ghastly. They took off a door of the van and carried her on it to the house. But when the doctor arrived she had died without regaining consciousness.

The author of the catastrophe had slunk away. Frightened, perhaps, at what she had done, she slipped into her cottage and packed her belongings and left. She went straight off to Liverpool.

'And the law can't touch her,' said Haydock bitterly.

He was speaking to Miss Marple who had paid him an unexpected visit.

He went on, his tone reflecting the deep anger and discouragement of his mood.

'You couldn't make out a case against her. A clever counsel would tear her to pieces. She didn't even threaten. She never touched the horse. It's a case of malevolent will power, that's all. She terrified that poor child, and she scared the horse and he bolted with her. It's an *accident* – that's all. But in my opinion, Louise Laxton was murdered as truly as I stand here talking to you.'

Miss Marple nodded her head.

'I agree with you.'

'And that half witted malevolent old crone commits murder and gets away with it! And all for no reason as far as I can see . . .'

Miss Marple was twisting her fingers nervously.

She said:

'You know, Dr Haydock, I don't think she did murder her.'

'Not legally, perhaps.'

'Not at all.'

Haydock stared.

'But you just said—'

'You see, we are talking at cross purposes. I do think Louise was murdered – but not by the person you think.'

Haydock stared. He said:

'My dear old friend, are you mad, or am I?'

'Oh I know it may sound *quite* ridiculous to you, and of course it is entirely an *idea* on my part, only, if it *is* so, it is most important that the truth should come out, because one doesn't want to see another young life ruined and it might be – in fact, it probably would be. Oh dear, how incoherent I sound, and it is necessary, I know, to be calm and *businesslike* in order to convince you.'

Haydock looked at her attentively. He said:

'Tell it your own way.'

'Oh, *thank* you. Well, you see, there are certain facts that seem so at variance with the whole thing. To begin with – Mrs Murgatroyd always hated Kingsdean House – they only stayed there because Murgatroyd drank and couldn't keep any other job. So you see it seems very unlikely that she'd feel leaving so keenly. Which means, of course, that somebody *paid* her to act that way she's done . . . *putting on an act,* they call it nowadays.'

Haydock drew a deep breath.

'What are you trying to say?'

'Poor little rich girl,' said Miss Marple unexpectedly. 'Gentlemen, so I have noticed, are nearly always attracted by the same *type*. Not always in the same class of life, of course, but there's usually physical resemblance. Bella Edge, for instance, was a tall dark handsome girl with white teeth and a lot of spirit. Rather like your niece Clarice. That's why when I saw Louise I was quite sure that Harry wasn't the least bit in love with her. He married for money. And after that he planned to get rid of her.'

Haydock said incredulously:

'You think he paid that old woman to come and curse in order to scare his wife and finally induce her horse to run away with her. My dear woman, that's a tall order!'

'Oh yes, yes, put like that. Did she die of the fall?'

'She had a fractured arm and concussion, but she actually died of the shock.'

'You've not done an autopsy, have you? And has anyone examined the horse?'

'What's the idea?'

Miss Marple said:

'I'm suggesting, absurd or not, that it wasn't Mrs Murgatroyd who caused the horse to bolt. That was only the *apparent* cause – for the onlookers. Harry was always very good with a catapult. A stone may have struck the horse just as it came through the gate. Then it bolted and threw Louise. The fall might have killed her but when Harry came out she was still alive. I think that then, before you got there, he may have injected something to make certain.'

Haydock said: 'You terrifying woman![36] I suppose you'll tell me what he injected next?'

'Oh, really I have not the least idea. Probably some very swift heart poison.'

'Such things aren't easy to get hold of.'

Miss Marple said sharply:

'Bella Edge could have got it for him.'

'Well – er yes – perhaps, but why should *she* do such a thing?'

'Because, poor woman, she's always been crazy about Harry Laxton. Because I've no doubt he's been playing her

---

36 This handwritten addition to the typescript is, apart from 'Haydock' and 'you', illegible. This transcription seems the most likely exchange.

up and telling her after Louise was dead he'd take her away from her husband and marry her.'

'Marry Bella Edge!'

'He wouldn't, of course! But afterwards she couldn't give him away. She'd be too afraid for herself. Actually Harry plans to marry your niece Clarice. She's no idea. He fell in love with her at that party. That's why you've got to do something if you can. She's in love with him and you don't want her married to a murderer.'

'Not if *I* can help it,' said Haydock grimly.

Satisfied, Miss Marple went out into the clear sunshine of the morning.

She said under her breath:

'Poor little rich girl . . .'

THE END

Two interesting amendments that appear in the original typescript merit mention. The first time the name Clarice appears, in section ii, it has been inserted in handwriting and the following has been deleted: 'Griselda Clement, the young and pretty wife of the vicar . . .' This is the only appearance in the typescript of Griselda and by the top of the next page, and thereafter, 'Clarice' has been typed. Possibly as she wrote Christie decided to make Clarice part of the motive, something that she could not have done with happily married mother Griselda, whom her readers knew from *The Murder at the Vicarage*. The second change was to the scene in the chemist's shop (section vi), when Bella and Harry's conversation is witnessed by Clarice and Miss Harmon/Hartnell. Here again, 'Clarice' is inserted in handwriting and 'Miss Marple' is deleted. And the closing paragraph of this section, here reinstated, is omitted in Version A, to the detriment of the plot; the information given here is an indication of collusion between Harry and Bella.

Version A has the totally incredible account, given by Dr Haydock in the closing scene, in which Harry, the newly widowed murderer, drops a hypodermic syringe out of his trouser pocket. No murderer, regardless of circumstance, would resort to this potentially hazardous, not to mention probably painful, method of concealment. I cannot believe that Agatha Christie ever envisioned such a scene; this *must* be the invention of a (poor) magazine editor.

Despite her last-minute substitution and insertion in the two instances mentioned above, Clarice plays a more pivotal role in Version B. Although in both versions she provides part of the motive, it is more unequivocal and less covert in Version B than in the earlier version, where her interest in Harry is peripheral.

Overall, this newly discovered version is longer, more convincing and more coherent than its predecessor. The awkward, not to mention unmotivated, manuscript ploy is replaced by a more straightforward narration in which Miss Marple takes centre stage – where she belongs.

The Fourth Decade 1950–1959

'So I was happy, radiantly happy, and made even more so by the applause of the audience.'

---◄◊►---

SOLUTIONS REVEALED

After The Funeral • *Appointment with Death* • 'The Case of the Perfect Maid' • *Cat among the Pigeons* • *Death in the Clouds* • *Death on the Nile* • *Destination Unknown* • *Endless Night* • 'Greenshaw's Folly' • *The Mysterious Affair at Styles* • *The Mystery of the Blue Train* • *Sparkling Cyanide* • *Taken at the Flood* • *They Came to Baghdad* • *They Do It with Mirrors* • *Three Act Tragedy* • *The Unexpected Guest*

---◄◊►---

While she still produced her annual 'Christie for Christmas', the 1950s was Agatha Christie's Golden Age of Theatre. Throughout this decade her name, already a constant on the bookshelf, now became a perennial on the theatre marquee as well. In so doing she became the only crime writer to conquer the stage as well as the page; and the only female playwright in history to have three plays running simultaneously in London's West End. Other playwrights wrote popular stage thrillers – Frederick Knott's *Dial M for Murder* and

Wait until Dark or Francis Durbridge's *Suddenly at Home* – and some of her fellow crime writers wrote stage plays – Dorothy L. Sayers' *Busman's Honeymoon*, Ngaio Marsh's *Singing in the Shrouds* – but Christie is still the only crime writer to achieve equal fame and success in both media.

The decade began well with the publication, in June, of her fiftieth title, *A Murder is Announced.* This is a major title not simply thanks to its jubilee status but also because it is one of Christie's greatest detective novels and Miss Marple's finest hour. To celebrate the occasion Collins hosted a party in the Savoy Hotel; photos of the event show a relaxed and smiling Agatha Christie chatting with Billy Collins and fellow crime writer Ngaio Marsh as well as with actress Barbara Mullen, then appearing in the West End as Miss Marple in *Murder at the Vicarage.*

Her 1950s novels reflected the new social order of a post-war Britain. Elements of the plot of *A Murder is Announced* depend on food rationing, identity cards, fuel shortages, and a new social mobility. *They Do It with Mirrors* (1952) is set in a reform home for delinquents; *Mrs McGinty's Dead* (1952) finds Poirot staying at an unspeakable guest-house while he solves the murder of a charwoman. *Hickory Dickory Dock* (1955) is set in a student hostel and *Ordeal by Innocence* (1958) is a dark novel about a miscarriage of justice. The female protagonist of *4.50 from Paddington* (1957) makes a living, despite a university degree, as a short-term domestic help; *Cat among the Pigeons* (1959) combines a murder mystery with international unrest and revolution. And two titles – *They Came to Baghdad* (1951) and *Destination Unknown* (1954) – represent a return, after almost 30 years and *The Man in the Brown Suit*, to the foreign thriller.

In this decade the final Mary Westmacotts were published, *A Daughter's a Daughter* in 1952 and *The Burden* in 1956. And in April 1950 Agatha Christie began to write her

Autobiography, a task that would take over 15 years; it would not materialise in print until after her death. Despite this impressive range of projects, throughout the 1950s her output remained steady, although 1953, with *After the Funeral* and *A Pocket Full of Rye*, was the last year that saw more than one 'Christie for Christmas'. During the 1950s, to the probable chagrin of Collins Crime Club, Christie concentrated her literary efforts on the stage.

Exactly a year after her fiftieth title became a best-seller, *The Hollow*, her 1946 Poirot novel, made its debut as a play, despite the prognostications of Christie's daughter Rosalind, who tried to dissuade her mother from adapting what she saw as unsuitable dramatic material. The play was a success and buoyed by its reception Christie began in earnest to turn her attention to the stage. In her *Autobiography* she explains that writing a play is much easier than writing a novel because 'the circumscribed limits of the stage simplifies things' and the playwright is not 'hampered with all that description that . . . stops [the writer from] getting on with what happens'.

In 1952 *The Mousetrap* began its unstoppable run. Although it began as a radio play, written at the express request of Queen Mary, who celebrated her eightieth birthday in 1947, Christie subsequently adapted it as a long short story and, finally, as a stage play. After tryouts in Nottingham, it opened at London's Ambassadors Theatre on 25 November 1952. By the mid 1960s it had broken every existing theatrical record and it still sailed serenely on. The following year her greatest achievement in theatre, *Witness for the Prosecution*, opened and confirmed Agatha Christie's status as a crime dramatist. The year after that the play duplicated its London success on Broadway, earning for its author an Edgar award from the Mystery Writers of America.

The previous three plays had been her own adaptations of earlier titles, but she now began producing original work for the stage. *Spider's Web* (1954) was the first, followed by *Verdict* and *The Unexpected Guest* (both 1958). Although all three contained a dead body, something audiences had come to expect from a Christie play, in most other respects they were surprises and showed that her talents were not confined to the printed page. *Spider's Web* was another commission, this one written at the request of the actress Margaret Lockwood, and was a light comedy with a whodunit element. *Verdict,* the only failure of the decade, was, despite its title and the presence of a murdered body, not a whodunit at all; and *The Unexpected Guest* was a brooding will-they-get-away-with-it – or so it seems until the final surprise. In between these titles *Towards Zero,* an adaptation of her 1943 novel, opened to a lukewarm reception in 1956. It was her only collaboration and it was co-adapted by Gerald Verner, a now-forgotten crime writer with a long list of titles to his credit.

On radio Tommy and Tuppence, played by *The Mousetrap*'s husband-and-wife team of Richard Attenborough and Sheila Sim, appeared in a 13-part adaptation of *Partners in Crime* beginning in April 1953. The following year the BBC broadcast an original radio play, *Personal Call.* The artistically and critically acclaimed Billy Wilder version of *Witness for the Prosecution* arrived on screen in 1957 and remains the best film version of any Christie material. And in 1956 US television cast (the unlikely) Gracie Fields in the role of Miss Marple in *A Murder is Announced.*

The 1950s saw The Queen of Crime expanding her literary horizons from phenomenally successful crime novelist to equally impressive crime dramatist. And in 1956, in recognition of her exceptional contribution to both, Agatha Christie was awarded a CBE.

They Came to Baghdad
5 March 1951

————————◄◊►————————

After losing her job and falling for a young man she
meets in a London park, Victoria Jones travels to
Baghdad, where she becomes involved, not entirely
unwillingly, in murder, mystery and international
intrigue.

————————◄◊►————————

'It is difficult to believe that Mrs Christie regards this as
more than a joke.' This was the verdict from the first person
at Collins to read *They Came to Baghdad*. Phrases such as
'far-fetched and puerile . . . not worthy of Mrs Christie .
. . wildly improbable' pepper the report, but it goes on to
say 'it is eminently readable' and that 'its sheer vitality
and humour and the delightful . . . Victoria Jones carry it
through.' It should be remembered that this book followed
on from *Crooked House* and *A Murder is Announced*, both first-
class Christie detective novels; Collins, not unreasonably,
expected another in the same vein. *They Came to Baghdad*, the
first foreign adventure story since *The Man in the Brown Suit* a
quarter of a century earlier, was obviously a shock. And there
are, undoubtedly, far-fetched aspects to the plot.

Although published in March there had been a serialisation
in *John Bull* in January 1951. The manuscript was received by
Collins in late July or early August 1950 and Christie's agent,
Edmund Cork, wrote to her on 21 August asking for clarifi-
cation, for the Collins reader, of two small points – why does
Carmichael use the name 'Lucifer' instead of 'Edward', when
he is dying in Chapter 13; and the question of the scar on
Grete Harden's lip early in Chapter 23 which resulted in the

insertion of the sentence beginning 'Some blotchily applied make-up . . .' In the USA, a radio and TV version were broadcast in September 1951 and on 12 May 1952 respectively. For such an atypical Christie title it is surprising that it should have been adapted so quickly for other media.

The notes for this novel are contained in three Notebooks – 31, 49 and 56. The majority of them, 95 pages, are in Notebook 56, the opening page of which reads:

The House in Baghdad
A. A 'Robinson' approach. Disgruntled young man – turned down – by girl – light hearted
B. T and T
C. Woman about to commit suicide in Baghdad
D. Smell of fear

As can be seen, the working title of the book was *The House in Baghdad* and the planning of it, to judge from a letter dated 3 October of that year, went back as far as October 1947. The 'Robinson' reference is puzzling but the first notes otherwise reflect the basic set-up. But the biggest surprise in this list is B – the inclusion of Tommy and Tuppence. As we shall see, they also feature in the more detailed notes later in the same Notebook, although all of their published adventures (both in novel and short story form) are firmly based in the UK. Idea C is clearly the forerunner of *Destination Unknown*, which was to follow three years later, and throughout the notes for *They Came to Baghdad*, the name Olive, the main protagonist of *Destination Unknown*, appears frequently, together with some of the plot of the later novel. The phrase 'smell of fear' runs like a motif throughout the notes, where it occurs 17 times, and it appears in the novel in Chapter 6.

Notebook 31 continues the Tommy and Tuppence idea:

Baghdad Mystery May 24th
T and T – went into Consulate – didn't come out
Points
At Consulate – Kuwait chest – Tup. looks inside – nothing
– but something showing that gunman had been there. He
hid in the chest?
Sir Rupert Stein – great traveller – was to meet S. He came
from Kashmir – found dead in Baghdad later – really
kidnapped before?
They went to Baghdad
Beginning in Basrah – the hunted man – into the Consulate
– the man through – up the stairs – meets man coming
down – through door to bedroom.
Miss Gilda Martin – attention paid to her – goes to the Zia
hotel – she has a little red book.
Archaeologists – including Mrs. Oliver and her brother
– latter is learned gentleman horrified by her inaccurate
Professor Dorman. A question of poison arises – Mrs O.
tries to get it – finally does get it – then it disappears – she is
very upset.

The 'May 24th' reference is less definite than it might at
first seem. It is most likely to be 1949. If Christie was correcting the text in September 1950, after the manuscript
had been read and discussed at Collins, it is unlikely that
the rough notes for the novel had been first sketched at the
end of May, three months earlier. (A page of Notebook 56 is
dated unequivocally 'Oct. 1949'.) At this point Tommy and
Tuppence are still in the book and there are certainly some
similarities between Victoria and Tuppence – resourceful-
ness, courage, determination and a sense of humour. There
is no mention of Tommy in any of the notes. Perhaps the
inclusion of the Beresfords is not that surprising when you
remember that they had not appeared in print since *N or M?*

in 1941 and would not actually appear again for another 17 years, in *By the Pricking of my Thumbs*.

There is a definite foreshadowing of Sir Stafford Nye from *Passenger to Frankfurt* in the sketch of Sir Rupert Stein and, indeed, in the eventual Sir Rupert Crofton Lee in the novel. Both characters, each with an international reputation, make their appearance in airports and both favour the dramatic look by wearing long cloaks with hoods. Sir Stafford survives his airport adventure but Sir Rupert is not so lucky.

The second shock is the mention of Mrs Oliver; and not just Mrs Oliver but her brother also. This could have been a very amusing pairing and would have probably given Christie herself an opportunity to vent her spleen on some of the nit-picking observations of critics and readers. The 'question of poison' would suggest a more traditional whodunit rather than a spy adventure.

The 'Kuwait chest' has echoes of the earlier short story 'The Mystery of the Baghdad Chest' and its more elaborate form 'The Mystery of the Spanish Chest', and *The Rats*, the one-act play from *Rule of Three*. In each case a body is discovered in such a chest. Gilda Martin may have been an early version of Victoria.

To judge from the amount of notes (well over 100 pages, many more than for any other title) and the amount of repetition in those notes, this book gave more trouble than other, more densely plotted whodunits. Again and again in Notebook 56 the opening chapters are sketched, each of them with only minor differences. This is unique within the Notebooks. These are not alternatives or an example of her usual fertility of invention – this is repetition of just one scene, which, apart from the name change, remains substantially the same throughout. Victoria Jones does not appear until 50 pages into the planning, at which point Olive is put aside until *Destination Unknown*. The following nine examples are some of the notes for the opening of the book and, as can be seen, there are only minor differences between them.

They Went to Baghdad
Quotation from girl's book – Western approach – Olivia in plane – Sir Rupert Crofton Lee – great traveller and orientalist – his traveller's cape and hood

Olive in the plane – behind Sir Rupert – his cape slips back – boil on neck – (perhaps he is flown on by RAF plane to Basrah)

Sketch (rough) – Olive arrives in Baghdad

Approaches
A. Olive – plane – Crofton Lee – boil
Tentatives
Olive arrives in Basrah – welcome by Mr. D – ordinary life – Sir Rupert – does not recognise her – supercilious she thinks

Start with A
Olive leaving England – Heathrow – Sir Rupert in plane – her thoughts – divorce – future – Baghdad – sensible – happy free life – uneasy feeling of something she doesn't want to remember – then sees back of Sir R's neck

Victoria Jones – a plain girl with an amusing mouth – can do imitations – is doing one of her boss – gets sack – finds young man – also sacked? Edward – ex-pilot – given me a job in an office

Parts settled – Victoria Jones in London and Edward

Vic. – Journey out – Sir Rupert – Cairo? Air hostess? – arrival in Baghdad

(A) Journey out – Victoria Mrs HC Sir R changes at Heliopolis – arrive Baghdad Aerodrome

Running alongside the Olive/Victoria approach was what Christie called the Eastern approach, in other words the events leading up to the scene in the consulate that sets the plot in motion:

> Eastern approach – in the Market – Arabs – young man's feelings – goes to Souk. In Consulate's office waiting room – smell of fear – Richard knows it well – in war – looks around waiting room
>
> 2. Carmichael ~~Stewart~~ in Marshes – with Arabs – coming into civilisation
>
> B. Carmichael – with Arabs – bazaar – something wrong
>
> Approach B. Carmichael gets to Basrah – everything as planned – to South – passwords – all OK – to Consulate – fear – then along passage – upstairs – Richard watches him go – last time ever seen alive. Idea is for false Rupert to extract information from him
>
> Richard – off boat at Basrah – waiting room – smell of fear – ~~man stumbles puts in his pocket – What~~?
>
> Start
> A. Richard off boat – smell of fear – somehow or other something is passed to him (washing bag) – finds afterwards wonders what it is
> B. In from Marshes – something wrong – does he put half – Message in Kuwait chest – specially made secret drawer – has been a conjurer – goes up steps – vanishes

Notebook 56 speculates about bringing the various strands of the plot together, although Janet McCrae does not feature in the novel. The illustration below, from the same Notebook, is similar to that drawn by Dakin in the first chapter of the book and is also the idea behind the well-known Tom Adams Fontana paperback cover from the late 1960s.

At the end of Chapter 1 of They Came to Baghdad *Dakin doodles a sketch like this but the above is Christie's own interpretation of the title from Notebook 56. The Tom Adams painting for the 1970's Fontana paperback edition is a more elaborate and sinister version.*

4 people bringing four parts of the puzzle
Schute's [Scheele] evidence from America
Carmichael's from Persia(?) Kashgar(?)
Sir Rupert's from China
Janet McCrae's from the Bahamas

1. Olive in the plane – behind Sir Rupert – his cape slips back –
boil on neck (perhaps he is flown on by RAF plane to Basrah)
2. Carmichael Stewart in Marshes – with Arabs – coming
into civilisation
3. Richard lands from ship – goes to Consulate – smell of fear
4. Crooks? In train? At Alep – Damascus? Stamboul –
agents everywhere

Notebook 56 also considers the identity of the villain:

Is Crosbie real villain? Does he send Olive (or Vic) to Basrah
on his own account?
Can Edward be young (Nazi) villain – uses Victoria. V.
resembles Anne Schepp – that is why Edward picks her up

A. Does Edward (IT!) deliberately select Victoria
Or
B Edward and Victoria allies
If A, Victoria pairs with Richard? Deakin ?
If B, is villain Mrs Willard (plaster on arm?)

Overall, as the Collins reader rightly noted, the novel has
great pace and readability and, if not taken seriously or
examined in any detail, is a pleasant read. But it must be
asked why Edward, in Chapter 2, should draw attention to
'something fishy' in the Baghdad set-up (thereby setting
the whole novel in motion) when he is the (very surprising)
villain of the piece. He could easily have invented another
reason to persuade Victoria to follow him. This very basic

flaw in the plot is, possibly, a reflection of the problems the book seems to have given in its creation. But as the Collins reader observed, the character of Victoria, as well as the depiction of life in Baghdad and on an archaeological dig, more than compensate.

❦

They Do It with Mirrors
17 November 1952

―――――――――◄○►―――――――――

Miss Marple goes to Stonygates, the reform home for young delinquents run by the husband of her childhood friend Carrie Louise. Although the atmosphere is tense, when murder is committed the victim is totally unexpected. More deaths follow before Miss Marple penetrates the murderer's conjuring trick.

―――――――――◄○►―――――――――

They Do It with Mirrors was serialised six months before book publication in both the UK and the USA and was Christie's second title of 1952, following a few months after *Mrs McGinty's Dead.* Leaving aside the unlikely background – a reform home – for Miss Marple, the conjuring trick at the heart of the plot is clever; although even the mention of a conjuring trick risks giving the game away immediately. The subsequent killings are, like similar deaths in later novels of the 1950s – *4.50 from Paddington, Ordeal by Innocence* – unconvincing and read suspiciously like padding. The principle behind the misdirection involving Carrie Louise's innocent tonic is similar in type to the misdirection in *After the Funeral,* the following year, concerning the death of Richard Abernethie. Having successfully deceived her readers for over 30 years, Agatha Christie

272

could still devise new and infuriatingly simple tricks. And her presentation of clues remained as devious and daring as ever. Read the description of Lewis Serrocold opening the door of the locked study after the quarrel – and marvel anew.

Most of the notes, almost 30 pages, for *They Do It with Mirrors* are contained in Notebook 17, with brief references to the main plot device in another seven. The central idea behind this plot, the fake quarrel, was one that Christie nursed for a long time before finally incorporating it into a book. She considered numerous variations and various settings and the plotting was entangled, at different times, with both *Taken at the Flood* and *A Pocket Full of Rye*. As can be seen, that attraction went back over many years and oddly, it would seem that it was the title, or at least a reference to 'mirrors', that attracted her:

Jan 1935
A and B alibi A has attempted to murder B – really they both murdered C

Ideas for G.K.C.
Alibi by attempted murder. A tries murder B and fails (Really A and B murder C or C and D)

They do it with Mirrors
Combine with Third Floor Flat – fortune telling woman dead, discovered by getting into wrong flat

Plans Nov. 1948 Cont.
Mirrors
Approach – Miss M. on jury – NAAFI girl[37] – Japp or equal

---

37 Navy, Army and Air Force Institute, founded in 1921 to run recreational establishments needed by the armed forces, and to sell goods to servicemen and their families.

unhappy about case – goes to Poirot. The fight between two
men – (maisonette) – one clatters down – goes up again
in service lift and through door – shouts for help – badly
wounded – thereby they prove an alibi

Mirrors
Basic necessity – two enemies who give each other alibi.
Brothers – Cain and Abel

A split B's head open once – A bad tempered cheerful ne'er
do well; B Cautious stay at home

Mirrors
The antagonism between two people providing the alibi
for one. Sound of quarrel overheard – struggle and chairs –
finally he comes out – calls for doctor

Mirrors
The trick – P and L fake quarrel – overheard below (actually
P. does it above) L. returns and stuns him – calls for help

The 'fake quarrel' trick extends back as far as Christie's first
book, *The Mysterious Affair at Styles*, where Alfred Inglethorp
and Evelyn Howard feign an argument in order to allay suspicion. *Death on the Nile* and *Endless Night* also feature this
deception. In *They Do It with Mirrors* the trick depends, like
that of a conjuror, on the misdirection of an audience's
attention while the murder is actually committed elsewhere.
As can be seen in the first example above, this brief note may
well have inspired *Death on the Nile* as it preceded that novel
by two years; and the 'G.K.C.' note was for a 1935 anthology
A Century of Detective Stories, edited by G.K. Chesterton. The
reference to 'Third Floor Flat' is to the 1929 Poirot short
story of the same name; its possible combination with the

'mirrors' idea is echoed again in the example following, with the mention of the service lift. This dated extract is from Notebook 14, directly after the main notes for 1949's *Crooked House*. The 'Cain and Abel' note is from the early 1950s; it appears a few pages before the rough notes for the adaptation of *The Hollow* as a play. The final example shows the connection with *A Pocket Full of Rye*, as the initials refer to Percival and Lancelot from that novel.

Notebook 63 confirms that Christie considered the title a promising one and shows an elaboration of the idea as she experiments with various combinations of male/female and A/B. The reference to 1941's *Evil under the Sun* shows that this version postdates 1937's *Death on the Nile*.

They Do it with Mirrors (Good title?)

Combine with AB alibi idea – A and B, apparently on bad terms, quarrel

(a) Man and Woman (?) Jealousy? He pays attention to someone else? or she does? or married couple? (too like Evil under Sun)

(b) Two men or two women quarrelled about a man (or woman) according to sex

Result – clever timing – B phones police or is heard by people in flat or being attacked by A (A is really killing C at that moment!). C's death must be synchronised beyond any possible doubt.

A stabbed by B – then B goes off to kill X – A does double act of quarrel – ending with great shout – 'he's stabbed me.'

A has alibi (given by the attacked B) – B has alibi (given by injury and A's confession) – [therefore] suspicion is narrowed to D E or F

Then she tries out completely different plots, while retaining the promising title. The first one has echoes – sisters masquerading as 'woman and maid' – of the Miss Marple story, 'The Case of the Perfect Maid', first published in 1942, and the second is somewhat similar to the Poirot case *Mrs McGinty's Dead*. The third is a resumé of 'Triangle at Rhodes', with the addition of a quarrel and the substitution of Miss Marple for Poirot; and the final one is an original, and confusing, undeveloped scenario:

They do it with Mirrors

Idea?
Adv[ertisement] for identical twins. Really put in by twins
– crooks who are <u>not</u> identical. Woman and maid (really
sisters). The maid gives alibi etc. and talks for the first one

Mirrors

Starting Inspector (?) The Moving Finger or one of
the others. Calls on Miss M – retiring – his last case –
doesn't like it – puts it to her – evidence to the P[ublic]
P[rosecutor] overwhelming but he isn't satisfied

Could Mirrors be triangle idea
Valerie – rich, immoral, man mad
~~Michael~~ Peter – Air ace – married to her
Marjorie – brown mouse
Douglas – her husband – rather anxious – keen on Valerie
Miss Marple
V[alerie] poisoned – it was meant for P[eter]. Could there
be quarrel overheard – M and D really M and P (pretending
to be D)

Mirrors

Randal and ~~Nicholas~~ Harvey Derek – brothers – violent
quarrel – over woman? N marries Gwynneth. Old lady
killed by H and R during time when R is attacking H or by
R and G

In Notebook 17 Christie arrives at the plan that she eventually adopted for the novel. She drafts the set-up twice in three pages and then proceeds to a list of characters which is remarkably close to that of the finished work:

Mrs. Gordon, old friend of Miss Marple at Ritz – asks her to
come. Same age but Mrs. Gordon all dolled up etc. – vague
curious woman. Worried about Loulou – married that man
– all efficiency and eye glasses. Fuss over young man who
attacked him – said he was his father – had previously said
to several people that Churchill was his father.

Mirrors

Miss M summoned by rich friend (at school together in
Italy? France?). 2 sisters – both married a good deal Mrs.
B and Mrs. E. Former vague but shrewd – knows how
to manage men – with Louie, Mrs. E. men know how to
manage her. She is committed to this cultural scheme – by
first husband. 2nd selfish artist. She has various children
by first husband; by second – selfish pansy young man
[and] by third. E. is hard headed character, accountant.
A big trust (by D) – E. is one of principal trustees – others
being old lawyer – old Cabinet Minister – later dead lawyer
replaced by son – C[abinet] M[inister] replaced by Dr's
son, young man – has come to college – taken and accepted
by E.

People in Mirrors

Carrie Louise – friend of Gulbrandsen
Lewis Serrocold
Emma Westingham [Mildred Strete] – daughter – plain –
married Canon W. now a widow come home)
Gina – daughter of Gulbrandsen's adopted daughter, Joy,
who married unsatisfactory Italian Count, name of San
Severiano – daughter back to Gulbrandsen
Walter – her young American husband – good war record –
but obscure origin
Edgar – a psychiatric 'case' young research worker? Or
secretary? a bastard and a little insane
Dr. Maverick – Resident physician under Sir Willoughby
Goddard leading psychiatrist
Jeremy Faber [Stephen Restarick] – Stepson of Carrie
Louise by second husband 'bad Larry Faber', a scenic
designer in love with Gina
'Jolly' Bellamy [Bellever] – a Carlo [Carlo Fisher, Christie's
devoted secretary and friend], devoted to Carrie Louise –
or is she?
Christian Gulbrandsen

The arrival of Miss Marple and her introduction to the
inhabitants of Stonygates is sketched in Notebook 17:

Miss M arrives – met at station by Edgar – introduces himself
– his statement – Winston [Churchill] is his father – C[arrie]
L[ouise] – charming greeting. They see Gina out of window
– with handsome dark man. 'What a handsome couple' says
Miss M – C-L looks disturbed – not her husband – Mike –
gives acting classes to boys – gets up plays etc.

Telegram from Christian

> Mike or Wally to Miss M about Edgar being Montgomery's
> son. Talk about Edgar – illegitimate of course – served a
> short prison sentence

Earlier in the same Notebook, and while Lance and Percival
were still possible characters in *They Do It with Mirrors*, she
sketched the following scenes, remarkable for their similarity
to the all-important scene in the published version:

> Procedure
> P. asks Renee to come into room – study – they start
> quarrelling – not married etc. Conversation continues – her
> voice high and clear, he goes out by window, kills father and
> comes back. She stabs him – shoots him etc.
> Or
> Same with two brothers – violent quarrel. P's voice heard
> first, then L's – L's continues – then P. knocked out. 'Oh
> God, I think I've killed him'

In Notebook 43 Christie outlines the events of Chapter 7
iii with only minor differences – in the published version
Dr Maverick leaves before the quarrel and returns after the
shooting; and it is Miss Bellever who discovers the body.

> After dinner, Gulbrandsen goes to his room – 'I have some
> typing to do.' Lewis takes medicine away from Louise –
> powder – calc. Aspirin – for arthritis – moment of strain.
> Tel[ephone] – Jolly goes – 'Alexis has arrived at station –
> can we send a car.' Lewis goes to his room – Edgar comes
> through window – 'My father' – makes scene. Goes into
> Lewis's room – shuts door behind him, locks it – voices
> raised. Ought to break down door – Carrie Louise very calm
> 'Oh, no dear, Edgar would never harm Lewis.'

Maverick says very important not to apply force – Maverick
goes. Jolly rather violent about it – leaves hall. Then – 'You
didn't know I had a revolver' – presently sound of shot –
somebody screams – no, not here – it's outside – far away.
Edgar shouting – things falling over. Then, shot inside room
– Edgar calling out – 'I didn't mean it, I didn't mean to.'
'Open this door' – Edgar unbolts it – Lewis ~~shot~~ not shot
– missed, two holes in parapet. Then Edgar breaks down.
Lewis asks Stephen to fetch Gulbrandsen or ask him for some
figures. They go – Gulbrandsen shot. Then Alexis walks in.

A page of Notebook 43 is headed with a straightforward
question. The possibilities are then considered, with those
characters ostensibly in the clear and those still under suspicion listed separately. But as we – and the police – discover,
things are not always as they seem:

Who could have shot Christian Gulbrandsen

Miss Bellever
Alexis
Gina
Stephen
Clear   Gina and Stephen – off
Lewis
Edgar
Dr. Maverick
Carrie Louise
Miss Marple

And the clue of the typewriter letter is drafted later on the
same page:

Bottom bit left in typewriter – or just left

Dear David
You are my oldest friend. Beg you will come here to advise
us on a very grave situation that has arisen. The person to
be considered and shielded is father's wife Carrie-Louise.
Briefly I have reason to believe . . .

As usual, Christie sketched ideas that never went further than
the Notebook, and the following page had a few interesting
ones. In the extract below, E is Lewis Serrocold of the novel;
none of this sketch is used, apart from the clever adaptation
of the well-known phrase, 'Abandon hope all ye that enter
here.' Note also the possibility of using Abney (see *After the
Funeral*) as a setting.:

Scene Abney
E's a fanatic about delinquent children – they take them

'Recover hope all ye that enter here' [Chapter 5]

Secret training school for thieves and embezzlers. Director
E. – under David clever master with forged credentials

C. Gulbrandsen finds out about it and goes to police – then
says he made a mistake. Then shot. Police suggest young
man Walters – a bit balmy – someone tells him E is his
father – incites him to attack him – so as to help as cover –
they do it with mirrors

After the Funeral
18 May 1953

————————◄○►————————

At the family reunion following the funeral of Richard
Abernethie, Cora Lansquenet makes an unguarded
remark about his death – 'But he was murdered, wasn't
he?' When she is savagely murdered the following day it
would seem that her suspicions were justified.

————————◄○►————————

After the Funeral appeared in the USA, as *Funerals Are Fatal*,
two months before its UK publication and in both countries
book publication was preceded by an earlier serialisation.
After the Funeral is typical Christie territory – an extended
family in a large country house, and the death of a wealthy
patriarch with impecunious relatives waiting for the reading
of the will. That family is also her most complicated, result-
ing in the inclusion of a family tree.

The book's dedication reads 'For James in memory of
happy days at Abney.' 'James' was Christie's brother-in-law
James Watts, the husband of her sister Madge. They lived
in Abney, a vast Victorian house built in the Gothic style,
exactly as Enderby Hall is described on the first page of the
novel. It was to Abney that Christie retired in 1926 to recover
from the trauma of her disappearance. The house is also
mentioned in the Author's Foreword to *The Adventure of the
Christmas Pudding*: 'Abney Hall had everything! The garden
boasted a waterfall, a stream and a tunnel under the drive!'
In Chapter 23 of *After the Funeral* Rosamund has a conversation with Poirot seated by such a waterfall in the garden.

There is a reference to *Lord Edgware Dies* in Chapter 12,
and the same chapter also contains two (coincidental)

references, in the space of four pages, to a *Destination Unknown* (the following year's book). The distinctiveness and recognisability of backs is discussed in Chapter 16 and this would also feature in *4.50 from Paddington*. And the attempted murder of Helen Abernethie, overheard down a phone line, in Chapter 20 has distinct similarities to the actual murder of Donald Ross 20 years earlier in *Lord Edgware Dies*, and to that of Patricia Lane in *Hickory Dickory Dock*, two years later.

The death of Cora is one of Christie's most brutal and bloody murders, rivalling those of Simeon Lee in *Hercule Poirot's Christmas* and Miss Sainsbury Seale in *One, Two, Buckle my Shoe*. But, unlike the murders in these novels, the reason for the savagery of the killing in *After the Funeral* is not justified by the plot and it is difficult to understand why this method was adopted by the killer or, indeed, by Christie. There is never any question about the identity of the corpse as there was in *One, Two, Buckle my Shoe* and there is no subterfuge about the time of death as there was in *Hercule Poirot's Christmas*. Stabbing or any other blunt instrument would have met the killer's requirement.

After the Funeral also includes one of Christie's most daring examples of telling readers the truth and defying them to interpret it correctly. At the end of Chapter 3 we fondly imagine we are sharing the thoughts of Cora Lansquenet but, on closer examination, her name is never mentioned. The description of 'a lady in wispy mourning' applies equally well to her impersonator. Although the thoughts we share are perfectly believable as those of a sister in mourning, they are also capable of a more sinister interpretation when we later realise whose thoughts they actually are. This subterfuge is shared in an equally daring, and yet perfectly truthful, manner in Chapter 2 of *Sparkling Cyanide*.

Notebook 53 contains all of the notes for *After the Funeral* and they are more organised than many. They alternate with those for *A Pocket Full of Rye*, published later the same year. Along with the title, the basic plot appears on the first page of notes exactly as it does in the novel, with no crossings out or alternatives. The only point to change is that the 'somebody' who speculates about the murder of Richard is, in fact, 'Cora'.

Throughout the notes it would seem that the plotting of this book went smoothly. Apart from one major deviation – the quick-change impersonation of housekeeper and householder – the notes accurately reflect the entire plot of the book. They proceed chronologically and there is very little deleting or revising or listing of alternatives. And, interestingly, there is no earlier brief jotting with the seed of the idea that was later to bloom into this novel. The encapsulation of the plot on the first page of Notebook 53 even includes the name of the artist of the concealed painting that provides the motive for the appallingly brutal murder.

The underlying misdirection of *After the Funeral* also featured in the previous year's novel, *They Do It with Mirrors*.

After the Funeral
Family returning from cemetery – a meal – deceased
younger sister – not been seen for many years or at all by
his grandchildren etc. – Cora Lansquenet – (Somebody says
– of course – he was murdered) Cora L murdered the next
day. Really the CL of funeral is not CL – CL is already dead
[actually drugged]. Companion kills C – Why? Contents of
house are left to her including a picture? A Vermeer – she
paints it over with another

As usual, one of the elements to change was the names:

Helen Leo's wife
Timothy & Maude. Stansfield Grange —?
                                    Yorkshire?
George Denman? Crosfield.
Michael Shane
Rosamond   "
Gregory Banks?
? Susan Banks.
? Elizabeth
? Jane

                Cornelius Abernethie — Coralie Bassington

Richard—Elinor Maude·Timothy m Maude Fox Gordon m Pamela Sdus/ Laura m Henri Crosfield
    Mortimer   Susan m Gregory   George
    (d.)   Banks.

Geraldine m Antony Carss   Cora m Pierre Lansquenet
    Rosamund m Michael Shane

                        Lytchett St Mary.

The family tree (with a few question marks) of the Abernethies from After
the Funeral, *one of the most complicated families in all of Christie.*

Characters

Cora Lansquenet – youngest ~~daughter~~ sister of old ~~Mrs~~ Mr
Dent (like James). Married a rather feckless painter – lived
abroad a lot

Pam and husband (actor)

Jean – Leo's widow (2nd wife?)

Judy and Greg (photographer)

Andrea – (Miles's wife) he doesn't come – too delicate

George – (Laura's son) in City

A look at the family tree shows minor differences in the
eventual make-up of the Abernethies. Leo's wife becomes
Helen and the '2nd wife' idea was discarded; Andrea and
Miles, the hypochondriac, become Maud and Timothy;
Pam becomes Rosamund with an actor husband, Michael
Shane; and Judy becomes Susan, while Greg has a change
of profession to chemist's assistant. Although the comment 'like James' (Christie's brother-in-law) appears after
Mr Dent (the forerunner of Richard Abernethie), there is
nothing to show that the character was, in fact, anything
like James Watts.

It is not until some pages into the notes that Poirot is mentioned, although in the novel it is Mr Entwhistle, the family
lawyer, who actually brings him into the case:

HP is got into case by doctor attending old Larraby –
exhumation requested – cannot see how it can be anything
but a natural death – only, of course, it <u>could</u> be an alkaloid
etc

Christie again employs her alphabetical sequence but this
time there is little rearranging. The main reordering, as it
appears in the book, is the poisoning of Miss Gilchrist *before*

she gets to Timothy's rather than afterwards. In fact, it is partly because of the poisoning that she agrees to go to Timothy's.

A. Mr E gets telephone call from Maude – agrees to go up [Chapter 5]
B. Before goes up – calls on George – Tony and Rosemary [Michael and Rosamund] [Chapter 5]
C. Visits Timothy and Maude [Chapter 6]
D. HP and Ent[whistle] Whole thing rests on E's belief in Cora's hunches – she thought it was murder – she had some basis for thinking it so she was quite willing to hush it up – therefore – murder [Chapter 7]
E. Susan finds a wig in Cora's drawer [Chapter 11]
F. Susan arranges for Miss G to go to Tim's [Chapter 10]
G. HP receives reports [Chapter 12]
H. HP goes to Enderby – meets Andrea [actually Helen] – her story of something wrong – (Point here is was looking at Cora) – HP represents himself to be taking a house for foreign refugees – Andrea [Maude] speaks of paint smell upsetting Timothy [Chapter 14]
I. At Timothy's Miss G gets into her stride – gossip with daily women – nun? Miss G very surprised – same nun she is almost certain who was at Cora's – ? Then wedding cake? To Miss G – she is delighted – taken ill – but not fatal [Chapter 15]
J. They all assemble at Enderby to choose anything from sale – some comedy? Miss G says something about wax flowers? Or something that she could not have seen [Chapter 19]

Points in conversation
A. Nuns – what they were like – same one – a moustache [Chapter 19]

B. R[osamund] asks about wax flowers on malachite table
   – Miss G says looked lovely there [Chapter 19]
C. Susan says Cora didn't really sketch Polperro from a
   postcard [Chapter 18]
D. Talk about seeing yourself [Chapter 19]

One major sequence in Notebook 53 does not appear in the finished novel. Christie referred to it as the Hunter's Lodge idea:

Idea like Hunter's Lodge? Housekeeper doubles with
someone else made up glamorous

This is a reference to one of Poirot's early cases, 'The Mystery of Hunter's Lodge' in *Poirot Investigates*. He solves this case while confined to bed with influenza while Hastings travels to Derbyshire, reporting back by telegram. The plot device, which bears more than a passing resemblance to *After the Funeral*, depends on the ability of the murderer to effect a quick change and to appear both as housekeeper and mistress of the house within minutes of each other. Similar impersonations are adopted by the killers in *The Mystery of the Blue Train, Death in the Clouds, Three Act Tragedy, Appointment with Death, Sparkling Cyanide* and *Taken at the Flood*.

Although in Chapter 15 this idea is briefly considered, it is never a serious possibility as a solution. But the underlying subterfuge is very much the same – a domestic successfully masquerades as both mistress and maid, fooling the family and the police (and the reader) into believing someone alive when they have already been murdered. The impersonation in *After the Funeral* is played over a longer period and is more elaborate. And as the reader is told very early in the novel that Cora had lived abroad for over 25 years, the masquerade is perfectly feasible. Lanscombe the butler 'would hardly have known her'; Mr Entwhistle, the family lawyer, was 'able to see little resemblance to the gawky girl of earlier days'; and none of the younger generation of Abernethies knew her at all. At first it seems as if Christie toyed with the idea of the quick-change routine and in Chapter 15 there is an opportunity for this when Miss Gilchrist answers the door in response to a bell that no one else hears and a caller that no one else sees. Pages 26–7 of the notes consider the ramifications of such a development. But this was subsequently subsumed into the nun motif and the impersonation took on a more leisurely aspect.

Does Helen, while with Jean, see woman who collects
subscriptions – herself – and immediately after appear as
herself – quick change owing to geography of house – such
as appearing at front door and in Hall – just calling to ask
you – one moment please – two voices. Helen hurries into
room where Jean is upstairs – she is in morning room. Jean
rings up police – then goes down – visitor is there
Or
Visitor coming in – J says will you wait – get my purse – goes
to phone tells police – comes out finds Helen. H goes down
to keep him in play – gone.
Appearance of all the people
Cora – blonde hair faded curls like a bird's nest – make up –
big? plump? or a hennaed bang
Miss Earle [Gilchrist] – grey hair brushed back – Pince nez
or iron-grey bob – very thin
The caller – blue grey hair well dressed – (transformation)
slight moustache – dark eyes (belladonna) deep voice –
well cut tweeds – large sensible feet. When Jean sees her
– difference in costume wig – coat and street shoes – all
removed – thrown in closet – overall and slippers – Gone!
What did she come for? Things have to be got rid of – taken
away in suitcase – left in train

Finally, most of Chapter 20 is sketched in the latter stages of the notes. In the first paragraph Poirot reviews all the important facts of the case as he tries to sleep (Chapter 20 ii).

> P goes to bed – feels something significant said – odd business about Cora's painting – paint – Timothy – smell of paint. Something else – something connected with Entwhistle – something Entwhistle had said – significant – and something else – a malachite table and on it wax flowers only somebody had covered the malachite table with paint. He sat up in bed. Wax flowers – he remembers that Helen had arranged them that day. A rough plan – Mr Entwhistle – the smell of paint – the wax flowers.

Although the necessary clues are here paraded for the reader, how many will appreciate their significance?

Immediately following, the scene where Helen realises the implication of what she noticed at the funeral is sketched, although this is broken into two scenes in the book (Chapter 20 iii and iv):

> Helen – in the room – to see ourselves – she looks – my right eye goes up higher – no it's my left – she made an experimental face – she put her lead on one said and said it was murder wasn't it? And with that it came back to her – of course – that was what was wrong – excited – goes down to telephone – (or in early morning) – Mr E – do you see – she didn't – CONK

After the Funeral contains what is probably Christie's simplest subterfuge and one that is, in retrospect, maddeningly obvious. Even without this ploy it remains a clever but conventional detective novel. The trick played on the reader puts it straight into the classic Christie class.

Destination Unknown
1 November 1954

————————◄○►————————

In order to solve the mystery of his disappearance,
Hilary Craven agrees to impersonate the dead wife
of scientist Thomas Betterton. She joins a mysterious
group aboard a plane bound for an unknown
destination and when it lands in the middle of nowhere
she needs all her courage and wits.

————————◄○►————————

The UK serialisation of *Destination Unknown* preceded book publication by two months, while US readers had to wait until 1955, when it was published as *So Many Steps to Death*. From this year onwards Christie produced only one title per year. This cutback in production is understandable when it is remembered that 1952 and 1953 each saw the publication of two books, as well as work on the scripts of *Spider's Web* and *Witness for the Prosecution*.

Following only four years after *They Came to Baghdad*, *Destination Unknown* is another adventure-cum-travel story and an even more unlikely one than the earlier title. Like all Christie titles, even the weakest, it has a compelling premise, but one that is not developed or resolved in a manner we have come to expect of the Queen of Crime. The opening section dealing with the state of mind of Hilary Craven as she considers suicide could have been more profitably developed at the expense of some of the interminable travel sequences, which merely pad out the novel. Unlike other one-off heroines in earlier titles – Anne Beddingfeld[38] in *The Man in the Brown Suit*,

---

38 Anne's surname appears in some editions, and in some books about
    Christie, as Beddingfield.

Victoria Jones in *They Came to Baghdad*, and, in a more domestic setting, Emily Trefusis in *The Sittaford Mystery* and Lady Frances Derwent in *Why Didn't They Ask Evans?* – Hilary is not looking for either adventure or a husband. She is a divorced woman and has been a mother; in fact, it is the loss of her husband through divorce and the death of her child that causes her to agree to the seemingly outrageous suggestion that she change her method of suicide from sleeping pills to a potentially fatal impersonation. Also unlike the others, she works alone once the impersonation begins because from then she can trust no one. *Destination Unknown* contains none of the light-hearted scenes of the earlier *They Came to Baghdad*, mainly due to the fact that Victoria and Hilary are totally different characters.

There are a mere dozen pages of notes, scattered over Notebooks 12, 53 and 56; and Notebook 12 has a page dated 'Morocco Cont[inued]. Feb 28th'.

The year is, in all likelihood, 1954. Collins were anxious as that year progressed and no book reached them. If Christie was still plotting it in February in the year of publication, this would indeed be a cause for alarm. This is somewhat reflected in Notebook 12, which has four scattered attempts to get to grips with the plot. The dated page goes on to discuss possible plot developments when Hilary has already arrived at her final destination, so it is safe to assume that most of the plotting was complete at that stage.

The notes for *Destination Unknown* are inextricably linked with those of *They Came to Baghdad* from three years earlier. Much of the sketching of *They Came to Baghdad* features a character named Hilary/Olive and it would seem that, to begin with, the ideas that were to be included in one novel eventually generated two. The earliest indication of this comes in Notebook 56, where four possible ideas for *The House in Baghdad* (an early title for *They Came to Baghdad*) were noted.

As we have seen in the discussion of *They Came to Baghdad*, three of these ideas were indeed used for that novel, and one broke off to become the basis of *Destination Unknown*.

Notebook 12 contains notes mainly for the first half of the book, before Hilary arrives at her destination. Although they are very sketchy, most of the following ideas appear in the novel with only the usual name changes:

Morocco – Hospital – Olive dying says 'Warn him – Boris – Boris knows – a password – Elsinore?

Ou sont les neiges – The snows of yesteryear. The Snow Queen – Little Kay – Snow, Snow beautiful snow you slip on lump and over you go. [Chapter 4]

She is vetted by Dalton . . . The instructions – tickets etc. She goes to hotel – her conversation with people. Miss Hetherington – stylish spinster; Mrs. Ferber [Baker?] – American [Chapter 5]

Hilary – goes to Marrakesh. Then to fly to Fez – small plane – or plane to Tangier. Comes down – forced landing – petrol poured over it – bodies

Fellow travellers

Young American – Andy Peters

Hilary

Olaf ~~Ericsson~~ [Torquil Ericsson]

Madame Depuis – elderly Frenchwoman

Carslake – business man – or could be German

Dr. Barnard [Dr Barron]

Mrs Bailer [Mrs Baker]

Nun [Helga Needham] [Chapter 8]

Morocco Cont. Feb 28th

The arrival

Start from a point or little later. Hilary is finishing toilet?

Dresses – her panic – no escape. 'That's not my wife' – sits

on bed – fertile brain thinking out plans – injure her face?
Story about wife – couldn't come? Dead? That journalist is
it Tom Betterton – the hostess comes for her – meeting with
Tom – 'Olive' [Chapter 11]

Notebook 53 contains the background that the reader learns
only at the end of the novel. Unlike her detective novels, the
reader is not given the information necessary to arrive at this
scenario independently. In these extracts Henslowe is the
Betterton of the novel and the American professor is Caspar
instead of the Mannheims of the novel. Confusingly, in the
book the real wife is Olive and Hilary is the impersonator,
but in the Notebook Olive appears as the impersonator.

Morocco
Henslowe – young chemist – protégé of Professor Caspar –
(a world famous Atom scientist – refugee to USA). H marries
C's daughter Eva Caspar – Eva dies a couple of years after the
marriage. Argument – Eva inherits her father's genius – is a
first-class physicist and makes a discovery in nuclear fission.
H. murders her and takes discovery as his.

The idea of a plastic surgeon altering fingerprints is an interesting but unexplored possibility:

This disappearance business is an agency run by an old
American – a kind of Gulbenkian[39] – he pays scientists
good sums to come to him – also plastic surgeons – who
also operate on finger prints. A suspicion gets about that
Henslowe is not Henslowe because he is not brilliant

---

39 Calouste Gulbenkian, an Armenian businessman and
    philanthropist, founder of The Gulbenkian Foundation for
    charitable educational, artistic, and scientific purposes.

And the devious Christie can be seen in the last note ('Because he is <u>not</u> Henslowe?'). The obvious explanation is not the one she adopts: it is not that 'Henslowe' is really someone else, but that he is not the scientist that he purports to be, because his reputation was built on the genius of his dead first wife:

> Olive sees real wife dying in hospital – dying words – enigmatic – but they mean something. Olive and Henslowe meet – he recognises her as his wife – why? Because he is <u>not</u> Henslowe?

Christie also toyed with a more domestic variation concerning the earlier murder that set most of the plot in motion:

> Conman finds out about murder [of Elsa] and has a hold over him
> Communist Agent?
> A woman?
> Just an ordinary blackmailer?
>
> Henslowe marries again
> Deliberately a communist?
> Just a devoted woman?
>
> His disappearance and journey to Morocco is planned deliberately by him. [Therefore] Olive when on his trail will eventually discover that the dead body they come across (actually the blackmailer) is a private murder by Henslowe and all the Russian agents stuff is faked by Henslowe

After four very traditional whodunits in the previous two years – *Mrs McGinty's Dead, They Do It with Mirrors, A Pocket Full of Rye, After the Funeral* – *Destination Unknown* is a disappointment. Despite a promising opening the novel ambles

295

along to a destination that is more unbelievable than unknown, with little evidence of the author's usual ingenuity. The denouement of *They Came to Baghdad* unmasked an unexpected (if somewhat illogical) villain but there are no surprises at the climax of *Destination Unknown*. It is undoubtedly the weakest book of the 1950s.

The Unexpected Guest
12 August 1958

When Michael Starkwedder stumbles out of the fog and into the Warwick household, he finds Richard Warwick shot dead and his wife, Laura, standing nearby holding a revolver. Between them they concoct a plan to explain the situation before ringing the police. But who really shot Richard Warwick?

During the 1950s Agatha Christie reigned supreme in London's West End. *The Hollow* led off the decade in June 1951, followed by *The Mousetrap* in November 1952. October 1953 saw the curtain rise on *Witness for the Prosecution*; *Spider's Web* opened in December of the following year and *Towards Zero* (co-written with Gerald Verner) in September 1956. In 1958 two new Christie plays appeared – *Verdict* in May and *The Unexpected Guest* in August. With the exception of *Verdict* all were major theatrical successes, two of them at least, *The Mousetrap* and *Witness for the Prosecution*, assuring Agatha Christie's eternal fame as a playwright.

Spider's Web had been the first original Christie stage play since *Black Coffee* in 1930. *Verdict* and *The Unexpected Guest* continued this trend for new, as distinct from adapted, material, although both of these scripts are considerably darker in tone than *Spider's Web*. To some extent all three feature attempts to explain away a mysterious death with less emphasis than usual on the whodunit element. And in *The Unexpected Guest* Christie sets herself the added challenge of portraying a 19-year-old who is mentally disturbed. On a more personal note, the description of the victim, Richard Warwick, has distinct similarities to Christie's brother, Monty. Both spent part of their adult life in Africa, both needed an attendant when they returned to live in England and both had the undesirable habit of taking pot-shots at animals, birds and, unfortunately, passers-by through the window of his home. In her *Autobiography* (Part VII, 'The Land of Lost Content') she recounts Monty's description of a 'silly old spinster going down the drive with her behind wobbling. Couldn't resist it – I sent a shot or two right and left of her'; this is exactly Laura's description in Act I, Scene i of Richard's behaviour. There, it must be emphasised, all similarities ended, as Richard Warwick is painted as a particularly despicable character.

Verdict, after a critical mauling due, in part, to a mistimed final curtain, lasted only one month but in August 1958, spirit unquenched, the curtain rose on the next offering from the Queen of Crime. *Verdict* was an atypical Christie stage offering; despite its title it is not a whodunit and has no surprise ending. With *The Unexpected Guest* she returned to more recognisable fare. Although it is, in part, a will-they-get-away-with-it type of plot, it also contains a strong whodunit element and a last-minute surprise.

Christie had, presumably, spent the intervening period, not in licking her wounds, but in setting out to prove her critics wrong by writing a new play to eradicate the failure of *Verdict*. Or so it seemed. But Notebook 34 shows, with an unequivocal date, that the earliest notes for this play had been drafted even before *The Mousetrap* had begun its unstoppable run. Three pages of that Notebook show that almost the entire plot of the play already existed. A more likely scenario, and one borne out by further notes below, is that the plotting of the play was already well advanced even before *Verdict* was taken off; it needed only a final polish.

1951 Play
Act I
Stranger stumbling into room in dark – finds light – turns it on – body of man – more light – woman against wall – revolver in hand (left) – says she shot him.
'There's the telephone –
Uh?
'To ring up the police'
Outsider shields her – rings police – rigs room
People Vera
        Julian (lover?)
        Benny (Cripple's brother)

Act II
Ends with S[tranger] accusing V[era] of lying. Julian killed him – you thought I'd shield you – (she admits it) or led up to by his realising she is left handed; crime committed by right handed person
Curtain as –
'Julian did it'
She – 'You can't prove it – you can't alter your story'
'You ingenious devil'!
Act III
Suspicion switches to Benny having done it. But actually it is woman. Ends with her preferring S[tranger] to Julian
Characters could be
Vera (Sandra)

Julian
Mrs Gregg   mother of victim
                  Stepmother
Barny feeble minded boy
Rosa   "   " girl
Miss Jennson – Nurse
Julian's sister
Lydia or niece of Julian's – hard girl

This is, in rough outline, the plot of the play; and the characters correspond closely to the eventual cast list. The only element missing is the development of the part played by 'the Stranger'; he does not even figure in the list of characters, although a 'stranger stumbling into room' is the opening of the play. And yet the part he plays is vital to the surprise in the closing lines of the eventual script. The explanation for this may be simply that the final twist had not occurred to Christie when she began drafting the play. This is in keeping with other titles; the shock endings to both *Crooked House* and *Endless Night* do not form a large part of the plotting of either novel and would seem to have emerged during, rather than being inspired by, the drafting of the book. But even without the final twist *The Unexpected Guest* is still an entertaining whodunit.

Notebook 53 also has a concise summation of the plot, this time including a list of possible murderers. These three pages appear, unexpectedly, between pages of extended plotting of *After the Funeral* and *A Pocket Full of Rye*, both of which were completed in the early 1950s and published in 1953. The general set-up here is reflected in the finished play, although neither victim nor killer has yet been decided. By now the part played by the 'stranger' has taken on a more important aspect; he is given a name, Trevor and is under consideration as the murderer.

Plan   The Unexpected Guest
Act I
Trevor blundering in – in fog or storm – Sandra against wall
– pistol. He and she – he rigs things – rings police. Scene
between them
Curtain – end of scene
Scene II
People being questioned by police
Julian Somers MP
Sandra
Nurse Eldon
Mrs Crawford
David Crawford – invalid
Or
David Etherington Sandra's brother
Act II
Further questions
Julian and Sandra – Trevor's suspicions. He accuses her –
having tricked her with revolver
Damned if I'll shield him
What else can you do – now? etc.
Act III
Mrs Crawford takes a hand. 'Who really did it' – (brightly)
Now who did?
1. Trevor the enemy from the past – his idea is to return and
   find body
2. Nurse? Told him about wife and Julian – his reaction is
   that he knew all about it – is brutal to her – she shoots him
3. Governess to child? Or to defective?
4. Defective has done it – or child
5. Mrs Crawford?

As further confirmation of the unpredictability of the
Notebooks, the following extract, clearly dated November

1957, appears in Notebook 28, preceded by notes for *By the Pricking of my Thumbs* and followed by notes for *Endless Night*, both published in the late 1960s. How this gap of ten years can have happened in the middle of a Notebook and how a title from the previous decade can appear between notes for two titles from a later decade, is inexplicable; but it shows, yet again, the danger of drawing deductions or making explicit statements about the timeline of the notes, unless supported by incontrovertible proof.

There seems to be confusion in the following extract in the naming of the main female character. Earlier notes refer to her as Vera, as do the initials in this extract, but in the course of the notes she is also referred to as Ruth and/or Judith:

FOG
Nov 1957
M enters – R dead
V. revolver in hand – admits – the build up – tells her of
MacGregor – dead man displayed in bad light – letter
written – printed – left – <u>then</u> (M. rings up police?) V goes
up stairs – paper bag trick – they come down – M. enters
– discovery – M rings up police. Does Ruth – make some
remark about lighter (Julian's)
Scene II
Police – then family
Julian comes – lighter – he picks it up etc.
Act II
Police again or a police station – or his hotel and V. comes
there?
Ends with Julian and V
His saying 'You did not kill him – didn't know even how to
fire a revolver'
Act III
(Cast?) V[era]

M[ichael and/or MacGregor]
Jul[ian]
Police Insp.
   "   S[ergeant]
Mrs Warwick
Judith Venn [no equivalent]
Bernard Warwick [possibly Jan]
Crusty [possibly Miss Bennett]
Angell – Manservant (Shifty)
Crusty works on Bernard or Judith or Bernard begins talking
Points to decide
Judith (angry because R. chucks her out). If so, Bernard is
induced by her to confess or even boast. He is taken away.
M. clears him and breaks down J. [M] says to V. (good luck
with J.) he is M[acGregor]
Or
Bernard boasts to killing him – he is killed – cliff? window? etc.
Case closed. Then M springs his surprise

As can be seen, at this point the play is referred to as 'Fog';
and the same title appears in other Notebooks, once with the
addition of 'The Unexpected Guest' in brackets. As a title
'Fog' has its attractions. In both the physical and metaphorical
sense fog plays an important part in the play. 'Swirls of mist'
are described in the stage directions and fog is necessary to
lend credence to Starkwedder's story of crashing his car; and,
of course, the other characters, and the audience, are in a fog
of doubt throughout the play. Unusually for a Christie play
(with a UK setting) the scene is specifically set near the Bristol
Channel, and the fog-horn sounds a melancholy note periodi-
cally throughout the action of the play. The stage directions
specify that 'the fog signal is still sounding as the Curtain falls'.

'Greenshaw's Folly'
December 1958

————◄○►————

Miss Marple uses her powers of observation and armchair detection to solve the brutal murder of Miss Greenshaw, owner of the monstrous Greenshaw's Folly. In doing so she uses her knowledge of theatre, gardening – and human nature.

————◄○►————

The history behind this short story was outlined in *Agatha Christie's Secret Notebooks*. Briefly, it was written as a replacement for the still unpublished novella 'The Greenshore Folly', which, in turn, had been written as a gift for the Diocesan Board of Finance in Exeter. Embarrassingly, it had proved impossible to sell the story (due, probably, to its unusual length) and Christie recalled the original and replaced it with one bearing the similar-sounding title 'Greenshaw's Folly'. It was published in the UK in the *Daily Mail* in December 1956; in the USA, *Ellery Queen's Mystery Magazine* published it in March of the following year, referring to it as Christie's 'newest story'.

Unusually for a short story, there are 25 pages of notes in two Notebooks. Those in Notebook 3 are alongside notes for *4.50 from Paddington*, published in 1957, and *The Unexpected Guest*, first staged in 1958. Notebook 47 contains many of the notes for *Dead Man's Folly* as well as preliminary notes for the expansion of 'Baghdad Chest' (as Christie refers to it) and 'The Third Floor Flat'. The former, as 'The Mystery of the Spanish Chest', appeared alongside 'Greenshaw's Folly' in *The Adventure of the Christmas Pudding* but the latter was never completed.

Many themes and ideas from earlier stories make brief and partly disguised appearances in 'Greenshaw's Folly'. The mistress/housekeeper impersonation appeared 35 years earlier in 'The Mystery of Hunter's Lodge' and more recently in the 1953 novel *After the Funeral*. The weapon normally used from a distance but employed at close quarters featured in *Death in the Clouds*, the fake policeman appeared in *The Mousetrap* and 'The Man in the Mist' from *Partners in Crime*, and unsuspected family connections had been a constant element of Christie's detective fiction for years. And below, we see the reappearance of an old reliable idea – that no one looks properly at a parlour maid or, in this case, a policeman.

The main plot device, as well as the choice of detective, is briefly outlined at the beginning of Notebook 3, while Notebook 47 sketches the opening pages as well as unequivocally stating the title:

Miss M
Hinges on policeman – not really a policeman – like parlourmaid one does not really look at policemen. Man (or woman) shot – householder rushes out – Policeman bending over body tells man to telephone – a colleague will be along in a moment

Greenshaw's Folly
Conversation between Ronald [Horace] who collects monstrosities and Raymond West – photograph – Miss Greenshaw

Notebook 47 considers two possible plot developments. The first is clearly the seed of the Poirot novel *The Clocks*, to be written five years later. Most of the ideas noted here were incorporated into that novel apart from the reason for the presence of the clocks. 'The Dream' is a Poirot short story from 1938 and it contains elements of the plot of 'Greenshaw's Folly' – the impersonation, by the killer, of the victim and the consequent faking of the time of death.

> Typist sent from agency to G's Folly alone there – finds body – or blind woman who nearly steps on it. Clocks all an hour wrong. Why? So that they will strike 12 instead of 1.

> The Dream
> Wrong man interviews woman – girl gives her instruction – she goes into next room to type. Then finds apparently same woman dead – really dead before – has said secretary is out or faithful companion – faithful companion seen walking up path. Combine this with policeman – girl is typing – looks up to see police constable silhouetted against light.

The Notebooks show vacillation between Alfie and the nephew as murderer or, at least, conspirator. As can be seen, much thought and planning went into the timetable of the murder and impersonation, and this element of the plot is undoubtedly clever.

> Are Mrs C. and Alfie mother and son?
> Are Mrs C. and nephew mother and son?

> Mrs C. and Alf do it. Get Miss G. to make will – then one of them impersonates Miss G.

> A. Alfie then is seen to leave just before real policeman appears
> e.g.   11.55 Alfie leaves whistling or singing
>   12   Alfie as policeman arrives. Fake murder – Mrs C. yells Help etc. Alfie then in pub
>   12.5   Alfie as policeman

B. Nephew is the one who does it. An actor in Repertory –
Barrie's plays

   Alfie leaves ~~11.55~~ 12 o'clock. Nephew steals in, locks
doors on Lou and Mrs. C, kills Aunt, then strolls, dressed as
Aunt, across garden – asks time.

Mrs C. and N[at or nephew]
   12.15 – Fake murder – with Mrs C.
   12.20 – Policeman
   12.23 – Real police
   12.25 – Nephew arrives
Alfred gets to lunch – so he is <u>just</u> all right – or meets pal
and talks for a few minutes
Or
Mrs C. and Alfred
Fake murder Mrs C. 12.45 (Alfred in pub)
Policeman (Alfred) 12.50
Real police   12.55
Alfred returns   12.57
Nephew   1 o'clock   (has been given misleading
directions)

The following very orderly list has a puzzling heading; why
'things to *eliminate*'? Few of them actually are eliminated;
most of them remain in the finished story:

Things to eliminate

Will idea (Made with R[aymond] and H[orace] as witness)
left to Mrs C. or Alfie too
Policeman idea
Alfie is nephew
Alfie Mrs C.'s son
Alfie is not nephew but pretends to be – Riding master and
Mrs C.'s son)

Nephew and policeman's uniform (Barries' plays)
Nephew and Alfie are the same
Mrs C. plays part of Miss G.

As we have seen, Christie toyed with alternative versions of the plot and solution before she eventually settled on one that is, sadly, far from foolproof; the mechanics of the plot do not stand up to rigorous scrutiny. Would the 'real' police, for example, not query the presence and identity of the first 'policeman', despite Miss Marple's assertion that 'one just accepts one more uniform as part of the law'? And we have to accept that someone would work for nothing on the basis of expectations from a will. The will itself poses more problems. The conspirators assume it leaves the money to them, either to the housekeeper, as promised, or to the nephew, as inheritance. But, in reality, the estate is left to Alfred, thereby ensnaring him in the fatal trio of means, motive and opportunity. But if the conspirators knew this they had no motive; and if they didn't know it, framing Alfred was never a possibility.

Cat among the Pigeons
2 November 1959

As the headmistress, Miss Bulstrode, welcomes the pupils for the new term at Meadowbank School she little realises that before term ends a pupil will be kidnapped, four staff will be dead and a murderer will have been unmasked. It's just as well that Julia Upjohn called in Hercule Poirot.

With a serialisation beginning the previous September, *Cat among the Pigeons* was the 1959 'Christie for Christmas'. It is a hugely readable mixture of domestic murder mystery and international thriller with a solution that reflects both situations. In this, the unmasking of two completely independent killers, it is a unique Christie. It was the first Poirot since 1956 and there would not be another one until *The Clocks*, four years later. The reader's report on the manuscript, dated June 1959, was enthusiastic ('highly entertaining') rather than ecstatic ('not a dazzling performance'). Described as having 'enough of the crossword puzzle element towards the end to satisfy the purists, even though the solution shows that plot to be rather far-fetched' and to be 'more saleable than [the previous year's title] *Ordeal by Innocence*', the reader recommended including the book in a new contract. Although the reader was viewing the manuscript in purely commercial terms, few Christie aficionados would agree with the view that it would outshine *Ordeal by Innocence*, a far superior crime novel.

As will be seen, Christie toyed with the idea of having Miss Marple solve the murders at Meadowbank School and this might not have been such a bad idea. Miss Marple having a relative in the school is more credible than a school-girl 'escaping' to consult Poirot; and Meadowbank is a girls' school. That said, Miss Marple had already had a busy decade with four major investigations, and another minor one; and she would not, perhaps, have been as adept with the international segment.

In the opening chapter there is a variation on the ploy of a character seeing something momentous – '"Why!" exclaimed Mrs Upjohn, still gazing out of the window, "how extraordinary!"' – that has an important bearing on subsequent events. This has often taken the form of seeing something over the shoulder of another character, as do Lawrence

308

Cavendish in the bedroom of the dying Mrs Inglethorp in *The Mysterious Affair at Styles*, Mrs Boynton in the hotel foyer in *Appointment with Death* and Satipy on the path from the tomb in *Death Comes as the End*. In each case a death soon follows and the unidentified sight forms part of the explanation. If Miss Bulstrode had been listening properly to Mrs Upjohn, much of the ensuing mayhem might have been avoided. Two further telling examples of this ploy would appear within the next five years: when Marina Gregg, in *The Mirror Crack'd from Side to Side*, looks down her own staircase and sees something that transfixes her, and when the unfortunate Major Palgrave, in *A Caribbean Mystery*, recognises a killer over Miss Marple's shoulder, just before his own murder. As with other novels from Christie's later period – *Hickory Dickory Dock*, *4.50 from Paddington*, *Ordeal by Innocence*, *The Mirror Crack'd from Side to Side* – there is an unnecessary and 'rushed' murder in the closing stages. It features the future victim talking to an unseen, and unnamed, killer, also a feature of *Hickory Dickory Dock*.

There are over 80 pages of notes devoted to *Cat among the Pigeons* in three Notebooks, 70 of them in Notebook 15. The intricacy of the plot, with an unusually large cast of characters, two separate plot strands and scenes set in Ramat and Anatolia, as well as some beyond the grounds of Meadowbank, account for these extensive notes.

The first page of Notebook 15 is headed 'Oct. 1958 Projects', and goes on to list the ideas that would become *The Pale Horse*, *Passenger to Frankfurt* and *Fiddlers Five/Three*, along with the possibility of plays based on either *Murder is Easy* (or, as it appears in the Notebook, 'Murder Made Easy') or 'The Cretan Bull', from *The Labours of Hercules*. Idea C on this list became *Cat among the Pigeons*.

The earliest notes show Christie considering basic possibilities, which detective to use and how they might be brought into the story. At this stage also the princess/schoolgirl impersonation is under consideration, carrying echoes of a similar plot device in 'The Regatta Mystery'.

Book
Girl's school? Miss Bulstrode (Principal)
Mrs. Upjohn – or parent – rather like Mrs. Summerhayes in
Mrs. McGinty, fluffy, vague but surprisingly shrewd
Miss Marple? Great niece at the school?
Poirot? Mrs. U sits opposite him in a train?
Someone shot or stalked at school sports?
Princess Maynasita there or an actress as pupil or an actress
as games mistress

There were two contenders for the book's title. The rejected one, which is not at all bad, is briefly mentioned at the start of Chapter 8 when the two policemen first hear of the murder:

Death of a Games Mistress
Cat among the Pigeons

A list of characters in Notebook 15 is remarkably similar to those in the published novel, although the number of characters would increase considerably:

Possible characters
Bob Rawlinson
Mrs. Sutcliffe (his sister)
Frances [Jennifer] Sutcliffe (her daughter)
Angele Black
Fenella (pupil at school)
Mademoiselle Amelie Blanche
Miss Bolsover [Bulstrode] Principal of School

'Meadowbank'
Miss Springer – Gym Mistress
Mrs. Upjohn (rather like Mrs. Summerhayes)
Julia Upjohn
Mr Robinson

It seems likely that Angele Black and Amelie Blanche were amalgamated into Angele Blanche. It would seem that the character 'Fenella' was originally intended to be another agent, but masquerading as a pupil, possibly as well as Ann Shapland, within the school. The comparison of Mrs Upjohn with Maureen Summerhayes refers to Poirot's inefficient landlady in his disreputable guest house in *Mrs McGinty's Dead*, and it is an apt one. Both are disorganised, voluble and immensely likeable; and each is the possessor of a valuable piece of information which imperils their safety.

The set-up on the opening day of the new term is sketched, including the all-important Mrs Upjohn and her sighting, although at this stage what, or more strictly, whom she sees is still undecided:

Likely opening gambit
First day of summer term – mothers etc. – Mrs. U sees someone out of window. Could be New Mistress? Domestic Staff? Pupil? Parent?

The letters that constitute Chapter 5, and that contain much that is later significant, are considered in Notebook 15:

Letters

Julia
Jennifer
Angele Blanche
Chaddy

The 3rd weekend of
term –
        About what happens.
Miss Bullstrode. Say
for weekend to Duchess
of Arlington – to
I met Professor Bamilton
Leave school in Sleam
Cheque – Jm v Chaddy
Fenella – your uncle
has an — in London
will Ball you off to – women
Mary Greg – Elizabeth —
Princess Gulind. Veronica –
28 girls – Ann shape..
off – Miss Johnson — his
sister how from Kenya —
Can Call for Fenella
Vansittart v Chaddy – useful –
words –
Can Call for Fenella.
Then 2nd one —

Two pages from Notebook 15 with a lot of plotting and speculation for Cat among the Pigeons. *Note the incorrect spelling of Miss 'Bullstrode'.*

Gardner sees Bob — etc.

Meets Crooks at Savoy —
a name & address —

found drowned —
———

Ann sent on job - Scanning
Sports Pavilion — Miss S interrupts -
Shot -
———

who is other woman? Who calls for
Jacqui?
———

Eleanor Vanstittart
Anonymous to ??
Well, I've settled in all right – you'd have laughed like a
drain to see the reception committee. I've settled in – in this
I look the part all right. Anyway, nobody seems to have any
doubts of my bona fides – then we shall see what we shall
see – I hope!

The letter from Miss Chadwick ('Chaddy') did not materialise and although there is an anonymous one it is clear to the reader that the writer is Adam, the gardener. The inclusion of the one sketched here would have been tantalisingly mysterious and it is a shame that it was never developed.

Christie devotes a lot of space to the progress of the tennis racquet:

History of Racquet
A. Brought home by Mrs. Sutcliffe by sea (Does she see
A[ngele] B[lanche] at Tilbury?)
B. Her husband meets her – drives them straight down to
country or they go down by train and it is left in train?
C. House is entered – tennis racquets taken and a few other
things, later recovered by police

In effect, it is this unlikely object that sets the plot in motion. In this, it has echoes of the ninth Labour of Hercules, 'The Girdle of Hippolita', where Poirot investigates the disappearance of the schoolgirl Winnie King; she also was the unwitting smuggler of contraband in her otherwise innocent luggage. The initial swapping of the tennis racquets is acceptable but the scene in Chapter 12 ii, when a total stranger approaches Jennifer and asks to exchange them (again), is less than convincing. Christie considers possibilities, discarding those such as the use of a lacrosse stick; note also her practical concerns about how long lost property offices retain items:

> Motive? Motive? Jewels bound for Near East country – prior to abdication – perhaps shirks plan turns back. Pilots sister takes them out of country concealed in schoolgirl's 'kit.'
> Lacrosse stick?
> Tennis racquet? Where they lie concealed. Mother (or aunt?) killed – her room at the hotel ransacked – dies of shock?
> Racquets swopped by girls – Jennifer? Julia?
> Woman who comes – New lamps for old. Exchange tennis racquet for new one but it has already been swopped. Lost property office – how long – find out

She then sketches the scene more or less as it appears in the book:

> A lady calls – tweedy, county, vague – asks girl 'Can you tell me where I can find Janet McGrane? It's Janet McGrane. What a coincidence' Story about bringing a new tennis racquet 'As I was coming here anyway to ask about the school for my niece.' Takes old racquet to be restrung etc. J. gives her old tennis racquet but it's not really hers – she has done a swap (with Julia?). Hers wasn't 'balanced.' She exchanges it for one that needs restringing. Does woman say 'It needs restringing – that's what your aunt said.' But her's had been restrung for going abroad – a sort of 'New lamps for old' touch

The enterprising Julia brings Hercule Poirot into the case in Chapter 17, and Notebook 15 summarises her efforts:

> Julia leaves French class – goes to London – contacts
> Hercule Poirot – Maureen Summerhayes (from Mrs

McGinty) is her godmother. Tells about Mrs. U's letter and her own observations. HP takes it seriously – goes to school. Interview with Miss B – they get on well – Miss B tells about Mrs. U and HP tells her about Mrs. U's letter to India.

And the killer appears in Notebook 15 with a change of name. An earlier note shows some indecision, but no lack of ideas, about the possible identity of this killer:

Games Mistress, school maid, parent recognised by Mrs. U[pjohn] as espionage agent.
Ann Shelbourne [Shapland] – a criminal by choice – as a girl wild – gives herself an alibi. In studying her career – a double life – like a drunk who has occasional 'benders.' Very able – good jobs – first on stage – then sec. to Sir Dawson Kops – over Oil Company? or Industrial Magnate, in between other things

There was always going to be more than one murder; in the Notebooks the second murder seems to have been definite from the early stages. Although most Christie novels feature more than one death, the later deaths are usually as a result of the earlier one. Here, because of the two separate plot strands, the second murder is independent of the first; but, of course, the reader is unaware of this until the explanation. And the setting of the Games Pavilion seems to confirm the connection, as was Christie's intention. But the identity of her third victim was still undecided at this stage:

3 deaths
1. Miss Springer's games mistress (she surprises someone in sports pavilion)
2. Miss   ?   Miss Bulford's probable successor
3. ?

1st murder because of jewels. 'Angelina' is in Springer part –
interrupted by Games mistress – kills her. Then Chaddy kills
Rich

Miss Bulstrode retiring. Going to take someone into
partnership. Chadwick? Margaret Rich (Mathematical
mistress?). But really Mary Templar – young – only there a
few terms. But the stuff that's needed.
Second murder is committed by Miss Chadwick – sees light
in Sports pavilion and finds Miss V there – also sees light –
Chaddy has taken sandbag with her as weapon. Tempted
– hits

She lists alternative scenarios, some of which – Miss Springer
in Ramat, the art room attack – were rejected and others –
Julia and her missing mother, Miss Rich in Ramat – incorporated into the novel.

One possible sequence
B [Ann Shapland] does not recognise Mrs. U[pjohn]
until Sports Day – does not know Mrs. U has seen her
before. Manages an attack from behind (in the Arts Display
Room?) Mrs. U concussed badly – taken to hospital

Alternative
(A) Rich is school teacher in Ramat. Pregnant – absent that
term – not the woman who sees Bob [therefore] Dancer is
the woman on balcony – Either Fenella Angele or Fenella or
Ann
B. Springer was schoolteacher in Ramat she saw Bob – got
job at M[eadowbank]. Goes out to Pav[ilion] followed by
? Ann – member of organisation who shoots her
Points to be fitted in and retained
A. Julia comes to consult Poirot – mother missing? in

317

hospital with concussion? Gone abroad – E. Africa? Safari?
B. Recognition by Mrs. U of somebody at school. Is that
somebody the victim or the murderer. Does an incident
happen at some other school?
C. 3 people on the job – (1) Knows about racquet (2) Relies
on Fenella – (impersonates?). Believes Mrs. S. – has been
instructed to give jewels to Fenella. (3) A woman who is put
on to following whoever knows about racquet (S.T. or D)
[school teacher or domestic]

Overall, the two distinct strands of *Cat among the Pigeons*, the
international and the academic, coalesce convincingly. And
what seems like cheating, the transition between Chapter 14
i and ii, is shown in retrospect to be perfectly fair and acceptable. If there is a fault with the book it is the excess of female
characters. Apart from Adam, the gardener, all the other
male characters are peripheral; this applies even to Poirot
– although he would doubtless disagree! Despite this abundance of femininity, there is never any difficulty in differenti-
ating between the characters.

UNUSED IDEAS: FOUR

SOLUTIONS REVEALED
4.50 from Paddington • *Five Little Pigs* • *The Mirror Crack'd
from Side to Side* • *Three Act Tragedy*

This selection features a number of relatively short but intriguing possibilities.

THE 'HANDED TO' IDEA

Interesting idea that many murderers are loose. Experiment
by saying to people 'Getting away with murder' etc.
Dropped teacup just as it is being handed to someone.
Inference – the hander has dropped it (wife or husband
recently conveniently dead) – really the 'handed to.'
Experimenter shortly after has near escapes – being gunned
for. Result – investigation – more near escapes – actually
investigations also apply to 'recipient' this not seen till by
surprise at end

This outline seems to date from the early 1950s, as it appears on a page in the middle of plotting 1952's *They Do It with Mirrors*. Here Christie experimented with yet another variation on misdirecting the reader. In many of her poisoning dramas – *Three Act Tragedy*, *The Mirror Crack'd from Side to Side*, *Five Little Pigs* – the 'hander', not surprisingly, was the killer, but the 'handed to' is a new twist. This would have needed careful setting-up on the part of the writer, not to mention careful stage-managing on the part of the murderous 'recipient'. Two novels of the early 1950s feature a misdirection of the reader from the very start. *After the Funeral* and *They Do It with Mirrors* both mislead the reader into believing something that is completely false, although the author never explicitly states it. The above scenario is similar in design.

––––––•◆•––––––

THE LOCUM DOCTOR

Next Detective novel
Villain is doctor (locum) – Lies about time of death. But he
is the one to suspect murder – not satisfied with cause of
death – therefore he is free of suspicion and can add poison
to a 'sample' he has taken – and which can only have been
prepared by
wife
foreign girl in house
etc.
Actually that preparation was harmless – poison was
administered by doctor himself in something else – before
– or later (capsule?). Motive – will marry daughter – plain –
devoted. 2 person crime – he and daughter?

Book – Dr. Scofield – called in after discovery of body
– gives time of death incorrectly. Dr. S (who is locum)

suspects what real doctor (busy careless chap) has not – chronic poisoning by member of household. Takes sample of food (or vomit) – sends for analysis – sure enough there is poison – he gives a warning to household – that night the old man dies – Poison? Bashed? Appearance of robbery – doctor fixes time of death at such a time (wrong). Police surgeon arriving later can only give wide latitude of time

The first of these notes appears in Notebook 53 alongside notes for the 1954 radio play *Personal Call* and the novels *They Do It with Mirrors, After the Funeral* and *Destination Unknown*, all published 1952–4. So it is reasonable to assume that the notes date from the early to mid 1950s. And some of the ideas do feature in 1957's *4.50 from Paddington*. Dr Quimper adds poison to the curry sample, having doctored the drinks jug earlier, with the intention of marrying the devoted daughter (and heiress), although in the book she is unaware of his plan. But it has to be asked why the villainous doctor of the first extract should draw attention to a murder instead of certifying it a 'natural' death.

The 'foreign girl in house' scapegoat appears in 'How Does Your Garden Grow?', and will surface again in *Hallowe'en Party*. Oddly, the second sketch directly precedes the main plotting for *4.50 from Paddington*, although there is less connection between the two.

———•◆•———

THE BRITISH MUSEUM

British Museum Story
S.S., Keeper of Babylonian Dept., has been stealing objects and replacing them with electrotypes in parchment unheard of in B.M. laboratories. Sir James Dale, director, gets wind of this but decides to hush the matter up. Dobson who has

been passed over for director is suspected as he has been
very bitter – he went to see Sir James last thing with a dagger
he wanted to buy for the Museum – wound is like one made
by such a dagger.
Slightly batty old gentleman (Olin?) gives show away by
handling some stuff of his and saying it didn't feel right

The idea of a short story set around the British Museum
appears in three other Notebooks but this, from Notebook
30, is the most elaborate version. The setting had an obvious
appeal for Christie because of her connection, via her husband Max Mallowan, with the Museum and it might have
been possible to have had some quiet fun with the characters.
The idea of 'electrotypes' surfaced in *Murder in Mesopotamia.*

———•◆•———

THE BOMBED BUILDING

Man trapped under bombed building – Nurse at AT crawls
in and rescues him. He says do you want to be rich? She
thinks funny idea.
Now!
He presses something into her hand – paper? Formula?
Afterwards man visits her – asks – she senses danger – the
paper? Hides it.

This dates from early in the Second World War, appearing
on a list between the ideas for *The Moving Finger* and *Towards
Zero*. It sounds more spy story than detective story with its
overtones of secret formulas, and the Nurse may well be a
prototype for Hilary Craven in *Destination Unknown* and
Victoria Jones in *They Came to Baghdad*. The 'bombed building' idea is the starting point for *Taken at the Flood.*

Agatha Christie and Poison

'Since I was surrounded by poisons, perhaps it was natural that death by poisoning should be the method I selected.'

From her experience as a hospital dispenser in both world wars, Agatha Christie had a professional knowledge of medicines and poisons. Starting with her first book, she used poison as a murder method more often than any of her contemporaries. The use of strychnine in *The Mysterious Affair at Styles* is a vital element of the murder plot; in fact the success of the conspirators depends on it. She uses not just the usual poisons – arsenic (*Murder is Easy*), morphine (*Hickory Dickory Dock*), cyanide (*Sparkling Cyanide*), but also the more esoteric – nicotine (*Three Act Tragedy*), thallium (*The Pale Horse*), taxine (*A Pocket Full of Rye*).

Notebooks 52 and 53 both include notes on the properties of a number of poisons. The former Notebook, dating from the early 1960s, contains notes for *The Mirror Crack'd from Side to Side* and *The Clocks*; the latter, from ten years earlier, has notes for *After the Funeral* and *A Pocket Full of Rye*, both published in 1953. Despite the fact that she had been dispatching her victims with poison for over 30 years, these notes show that Christie still researched new and ingenious methods of literary murder.

The notes are telegrammatic in style but most of the detail is scientifically accurate; I imagine that she was taking notes from a textbook. I have had to omit a few words whose illegibility defeated me and I include brief comments on some of the entries. The first list is from Notebook 53:

Notes on Poison
Taxine from leaves and berries of yew tree – salts soluble in water
Symptoms
Suddenly taken ill – fainting – face pale – pulse almost imperceptible – pupils contracted – eleptiform [resembling epilepsy] convulsions – stertorous breathing – slowing of respiration. Died within hour of illness, 2 hours after taking leaves. In another case died in eleptiform fit.
Possible sequence – quick pulse – fainting – collapse – nausea, vomiting; convulsions, slow respiration, death sudden and unexpected – death due to rigid paralysis of respiration and suffocation.

Taxine is used in *A Pocket Full of Rye*, the notes for which are contained in the same Notebook, and the details of Rex Fortescue's death follow this outline.

Arsenic
Acute form similar in action to cholera; in district where cholera epidemic – no suspicion. Diarrhoea absent sometimes and death from shock
Rare form – nervous form – no diarrhoea or vomiting – narcotism – delirious – acute mania even eleptiform convulsions
Rare cases – symptoms delayed for 9 hours – fell suddenly and expired.

Murder is Easy features the use of arsenic and, in the 1950s, Alfred Crackenthorpe succumbs to arsenic poisoning in *4.50 from Paddington*.

Ouabain
Arrow poison – of extract of root of ouabai tree [found in Africa]
Tasteless, odourless, sol[uble] boiling water – almost insol[uble] in cold. V[ery] poisonous if injected – (Diabetes?)

Colchicine
Colchicine (meadow saffron) – Colchicine wine (sherry) or schnapps or madeira – leaves consumed with salad – less than a 1 gr. fatal. Mrs. Soames killed by Margaret [should be Catherine] Wilson 1862). Burning pain in throat and tummy
Death 2nd day to 5th

Although colchicine was not adopted as a murder method by Christie, the true-life Wilson case is mentioned in Chapter 12 of Anthony Berkeley's *The Wychford Poisoning Case* (1926).

Digitalis
Symptoms appear not less than 3 hours after. Red coal fire appears to be blue – sometimes blindness.

Digitoxin is the poison used to despatch Mrs Boynton in *Appointment with Death*.

Helleborus
From root of Christmas Rose, Helleborus Niger and other hellebores. Death under 8 hours – root boiled in wine?
Heart poison – symptoms as digitalis

Oleandrin from oleander leaves

Saponin
40 grams subcutaneously – lethargy – weakness of heart –
extracted from bread or flour. Sol[uble] in water – frothy –
in lemonade? Sherbet? Etc.

As can be seen, even as she jotted the above notes Christie
was thinking of a plot involving a frothy drink to camouflage
the poison, although she never used it in a story.

Santonin (for worms?!) Max dose . . . 6 gr.
Tetanic convulsions and death – 15 to 48 hours; everything
looks yellow (sometimes violet). 'Woman in yellow dress?'

Daphne Mezereum
Burning taste in mouth – sudden narcosis – convulsion –
dev[eloped from] fresh leaves? Berries?

Water hemlock
In flower in August – root like parsnip – stalk like celery.
Semi-comatose – legs dragged

Coniine, another name for hemlock, is the poison stolen
from Meredith Blake's laboratory and used the following day
to kill Amyas Crale in *Five Little Pigs*.

Hyoscyamine
1 gr. fatal – quiets excitement – muscular motion enfeebled
– flushed face – pupils dilate. Distinction from atropine as
latter causes delirium and excitement

The following list is from Notebook 52. In the 15 years
between use of this Notebook and the end of her career,
Christie used poison as a murder method in a further seven

novels, and mood-altering drugs are a major plot feature of *Third Girl.*

> Poisons   Possibilities for book
> Pentanol (Amyl Alcohol) $C_3H_{11}OH$ [should be $C_5H_{11}OH$]
> Ethylene Glycol CH_2OH [formula should be twice this $(CH_2OH)_2 = C_2H_6O_2$]
> Colourless sweet taste – substitute for glycerine – freeze – preserving substance – 100 grams drunk in "Schnapps" was fatal
>
> Diethylene alcohol
> Solvent for paints – Sol. of sulphanilamide in diluted diglycol caused 100 cases poisoning in America
> Look up veronal, phanodorm, curral, somnifen, noctal, phenocton [more probably phenytoin], nirvanol (phenyelhydantoin) – (barbiturate derivatives)
> Look up pyrazolone derivatives – in partic[ular] pyramidon (sol. 1 in 2 alcohol central paralysis) cardiazol – coramine etc.
> Strophanthin (Heart tonic)

Strophanthin is used and identified in 'The Case of the Caretaker' and 'Triangle at Rhodes' as well as *Verdict.*

> Nitrobenzene
> 1 gm. fatal
>
> Tri-ortho-cresyl phosphate
> Paraffin-like, colourless, odourless tasteless – insol. in water – used as adulteration of ginger extract – produces similar sensation to alcohol. In 1929 20,000 died of ginger paralysis – ten weeks before symptoms developed – ending with paralysis of arms and legs – (taken as liquid paraffin).

This adaptation of a patent medicine, popular during Prohibition because of its 'alcohol' effect, was later shown to have an adverse effect on some nerve cells in the spinal cord. The paralysis Christie notes was not fatal, although in many cases it was permanent.

Sodium fluosilicate
Sometimes mistaken for baking powder or sod[ium] bic[arbonate] – suicidal agent

E.605 plant protection agent – freely sold to public – epidemic of suicides in Germany
Neurotoxin affects regulation of parasympathetic system. Death through cardiac and respiratory paralysis after agonising pain and convulsions – a few minutes or up to half an hour. Christa Lehman poisoned a number of people

Christa Lehman was convicted in September 1955 in Germany of the murder of two members of her own family and a neighbour, using E605. Incongruously, it is thought that the publicity surrounding the case caused the 'epidemic of suicides', as the chemical, now banned, was then freely available.

Kava-kava
Narcotic pepper – peaceful joyous sensation – drowsiness

In her *Autobiography* Agatha Christie writes: 'Dispensing was interesting for a time, but became monotonous – I should never have cared to do it as a permanent job.' Fortunately for the world of detective fiction it did not become a permanent job; but the knowledge gained in that Torquay dispensary not only stood her in good stead in her future career but also inspired the poem 'In a Dispensary', published in the 1924 edition of her poetry collection, *Road of Dreams*. In one prophetic verse she writes:

> *From the Borgias' time to the present day, their power has been proved*
> *and tried!*
> *Monkshood blue, called Aconite and the deadly Cyanide!*
> *Here is sleep and solace and and soothing of pain – courage and*
> *vigour anew!*
> *Here is menace and murder and sudden death! – in these phials of*
> *green and blue!*

The Fifth Decade 1960–1969

'After all, to be able to continue writing at the age of 75 is very fortunate.'

◄○►

SOLUTIONS REVEALED

After the Funeral • *The Clocks* • *Endless Night* • *Lord Edgware Dies* • *Third Girl* • *Three Act Tragedy* • "Witness for the Prosecution'

◄○►

As she entered her fifth decade of crime writing Agatha Christie continued experimenting with her chosen genre. The decade began inauspiciously with a collection of short stories, the title story of which, 'The Adventure of the Christmas Pudding', was a reworking of a 1923 Poirot case, 'A Christmas Adventure'; but the elaboration, unlike similar earlier experiments, added only words. 'The Mystery of the Spanish Chest', in the same collection, was a far more imaginative expansion of the earlier 'The Mystery of the Baghdad Chest'. In fact, at one point the collection was to be called *The Mystery of the Spanish Chest and other stories*.

Of the ten titles she produced in the 1960s only two are pure whodunits, the last examples of the genre that she was to write. *The Mirror Crack'd from Side to Side* (1962) and *A Caribbean Mystery* (1964), both Miss Marple novels, employ clever variations on a plot device she had used before, that of a character seeing something surprising, shocking or frightening over someone's shoulder. The other Marple novel of the 1960s was *At Bertram's Hotel* (1965), a nostalgic journey into the past for the elderly Marple and Christie, with a not wholly believable variation on yet another earlier plot device. Though all three Poirot novels of this decade are disappointing – the Christie magic is missing from the development of each one – the fundamental plot ideas are as inventive as ever: in *The Clocks* (1963), a stranger's body found in a room full of incorrect clocks; in *Third Girl* (1966), a girl who thinks she 'may' have committed a murder; and in *Hallowe'en Party* (1969), a child is drowned while bobbing for apples. The best novels of this decade were, ironically, the two non-series titles, *The Pale Horse* (1961) and *Endless Night* (1967). Both of them were innovative, experimental and sinister – black magic murder to order in the former and a wholly original reworking of the Ackroyd trick in the latter – each showing an aspect of the Queen of Crime not heretofore seen.

Some old friends make welcome reappearances. Mrs Oliver has a solo run in *The Pale Horse*, which affords us a glimpse into the creative process of a mystery writer and, perhaps, into that of her creator; and appears with her old friend Poirot in both *Third Girl* and *Hallowe'en Party*. Tommy and Tuppence solve their penultimate case in *By the Pricking of my Thumbs* (1968). Age has not withered their spirit of adventure and the case they investigate, the disappearance of an elderly lady from a retirement home, is dark and sinister.

The elderly Christie is reflected in many of the books of this decade. Poirot's appearance in *The Clocks* is almost a cameo as he emulates an armchair detective and reflects on his magnum opus, a study of detective fiction; and in *Third Girl* he does unconvincing battle with the London of the Swinging Sixties. Miss Marple has aged since her previous appearance and agrees to a live-in companion in *The Mirror Crack'd from Side to Side*. Tommy and Tuppence are middle-aged grandparents and most of the characters in *By the Pricking of my Thumbs* are similarly elderly. And this book, as well as *Hallowe'en Party* and *At Bertram's Hotel*, is a journey into the past.

While *The Mousetrap* continued its inexorable success story with another new record in 1962 (the longest running play in London), Christie's only new play of this decade was another experiment. *Rule of Three* (1962) consists of three one-act plays, each totally different in style and content. Two years earlier saw a dramatisation of *Five Little Pigs* as *Go Back for Murder*, but both offerings received a cool critical reception.

In the cinema the four Margaret Rutherford Marple films were released – or should that be 'escaped'? – much to Christie's horror; only one, *Murder She Said*, was based on an authentic Marple novel, *4.50 from Paddington*. Of the other three, two were based on Poirot novels and one was a completely original script; and in all of them Miss Marple is unrecognisable, literally and metaphorically, as the elderly denizen of St Mary Mead. As a direct result, the 1964 Marple novel, *A Caribbean Mystery*, carried on its title page the reclamation 'Featuring the original character as created by Agatha Christie.' The following year, 1965, found *Ten Little Indians* transposed from an island off the coast of Devon to an Austrian ski resort (but filmed in Dublin!), but with the innovation of The Whodunit Break – a ticking clock-face reprised the suspects and murders for one minute to help the audience decide on the villain. *The Alphabet Murders* appeared in 1966, bearing almost no similarity to its inspiration, *The A.B.C. Murders*, to the extent of including a cameo appearance from Miss Marple. (All five films came from the same production company.) A more faithful adaptation was the 1960 screen version of *Spider's Web*, from the play of the same name. Also in the world of cinema, Christie worked on an adaptation of the Dickens novel *Bleak House*, but although she produced a script ('I quite realise that a third or more of the present script will have to go') in May 1962 the film was never made. And Hercule Poirot debuted on US television in *The Disappearance of Mr. Davenheim* in 1962.

In 1965 Christie published *Star over Bethlehem*, a miscellany of Christmas poetry and short tales, and in October of that year she finished work on her *Autobiography*. This was a project she had worked at, on and off, for the previous 15 years and although the book would not be published until after her death she enjoyed reviewing her life; it fell to her daughter, Rosalind, to edit the vast amount of material to produce the 1977 book. As we know from the recent release of recordings of the 'writing' of her *Autobiography*, Agatha Christie used a Dictaphone for many years. It is difficult to say with any certainty when this practice began, but in a radio interview as early as 1955 she said, 'I type my own drafts on an ancient faithful machine I've owned for years. And I find a Dictaphone useful for short stories or for re-casting an act of a play, but not for the more complicated business of working out a novel.' The implication is that she was practised in the use of the machine; and, of course, as far back as 1926, her most infamous title, *The Murder of Roger Ackroyd*, featured that piece of equipment as a plot device.

The photograph showing Agatha Christie with the Dictaphone dates from the late 1950s. The resultant tapes, or to use the more accurate term, Dictabelts, still exist for many of the titles from the succeeding decades. By that stage, no doubt, the elderly Christie found it physically easier to sit in her chair and 'speak' her novels into a machine and then correct a draft typed by her secretary. The less detailed notes for the last half-dozen novels can be seen as reflecting this

Agatha Christie, photographed in Winterbrook House in the 1950s, using a Dictaphone.

procedure. The exhaustive plot experimentation and varia-
tions-on-a-theme of the Notebooks of yesteryear are replaced
by plot highlights which she considered sufficient for this
method of writing. This procedure meant that the later
novels were both more verbose in narration and less tight in
construction than the earlier, more compactly written books;
to echo her own words, the Dictaphone was not suitable 'for
the complicated business' of constructing a detective novel.

In 1967 she co-operated with the first book to be written
about her work, G.C. Ramsey's *Agatha Christie: Mistress of
Mystery*. Although a slight book viewed from today's stand-
point, it was the first to impose order on the chaos of title
changes, both transatlantic and domestic, and variations in
short-story collections; thus it was as welcome to Christie's
agent and publisher as it was to her fans. And it remains
the only book about Christie which received her personal
cooperation. In 1961 she received a doctorate from Exeter
University, where today an archive of her papers is held. That
was also the year in which Christie was declared by UNESCO
to be the world's best-selling writer.

~⌒~

The Clocks
7 November 1963

---◄○►---

A roomful of clocks showing the wrong time, a
blind woman, a dead man and a hysterical girl – when
Colin Lamb explains the story to his friend, Hercule
Poirot decides that the situation is so bizarre that
the explanation must be simple. Developments
prove otherwise.

---◄○►---

Appearing between two very typical Miss Marple whodunits – preceded by *The Mirror Crack'd from Side to Side* and followed by *A Caribbean Mystery* – *The Clocks* was the first Poirot novel since *Cat among the Pigeons* in 1959. Poirot appears in only three chapters and acts, literally, as an armchair detective, with Colin Lamb bringing him the information to enable them both to arrive at a conclusion.

The Clocks is an uneasy mix of spy story and domestic murder mystery with little in the way of clues to help the reader distinguish between the two. There are, as usual, clever ideas – the telephone call and the broken shoe, the adoption of a ready-made plot, the conversion of secrets to Braille – but the overall explanation is a disappointment. If the spy angle had been dropped and the inheritance plot elaborated the result would have been a tighter book. And, as she has done in many previous titles, Christie introduces an unsuspected and unnecessary relationship in the closing chapters.

A fascinating interlude with Poirot occurs in Chapter 14 when we read of his forthcoming study of detective fiction. He mentions several milestones of the genre: *The Leavenworth Case*, *The Adventures of Arsene Lupin*, *The Mystery of the Yellow Room*, *The Adventures of Sherlock Holmes*. He goes on to discuss a number of authors, some of whom, although fictional, are identifiable – Cyril Quain with his attention to detail and unbreakable alibis is Freeman Wills Crofts; Louisa O'Malley with her milieu of brownstone mansion in New York is Elizabeth Daly. Florence Elks is more difficult to identify but is perhaps Margaret Millar, a writer Christie admired, as she stated in an interview in 1974. A Canadian who set most of her novels in the USA, Millar has order, method and wit, although not the abundance of drink to which Poirot refers. Two other writers are mentioned but both are firmly fictional – Garry Gregson, who is an important element in the plot of *The Clocks*, and, of course, Mrs Oliver.

The other area for speculation is the parentage of Colin Lamb. When they meet, Poirot asks after Colin's father and wonders why he is not using the family name. In G.C. Ramsay's *Mistress of Mystery* (1967) Christie is quoted as confirming that Colin is Superintendent Battle's son.

In Notebook 4, on a page dated 1961, an alphabetical list of plot ideas includes the inspirations for *The Mirror Crack'd from Side to Side* and *A Caribbean Mystery*; on that list idea F is a brief outline of *The Clocks*. And a year later the tentative title appears on a listing of future books.

F. The Clock – as beginning – typist – dead body – blind old lady

1962
Notes for 3 books

Y. The Clocks (?)
Z. Carribean [sic] Mystery
X. Gypsy's Acre

But in fact the plot for *The Clocks* goes back a lot further than that. In late 1949 Agatha Christie set a competition for which she wrote the opening of a short story that competitors were asked to complete. It concerned a typist, Nancy, arriving at a house and letting herself in to the front room. There she finds a collection of clocks, a dead man and a blind woman. Twelve years later Christie herself resurrected the story and set about expanding it. The main difference between the two is that the clocks in the short story all show different, and wrong, times whereas the clocks of the novel all show the same, but equally wrong, time. Unsurprisingly the character names are also different, as is the street address; but the similarities are striking – the description of the clocks is identical and the 'Rosemary' clock is specifically mentioned;

the telephone call making the appointment is a mystery and the blind woman, it transpires, is Nancy's mother. Overall the explanation of the presence of the clocks is more convincing in the prize-winning solution than in the novel.

In its earlier incarnation the short story is called 'The Clock Stops'; this is also the title used in Notebook 8 where most of the plotting, about 50 pages, is contained. A list of possible characters, most of whose names will change, and a possible motive, are the first considerations:

Mildred Pebmarsh – fiftyish – blind – had been a librarian – now teaches Braille
Alice Dale – young stenographer (Is her second name Rosemary) Does Alice, flying out of house, collide with Colin
Dead Man
Miss Curtis   Head of typing firm
Colin Lamb – young man – journalist? Doctor? Investigator? On vacation

Christie sketches the motive scenario more than once. Elements of each sketch were used in the final version, which has much in common – an unexpected arrival from abroad endangering a criminal impersonation – with *Dead Man's Folly*:

Money involved – something with money (gain)

A middle aged woman inherits vast fortune from an uncle in Canada? (Advertised?) S. America? (or written to Mrs. Bristow?) Actually real Mrs. Bristow is dead and Bristow has remarried (or not?). He decides that he and his wife will claim – was he small builder? Bankrupt – settled in her place. Anyway no one knows he has a first wife. But senior partner of firm of solicitors knows real Mrs. B. So he comes down to (No. 6? 19?) is received, drugged and killed. Taken

across diagonal to No. 19 – 61?
Unsatisfactory person marries nice girl – goes abroad –
actually she dies and he marries again – a woman who was
sec[retary] to det. story writer – his wife poisoned but he
won't marry her. Fortune left her – she plays invalid. Papers
brought for her to sign – O.K. Later someone who knows
her well comes – they prepare – plot hers – (from favourite
employer) her name is Rosemary – uses old clock. Is girl's
name Alice Rosemary called after his mother? Mother is
dead – some mystery about her. A. is illegitimate

Further elaboration follows; the first possible explanation
of the clocks is (thankfully) discarded and the second one
adopted:

Point of various things

(1) Clocks – the time (Fast?) (Slow?) 3–25
 Possibly – Rosemary faded carriage clock – press 3 – 2 – 5
contains a secret compartment – clocks works have been
taken out (a reference to time of a murder – it took place on
a Saturday night in Oct. (daylight saving!)

(2) Rosemary – the name of someone connected with
Martindale – Alice or M. Pebmarsh

The whole is a plot – invented by Rosemary Western (a Mrs.
Oliver) now dead and adapted for use as camouflage by her
secretary who is – Martindale? Pebmarsh? Mrs. Bristow at
No. 61 Pam or Geraldine

Fortune left to Mrs X (Argentine? Australia? S. Africa?).
Actually she has died abroad and husband remarried
almost at once. Only one person knows Mrs X by sight. It
is this member of law firm who has come over. They plan
murder – but not to let him be identified. Elaboration and

clocks etc. is suggested by plot of an unpublished book.
Mrs X or Miss Martindale was private secretary to a Creasey
detective story writer.

The reference to 'a Creasey detective story writer' is unexpected. John Creasey was a hugely prolific writer – producing over 500 titles under a variety of pen names – of most types of crime novel, with the exception of detective stories. In Chapter 28 Poirot explains the original meaning of the clocks as they feature in the unpublished manuscript; it was a code to the combination to the safe, concealed behind a reproduction of the Mona Lisa, containing the jewels of the Russian royal family. He describes the plot as '*Un tas de bêtises,* the whole thing', in other words, nonsense.

The all-important story of Edna and her damaged shoe appears alongside the timetable for the fateful lunch-hour:

Edna in outer office with stiletto heel that has come off –
describing where and how she bought buns and came back
to office

Timing here to be consistent
1.30 – 2.30 Alice lunch interval
12.30 – 1.30 L[unch] interval for ?
Edna leaves office 12.30 o'clock – returns by
12.50 – no call comes through before 1.30
1.30 Miss M goes out
            or
Edna goes out 1.30 – back 1.50 – better
No call before 2.30
Miss M goes out 12.30 – 1.30

Christie experimented throughout the Notebook with various neighbours, some of whom made it into the novel. Aspects

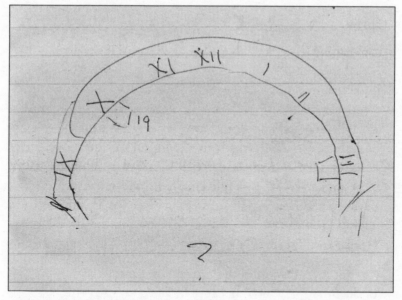

A sketch from Notebook 8 during the plotting of The Clocks. *Christie was experimenting with a combination of the numerals from a clock-face and a possible sketch of Wilbraham Crescent.*

of the following jottings – 'quiet gardening type', 'Cat lover woman', and the children – appear, but adapted and rearranged. Interestingly, the 'secretary to a bestseller writer' becomes a major plot feature; but the character chosen for this important role is not a resident of Wilbraham Crescent. Despite the alteration of house numbers between Notebook and novel, and the cryptic illustration in Chapter 6, these are not important elements. The use of a Crescent is a useful, though not entirely convincing, method of isolating the suspects:

Neighbours

No. 60 Man wife children – man sporty talkative, wife v. quiet
62 Couple of women – Pam and Geraldine – develop their characters

No. 18 Mainly cats?
No. 19 Middle aged man – a gardener – invalid wife? Got a blind spinster sister

Where is my murder and <u>why</u>

(1) Quiet gardener man – carries victim in sack
(2) One of the two women – Geraldine? – has been secretary to a bestseller writer (Mrs. O?!!) – has taken various details from one of her discarded plots
(3) Heart man with wife and children
(4) Miss Pebmarsh

Neighbours

16. Cat lover woman with draperies, accusative of one of the others (? which) because he killed my cat [Mrs Hemming at No. 20]
20. 2/3? awful children (later one of them says something) like B.B.'s children 10, 7, 3? Harassed fond mother children like Miss P [the Ramsays]
61. Mr. Bland – unimaginative man, sandy hair, freckled, commonplace – builder in small way near bankrupt – then wife comes into money. Thinking of living abroad – the wife would like it – I don't know myself – can't get any decent food abroad [no. 69]
62. 2 women? One former secretary to thriller writer or young man living with mother. He is weakly looking – she is really a man? Arty husband and wife – a son Thomas
~~69~~ 60. Middle-aged man – quiet gardening type – went with wheelbarrow sacks etc. [Mr McNaughton] Could have a flirty spinster sister

One of the problems with the book, though, is that there are too many neighbours and that they are not clearly enough

delineated to fix them in the mind, while the lengthy interviews with them offer little in the way of information, either
for the police or the reader.

Christie also toyed with ideas that were not pursued in the
finished novel, but some of which were to be used at a later
stage. The first has an element of the plot of the next Poirot
novel, *Third Girl,* where a female character has two distinct
'lives' miles apart, the family of each unaware of the existence of the other:

> Clocks
>
> Miss Pebmarsh – forty? fifty? blind – who is she?
>
> Idea – Really a Miss or Mrs X has a well authenticated life
> in small town Torquay or Wallingford; companion lives
> with her or perhaps she has a room as P[aying] G[uest]
> in people's house – goes away occasionally to stay with
> relations – 'Universal Aunt' sees her across London.
> Returns in due course – says she is a missionary – sister of
> a missionary. Came home with ill health – there <u>was</u> such a
> person – but lost track of.

And, as can be seen below, another early possibility was to
combine the 'Greenshaw's Folly' idea with *The Clocks*; in the
short story a secretary does indeed go to Greenshaw's Folly
to begin work:

> Typist sent from agency to G's Folly alone there – finds body
> – or blind woman who nearly steps on it. Clocks all an hour
> wrong Why? So that they will strike 12 instead of 1

Further ideas followed, some of which – the 'thriller' plot,
the claimed husband, the postcards from abroad – found
their way into the book:

Man next door does murder of blackmailer. Takes
advantage of Miss P's blindness – kills man with dagger?
Or strangles? – carries him in through window – then rings
up typewriting agency. Some reason for asking for that
particular girl? Is her name Rosemary – clocks just a fancy
touch (obvious really – contrived) mistake – one clock is at
a quarter to nine

A 'thriller' plot – some secret process – man almost gets it –
is killed – scrawls a few words – 61 – L

A woman whose lover is murdered
    "   "   daughter "   A 14
    "   "   son   "   (revenge)

Idea put about is that a woman Mrs U meets Mr C at
hotel – is to take him down in car. Later she calls for
baggage – goes to Victoria . . . and travels with man like him
(passport?) latter sends p.cs from abroad or his luggage is
in hotel unclaimed. Mr C at Cresc. is killed . . . taken across
to 19 – Mr Curry – later woman will turn up and claim him
as husband. Mr C disappears

Vasall like – plans photographed during [lunch?] hour
– 2 overcoats alike? – or bus or train. Miss Pebmarsh –
(caraway seed? aniseed?) Found by agent – or agent writes
it as dying

This last outline is very cryptic. 'Vasall' is a reference to
the real-life spy John Vassall, a British civil servant who was
arrested as a spy in September 1962 and subsequently convicted. This would have been a high-profile event during
the genesis of *The Clocks*. The '2 overcoats' is probably a
ploy used to effect a quick change of appearance in order to

avoid detection; the bus/train possibility is probably another escape route plan. The caraway seed/aniseed reference is probably to the hoary old plot device of using either as a means of tracking a quarry, a variation of which is used in the denouement of *N or M?*

The Mirror Crack'd from Side to Side, published the previous year, and *A Caribbean Mystery*, the following year were the last 'pure' whodunits Christie was to write but *The Clocks*, despite its promising opening, remains an inexplicably disappointing offering.

✦

Third Girl
14 November 1966

──────◄○►──────

When 'third girl' Norma Restarick approaches
Poirot with a story of 'a murder that she might have
committed', he is intrigued. When she disappears,
and a murder is committed at her apartment block
and his friend Mrs Oliver is coshed, Poirot enters the
unfamiliar world of Swinging Sixties London.

──────◄○►──────

Having made little more than a cameo appearance in his previous case, *The Clocks*, Poirot tackles old problems in a new setting in *Third Girl* and this time his involvement is more active. Like some other novels from Christie's last decade, *Third Girl* is wordy; there are many passages, and indeed chapters, which could, and arguably should, have been omitted, such as the detailed description of Long Basing (Chapter 4) and much of Mrs Oliver's trudge around London (Chapter 9). The plot itself, despite its promising beginning, requires a considerable suspension of disbelief, while the Swinging Sixties background is largely unconvincing. The impersonation disclosed in the final explanation is difficult to accept, calling into question the entire basis of the novel. *Third Girl* is the weakest book of the 1960s.

This uncertainty is mirrored in the notes. They are scattered over six Notebooks and 90 pages but they are repetitive, unlike the Christie of yesteryear. There are nevertheless ideas that she considered but ultimately rejected, although, as we shall see, some of them were utilised, three years later, in *Hallowe'en Party*.

When we meet Poirot in the opening chapter he has just completed his magnum opus on detective fiction, a project on which he had previously been working during *The Clocks*. Mrs Oliver makes her second appearance of the decade having already featured, sans Poirot, in *The Pale Horse*. She would appear again in *Hallowe'en Party* and for the last time in *Elephants Can Remember*. It can be no coincidence that Mrs Oliver, and the now very elderly Miss Marple, both characters with which Dame Agatha had now much in common, appear in over half of the last dozen novels.

A major element of the plot of *Third Girl* concerns the drugging of Norma Restarick. This has echoes of *A Caribbean Mystery* when Miss Marple discovered that Molly Kendal was the victim of a similar plot; and 25 years earlier the poisoning of Hugh Chandler in 'The Cretan Bull', the seventh Labour of Hercules, is undertaken for a similar sinister reason.

Mr Goby from *After the Funeral* makes a brief appearance. And is Chief Inspector Neele the same policeman, though not of the same rank, who investigated, alongside Miss Marple, the deaths at Yewtree Lodge in *A Pocket Full of Rye*? Is Dr Stillingfleet, moreover, the medical man who featured in 'The Dream'?

The intriguing opening scene is sketched over half a dozen

times, with little variation, in four separate Notebooks. This premise would seem to have been the starting point of the novel and the one unalterable idea throughout the notes.

> Poirot breakfast – Girl – Louise – I may have committed a murder. 3 girls in a flat Louise and Veronica – Judy – (Claudia Norma Townsend). One of these three girls. What does she mean by 'she thinks she may have committed'

> Poirot at breakfast – girl calls 'She thinks she may have committed a murder.' 'Thinks' Doesn't she know? No clearness – no precision. 'I'm sorry – I shouldn't have told you – you're too old'
> Poirot at breakfast table – Norma (an unattractive Ophelia) says she may have committed a murder – then tells Poirot he is 'too old.'

> Suggestions – Chap I – P. at breakfast

> Poirot at the breakfast table – thinks she may have committed a murder. Disappointed by P – too old – recommended by Mrs. Oliver – makes excuse – goes. Poirot worried

> Idea A   July – 1965
> Poirot at his breakfast table (The Late Mrs. Dane). P. at breakfast – George[40] announces – a – pause – young lady. I do not see people at this hour. She says she thinks she may have committed a murder. 'Thinks? It is not a subject on which one should be in doubt.' Girl – unkempt – Poirot regards her with pain etc. G[eorge] and P discuss – neurotic?

---

40 George appears as both George and Georges in *Third Girl.* In the Notebook he appears without the 's'.

This last sketch merits discussion. It appears in Notebook 27 a page after the final notes for *At Bertram's Hotel*, the previous year's book. To judge by the date heading this note, Christie was mulling over ideas for her 1966 book having just despatched the 1965 Christie for Christmas to Collins. In the notes that follow we find, using an alphabetical sequence, the germs of *Endless Night*, *Nemesis* and *Hallowe'en Party*.

Idea B, four pages later, is 'Gypsy's Acre – place where accidents always happen' (this became *Endless Night*). Idea C is a variation on 'The Cornish Mystery', though it did not generate a subsequent novel: 'Wife thinks her husband is poisoning her . . . niece's young man writes love letters to her – but to Aunt also'. Idea D toys with the possibility of a 'National Trust Tour of Gardens', later developed into *Nemesis*. And Idea E, headed 'Mary, Mary, Quite contrary', concerns a foreign girl who is left everything in the will of her wealthy employer. Christie urges herself at the end of this note, 'Good idea – needs working on'; after further work this became *Hallowe'en Party*.

The other interesting point concerns the reference to 'The Late Mrs. Dane'. The first page of Notebook 19, during the planning of what was to become *Sleeping Murder*, is headed:

Cover Her Face
The Late Mrs. Dane
They Do It with Mirrors

The promising title 'The Late Mrs Dane' was not pursued although the name itself appears in the early sketches for *Sad Cypress* and *The A.B.C. Murders*. Thirty years later, in 1965, we can see that the elderly Christie was still toying with it; and it is a great title.

Mrs Oliver's visits to Borodene Mansions in Chapters 3 and 7, and Poirot's to High Basing in Chapters 4 and 5, are sketched thoroughly in Notebook 26:

> Mrs Oliver visits Borodene Court – a flat – 3 girls
> Claudia – confident, efficient good background
> Frances – Arts Council or Art Gallery.
> Norma
> Milkman mentions to Mrs O. Lady pitched herself down from 7th floor. Mind disturbed – had only been in flat a month
> Decoration of flat – all similar built-in furniture and wallpaper – one wall with huge Harlequin
>
> Poirot at High Basing – visits Restaricks – pretends to know Sir Rodney. On leaving has a snoop before he and Mary encounter the Peacock (David) also snoopy. Later Poirot gives lift to David

And the essence of the plot is captured in the following paragraph from Notebook 42:

> Frances in an art racket – David works with her – gallery 'in' it. She runs picture shows abroad – he forges pictures. She meets McNaughton, he and Restarick whose brother dies suddenly – he takes R's place – R's passport faked by her. She goes back to England – once there assumes part of Mary – blonde and wig – Mrs Restarick – visit Uncle Rodney – furniture in store – picture 'cleaned' – substitute painted by David of McNaughton. Katrina found by Mary – dailies – Mary up and down to London, Frances to Manchester – Liverpool – Birmingham etc. Frances gets Norma to Borodene Court – she seldom sees F – but thinks she is going mad because she <u>dreams</u> F is M

Most of the salient points of the plot are covered but the words 'assumes part of Mary' are easier to read than to imagine. They involve a character playing a continuing dual role. It is difficult for the reader to believe that, even in Norma's drug-induced twilight existence, the same person could have been accepted as her flatmate and her stepmother. Impersonation has frequently played an important part in Christie's fiction – Carlotta Adams in *Lord Edgware Dies*, Sir Charles Cartwright in *Three Act Tragedy*, Miss Gilchrist in *After the Funeral*, Romaine in 'Witness for the Prosecution' – but in each of these cases the impersonation is a one-off episode and not a long-term arrangement. And in three of these instances the impersonator is a professional actor.

The sequence of events in Chapter 22 is outlined in Notebook 42:

> Frances speaks to porter, goes up in lift – inserts key etc.
> Hand rises slowly to throat – sees herself in glass – her look
> of frozen terror. Then screams and runs out of flat – grips
> someone – killed – she has just returned from Manchester?
> Dead body – 2 hours dead. F. comes by train from
> Bournemouth? – changes to Mary – meets David – where
> are Claudia? Andrew? Mary?

And there are flashes of Christie's old ingenuity – the odd/ even numbers, the different/same room scenario – in this extract from Notebook 49; elements of this note surfaced in the book although the practicality of the idea is questionable. The reference to 'Swan Court' is to the actual apartment block in which Christie had a flat for much of her life:

> An idea
> Girl or (dupe of some kind) taken to flat – go up in lift –

one of kind you can't see or count floors. Room has very
noticeable wall paper – Versailles? Cherries? Birds? She
swears to this – believing it – describes it minutely. Actually
that room and wallpaper is <u>somewhere else</u>. Wallpaper is
put on same night – it is all prepared – cut etc. – pasted
on – would take a couple of hours not more – <u>but</u> it would
have to dry off and therefore would be described as a
damp room – 'had patches' of damp on it <u>or</u> a room with
the noticeable paper would be papered over with another
paper. The similarity of rooms in a block like Swan Court in,
say, opposite sides of building – odd and even numbers if
some flats furniture would be the same

Much of the detail explored in the following extract from
Notebook 50 was to change but some concepts – the drugging and scapegoating, the fake portrait and the subterfuge
with regard to flat numbers – remained:

Girl doped by other girls (Claudia? Frances?) ~~friends~~ hears
a shot – comes to find herself shooting out of window –
other girl supporting her and pistol really discharged by her
– Lance they get in and fix him up – bandages etc. He and
(Cl?) (Frances?) are 'in it' together against simple Norma.
Later she is again 'doped' a second brain storm – result – a
young artist is shot – girls give evidence for Norma – police
can't shake them but don't believe them.
(B)? The Picture by Levenheim A.R.A. is of her mother ~~Lady~~
~~Roche~~ in country house. Actually picture is copied by young
David McDonald – only face of (Mary?) is substituted –
then David is shot. Norma suspected and believes herself
she did it. Thought to be a sexy crime.
C. <u>Or</u> is Arthur Wells – Mary's husband – painted into
picture
D. <u>Or</u> Arthur and Mary – Sir R – can't see A very well but

believes he is his nephew. A man with a stroke – is bribed to impersonate Arthur at a specialist.

[E] Painting – a Lowenstein – (L is dead) worth £40,000 – insured. Copy false – seen on one evening – party

Points of interest
Double flat – 71 7th floor (faces W), 64 6th floor (faces E)
Police called to which?

Finally, in the following extracts, all from Notebook 51, there are glimpses of the Christie of yesteryear with the listing of ideas and the consideration of possible combinations of conspirators (throughout these sketches the David of the book appears as Paul):

Norma – are her words connected with home – stepmother?
Her own mother – Sonia – old boy?
Or
3rd girl activities – is boy friend (Paul) a Mod – like a Van Dyk [sic] – brocade waistcoat – long glossy hair – is he the evil genius – is he in it with Claudia? with Frances? Narcotics?
Does Norma get keen on him – she acts as a go between for them? A girl – an addict – dies really because she is found to be a police agent getting evidence – killed by Paul or Claudia – (Frances) – they make Norma believe that she brought her an over strength dose of purple [hearts] (some new name) Technically she might be accused of murder – they do this to get her finished and say they will protect her – she really is fall guy if necessary – she thinks of getting help from Poirot – they decide she is danger – they'll get rid of her. What is Norma's job? Cosmetics Lucie Long powders etc. N[orma] packs things

2nd idea
Paul is really police spy – he tangles with the girls
3rd idea
Paul is in it with Sonia
4th idea
Paul is in it with Mary Wells. Sir Rodney – rich – his nephew
and wife come to live – or his niece and her husband. Niece
dies – widower is married – 2nd wife sucks up to old man –
then Sonia arrives also sucks up to him – he alters his will
5th idea
Sonia and Sir Paul linked together – he is impersonating real
Sir R
6th idea
Mary Restarick – her beautiful blue eyes – tells Poirot how she
got Norma to leave home – better for her – because she hates
me. Shows Poirot a chemist's analysis – arsenic? Or morphia.
Norma says – I hate her – I hate her – does boy friend ~~old boy
dies~~ see her (he says) walking in sleep – puts something in
glass. He tells her – will of old Rodney forged – by Norma?
7th
Poirot and Mary – her beauty – blue eyes – about Norma
– glad she went – I didn't know what to do – takes from
locked drawer an analyst's report – Arsenic? Or morphia? –
hated me because of her mother

Sadly Christie's former ingenuity is missing from these scenarios (note, for example, that Ideas 6 and 7 are very similar). Even if some of the ideas here – Paul/David as a police
spy, Norma as a go-between – had been utilised, little difference would have been made to the fundamental situation.

By the Pricking of my Thumbs
11 November 1968

———————◄○►———————

On a visit to Tommy's Aunt Ada in Sunny Ridge
Nursing Home, Tuppence meets Mrs Lancaster. Her
subsequent disappearance intrigues Tuppence, who
decides to investigate. This quest brings her to the
village of Sutton Chancellor where the mystery is finally
solved, but not before Tuppence's own life is in danger.

———————◄○►———————

By the pricking of my thumbs,
Something wicked this way comes.

William Shakespeare, *Macbeth*

Tommy and Tuppence Beresford are the only Christie characters to age gradually between their first appearance and
their last. In their first adventure, *The Secret Adversary* from
1922, they are 'bright young things', in 1941's *N or M?* they
are worried parents and by the time of *By the Pricking of my
Thumbs* they are middle-aged. The chronology of their lives
and ages does not bear close scrutiny, however, and gets even
more complicated and, in fact, inexplicable, by the time of
their final adventure *Postern of Fate* in 1973.

The notes for *By the Pricking of my Thumbs* are more unfo-
cused than usual. They repeat the same scene with only
minor variations, suggesting a lack of clarity as to where the
book was going. And although the scenes in Sunny Ridge are
intriguing, they are not enough to sustain an entire book.
When Tuppence embarks on her investigation, the novel
begins to flag and, unlike Christie's plotting in her heyday,

with a minimum of tweaking the final revelation could have been completely different with a totally different villain unmasked. Ironically, in Notebook 36 we find a note Christie wrote to herself: 'Rewriting of first half – not so verbose – 1st three or four chapters good – but afterwards too slow'.

Notes are contained in two Notebooks, 28 and 36, and extend to just over 50 pages. We have, in Notebook 36, a clearly dated starting point for the writing of this novel just over a year before it appeared in the bookshops. The early pages of this Notebook encapsulate the opening of the plot. The first and second sections of the novel, 'Sunny Ridge' and 'The House on the Canal', are then sketched between Notebooks 28 and 36:

> Behind the Fireplace – Oct. 1967
> Tommy and Tuppence go to visit disagreeable Aunt Ada
> – she takes dislike to Tuppence who goes and sits in the
> lounge – old lady in there sipping milk – says it's a very nice
> place – are you coming to stay here?
> It wasn't your poor child, was it?
> No – I wondered – the same every day – behind the fireplace
> – at ten minutes past eleven exactly.
> Then she goes out with her milk – Aunt Ada dies in her sleep
> four days later
> Possible ideas for this
> Is Mrs Nesbit the aunt or mother of a Philby or a Maclean
> [i.e. the British spies] – some well-known public character
> who defected to an enemy country. Were there papers?
> Hidden behind grate? Child knew secrets of Priest's Hole.
> Aunt Ada dies – funeral – call at the home – does Tuppence
> see picture

Notebook 28 begins again with, broadly speaking, the same scene and set-up. And in it, we find the only Notebook reference to one of the most sinister and incomprehensible motifs in all of Christie – that of the child's body behind the fireplace, a bizarre episode that also surfaces in *The Pale Horse* and *Sleeping Murder*. A possible explanation from within the plot of the novel, as distinct from within Christie's own life, is offered by the extract above; but it is not very convincing. The idea is repeated but not developed, and the suggested reasons are not utilised in the finished novel.

> Grandmother's Steps
> T and T – they visit nursing home for aged or slightly mental
> – Tommy's Aunt Amelia – (scatty? Tommy Pommy Johnnie?)
> Tuppence left in sitting room – old lady sipping milk
> 'Was it your poor child? It's not quite time yet – always the
> same time – twenty past ten – it's in there behind the grate,
> everyone knows but they don't talk about it. It wouldn't do'
> Shakes her head.
> 'I hope the milk is not poisoned today – sometimes it is – if
> so, I don't drink it, of course'
> Tuppence (on drive home) begins idly to think about it. 'I
> wonder what she had in her head – whose poor child? I'd
> like to know Tommy' [Chapters 2/3]
>
> The House – kindly witch – the jackdaw – heard through
> wall? They go in – jackdaw flies away – a dead one – the
> doll. Tuppence makes enquiries – goes to churchyard –
> vicar – elderly – a bossy woman doing flowers in church.
> Vicar introduces her to Tuppence – she invites Tuppence in
> to coffee. Tuppence goes to house agent in Market Basing
> [Chapters 7/8/9]

A month later more plot developments, as well as possible characters, are considered. Some of these ideas – the painted boats and the superimposed name – were adopted, while it is possible that 'The House by the Canal' was under consideration as a title:

Nov 1st [1967]
The House by the Bridge or the Canal
Some points
The picture is of a small hump-backed bridge over a canal
– across the bridge is a white horse on the canal bank –
there is a line of pale green poplar trees – tied up to the
bank, under the bridge are a couple of boats. An idea is
that boats are an afterthought added some time after the
picture was painted. Suppose a name was painted John Doe
– murderer – over that the boats were painted. Someone
either knew about this or someone did it

Ideas to pursue – or discard
1. Picture – boat superimposed – beneath it – 'Murder' [or]
'Maud'
'Come in to the garden, Maud' a clue
'The black bat, Night, hath flown' – who painted it?
2. Baby farmer idea (at Sunny Ridge? Before Old Ladies
Home?) Child really was dead and buried in chimney of
sitting room there
3. Could cocoa woman be the killer woman

Possible people involved?
The artist Sidney Boscowan
The friendly witch Mrs Perry
Big lumbering husband Mr Perry
Vicar Rev. Edmund Shipton
Active woman Mrs Bligh

Tommy features little in the book until Chapter 10 when he starts to track Tuppence. One of his first tasks is to find out more about the painting in Aunt Ada's room:

> How does Tommy start his search?
> Picture gallery – Bond St. – Boscowan – quite a demand for them again. Mrs. Boscowan lives in country. Tommy goes to see her – has Tuppence been there? Interested in her husband's pictures. Tells her how this picture was given him by aunt now dead – she was given [it] by an old lady, a Mrs. Lancaster – no reaction. [Chapters 10 and 12]

Some of the ideas Christie noted in November 1967 were not pursued at all; others were partially adopted. The first one below was rejected possibly because of its similarity to a plot device in *The Clocks*, five years earlier; the second has elements that were utilised – the pregnant actress and the name Lancaster – but the surrounding ideas were discarded:

> Does this really centre round a paperback – a thriller read by old Mrs Lancaster? Does Tommy find that out? He reads it in train, goes to Sunny Ridge, finds book was in library – Mrs L. very fond of crime stories – comes home triumphantly and debunks Tuppence

> Country small lonely house – to it comes down beautiful girl – actress – going to have child. Man marries her – but he now wants to marry rich boss's daughter so wedding is kept quiet (in local church) – under another name – he tells girl baby is dead? Or he kills girl. Who is Mrs Lancaster? Someone who lives near churchyard – sees body being buried in old grave

Five further sketches of the murderous back-plot appear; but as can be seen, each sketch is substantially the same, apart from a brief consideration of a homicidal Sir Philip Starke:

Nov. 12 [1967]
Alternatives
X Mrs Lancaster – alias Lady Peele – of batty family – barren – went queer. Husband loved children – she 'sacrificed' them. He gets his devoted secretary Nellie Blighe – sends her to ~~nursing~~ Old Ladies Home

Dec[ember]
Sir Philip Starke – loved children – his wife Eleanor – mental – (abortion) jealous of children – kills little girls. Nellie Bligh secretary – is also mental nurse.
Disappearance of child (Major Henley's) – Does Nellie and Philip bury one of them in churchyard – Lady S – in various homes. Friendly witch's husband was <u>Sexton.</u>

Was she Lady Peele – barren – had had abortion – was haunted by guilt – it was she, jealous, who killed any protégés of her husband. In asylum – released – then husband employs a faithful secretary to put her in old people's home – 'Miss Bates' the one who was doing the church – she adores Peele

Candidates for murder
Lady Sparke – neurotic – mental. Did she kill her children? She was released – Philip and Nellie Bligh hid her – took her to homes. Does an elderly woman go in also – does she die? Mrs. Cocoa?

Story gets about that Sir Philip's wife left him because he was the killer

Coming directly after the shocking and inventive *Endless Night*, *By the Pricking of my Thumbs* suffers, inevitably, by comparison. But although for the most part the book is a series of reminiscences with little solid fact, the opening chapters are certainly intriguing, conveying something of the old Christie magic, and the denouement is unsettling. The underlying themes of madness and child murder, combined with scenes set in graveyards and deserted houses, could well have justified, as suggested by the first-edition blurb which was written by Christie herself, the more appropriate title *By the Chilling of your Spine.*

UNUSED IDEAS:
FIVE

UNUSED IDEAS:
FIVE

All the Unused Ideas in this selection have strong connections with published works.

MURDER-DISCOVERED-AFTERWARDS

Mirrors or some other book
Murder discovered afterwards – 5 years or 2 years like
Crippen? Statements taken – all quite definite – no result.
(Poirot goes over it or Miss M) talk to people – or poison
case because poison is so difficult to trace (exhumation)
Possibility of husband being accused – liked a young woman
(secretary?)
Resented by his family – particularly eldest son – She is
~~marries him~~ going to marry him afterwards – son won't
speak to her – real rift (actually son and girl are in it
together)

This jotting immediately follows notes for *The Mousetrap* and *They Do It with Mirrors*, so it is reasonable to assume that it comes from the late 1940s or early 1950s. The phrase 'Statements taken' contains echoes of *Five Little Pigs*, the husband and secretary idea foreshadows *Ordeal by Innocence* and the proposed solution is somewhat similar to that of *They Do It with Mirrors*. The staged 'rift' has appeared before in Christie as early as *The Mysterious Affair at Styles* and in *Death on the Nile*, and would again in *Endless Night*. But while elements of the note appear in various titles, this combination of ideas does not appear in a finished work. The reference to *Mirrors* at the beginning is further evidence of the complicated genesis of that novel and title, as discussed in Chapter 8.

———•◆•———

THE VICTORY BALL

Victory Ball idea
Six people going to dance or dance in house
Murderer is Harlequin? Or Pierrot?
Possible people?
~~Janey facial surgeon (murdered?)~~
Columbine – sister S. American
Pierette – girl who might have married Monteith
Pulchinella – Mrs Carslake
Harlequin – brother S. American
Pierrot – Lord Monteith – in love with Lola [possibly Columbine]
Pulchinello – brother of Monteith (heir)

This was, presumably, to be a more elaborate variation on the very first Poirot short story, 'The Affair at the Victory Ball', published in *The Sketch* on 7 July 1923 and collected in *Poirot's Early Cases*. In this story the solution turns on the murderer assuming at different times the costumes of both Harlequin and Pierrot. And, of course, the Harlequin theme provided Christie with one of her other characters, *The Mysterious Mr Quin*. There are also brief notes dated 'June

1944' in Notebook 31, for a play, or possibly a ballet, based around the Harlequin figures. 'A Masque from Italy', one of the poems in *Road of Dreams*, her 1924 poetry collection, is based on the same characters. Inspiration for all of these came from the china figures in the drawing room of her home, Ashfield, and they can now be seen in the restored drawing room of Greenway House. Oddly, the plastic surgeon idea (see Unused Ideas – One) recurs here in somewhat unexpected surroundings.

———•◆•———

THE 'PRIME MINISTER' AND COMPANION

Man like Asquith or Burdett Coutts [both British MPs] – very ambitious – Junior clerk in firm – marries rich woman – head or daughter in firm – older than he is – she dies very conveniently for him. He becomes a big noise with the unreserved power she has left him.
Now – Did he really do away with her? Evidence of weird servant or companion acquits him absolutely but girl in question knows something. Say, e.g. like Gladys in 13 Problems she really committed crime quite unwittingly following his orders – later blackmails him. Or servant girl helped him – afterwards talking with friend – confidential friend etc. helps her in 2nd murder

Some of the ideas explored here did surface in a few later titles. Notebook 35, where these notes appear, also contains the notes for *One, Two, Buckle my Shoe* and there are distinct echoes of Alistair Blunt from that novel in the biographical sketch. The connivance, albeit unwitting, of a servant girl is an element of both the short story 'The Tuesday Night Club', the first of *The Thirteen Problems*, and the novel *A Pocket Full of Rye*. The variation of a friend helping the servant to commit a second murder is however a fresh, and distinctly original, development.

———•◆•———

THE FORTUNE TELLER

Fortune teller found dead   Japp and Poirot
Greta Moscheim found by some bright young people – one
of them's a friend of Greta
Michael O'Halloran – P. says saved him from a murder
charge – Ah, now a little matter of a defaulting bookmaker.
People – cocktail party
Jane Brown
John Colley B.B.C. young man
Lady Monica Trent
Greta Moscheim – last person to see her alive
Mrs. Edgerton – a letter (found in flat?) from her young
man in East Africa (but she hadn't heard from him for 4
months). Greta was helping her – so psychic – husband –
(suspicious) was reading her – Mrs Edgerton – says woman
with a deep melancholy voice – deep contralto voice

Death of Zenobia
P. visits Japp have found Michael O'Halloran – they go
along – flat – divisional surgeon and inspect the body

Fortune teller woman – Mrs De Lucia. She is very successful
because in partnership with young man (or girl) who tips
her off. If young man – he pretends to disapprove violently
– she also blackmails. Young man is in love with Sue – sister
to someone in a matrimonial tangle. De Lucia is really his
wife so he has to get rid of her. Stages quite a drama over
someone's fortune – something about letters? The post?
Brought in from door – puts her death after 6.30 pm or

whatever it is. So p[artner?] comes to flats – kills De L –
goes on up to Sue – they go out to cinema. Comes back –
no key – he goes up in lift – discovers body etc.

The murder of a fortune teller appears in four Notebooks but these are the two most detailed versions. As can be seen, it was to be a variation, or an elaboration, of the short story 'The Third Floor Flat', first published in January 1929. The second outline appears sandwiched between pages elaborating 'The Market Basing Mystery' into 'Murder in the Mews', so this idea seems to date from the early to mid 1930s. And the presence of Japp also indicates an early 1930s outline.

It may well be that Christie was toying with the elaboration of early short stories and this was her version of 'The Third Floor Flat'. If so, it is indeed an elaboration, as the only plot devices common to both are the use of the service lift and the 'finding' of the body. A fortune-teller is an aspect 'The Blue Geranium' from *The Thirteen Problems*. But the surrounding detail is completely different.

_____

The Dark Lady . . .

'Shakespeare is ruined for most people by having being made to learn it at school; you should see Shakespeare as it was written to be seen, played on the stage.'

———————◄○►———————

Agatha Christie was a lifelong fan of William Shakespeare. Some of her titles – _Sad Cypress, Taken at the Flood, By the Pricking of my Thumbs_ – come from his plays. _Macbeth,_ with its Three Witches, provides some of the background to _The Pale Horse_, in Chapter 4 Mark Easterbrook and his friends discuss the play after attending a performance and in the village of Much Deeping, Thyrza, Sybil and Bella have a reputation locally as three 'witches'. Iago, from _Othello_, is a psychologically important plot device in _Curtain_; a quotation from _Macbeth_ – 'Who would have thought the old man to have had so much blood in him' – follows the discovery of Simeon Lee's body in _Hercule Poirot's Christmas_; and _Appointment with Death_ closes with a quotation from _Cymbeline_ – 'Fear no more the heat of the Sun.' Her letters, written to Max Mallowan during the Second World War, include detailed discussions, instigated by nights at the theatre, about _Othello_ and _Hamlet_.

In _The Times_ of 29 January 1973, the historian and Shakespeare scholar A.L. Rowse claimed that he had positively identified the Dark Lady of Shakespeare's Sonnets as

Letter to Times — Jan 26 (of the interesting)

I have read with great interest (your) the article written by Dr A L Rowse on his discovery of the identity of Shakespeare's Dark Lady of the Sonnets. She has always had a peculiar fascination for me particularly in connection with Shakespeare's Antony and Cleopatra —

I have no pretensions to be in any way a historian — but I am one of those who can claim to belong to those for whom Shakespeare wrote — I have gone to plays from an early age and am a great believer that that is the way one should approach Shakespeare — He wrote to entertain and he wrote for playgoers — I took my daughter & her friends to Stratford when she was twelve years old — and later my grandson at about the same age — and nephews — One young schoolboy gave an immediate criticism after seeing Macbeth. I never would have believed that was Shakespeare — It was wonderful all about gangsters — So exciting & so real —

A page of Christie's handwritten draft of the 'Dark Lady' letter.

Emilia Lanier née Bassano, daughter of a court musician and a former mistress of the Lord Chamberlain. Although disputed since, this theory received much publicity. In Notebook 7, in the middle of the notes for *Postern of Fate*, Christie drafted her response to this discovery:

Letter to Times – Jan 26
I have read with great interest (your) the article written
by Dr. A. L. Rowse on his discovery of the identity
of Shakespeare's Dark Lady of the Sonnets. She has
always had a peculiar fascination for me particularly in
connection with Shakespeare's *Antony and Cleopatra*. I
have no pretensions to be in any way a historian but I am
one of those who can claim to belong to those for whom
Shakespeare wrote. I have gone to plays from an early age
and am a great believer that that is the way one should
approach Shakespeare. He wrote to entertain and he
wrote for playgoers – I took my daughter and her friends
to Stratford when she was twelve years old and later my
grandson – at about the same age – and nephews. One
young schoolboy gave an immediate criticism afterwards
seeing *Macbeth* – 'I never would have believed that that was
Shakespeare; it was wonderful, all about gangsters – so
exciting, so real.' Shakespeare was clearly associated in his
mind with a school lesson of extreme boredom, but the
real thing thrilled him. After *Julius Caesar* [he said] 'What
a wonderful speech Marc Antony made and what a clever
man.' Take children to <u>see</u> Shakespeare on a stage and
<u>reading</u> Shakespeare will be enjoyed all through their life.
    What I also particularly enjoy is to see different
productions of the same play. A character such as Iago
can lend himself to different renderings. But Cleopatra
has always been to me a most interesting problem. Is
Antony and Cleopatra a great love story? I don't think so.

Shakespeare in his sonnets shows clearly two opposite
emotions; one an overwhelming sexual bondage to a
woman who clearly enjoyed torturing him, the other was an
equally passionate hatred. She was to him a personification
of Evil. His description of her physical attributes, 'hair cut
like wire', was all he could do to express his rancour, in
those early times. But he did not forget. I think that, as
writers do, he pondered and planned a play to be written
some day – a study of an evil woman, a woman who would
be a gorgeous courtesan and who would bring about the
ruin of a man who loved her.

Is not that the real story of *Antony and Cleopatra*: Did
Cleopatra kill herself with her serpent for love of Antony?
Did she not, having tried to approach and capture Octavius
so as to retain her power and her kingdom was she not
tired of Antony? Anxious to become the mistress of the next
powerful leader, Augustus not Antony, and he rebuffed her.
And so, could it be that she would be taken in chains to
Rome? That, never [and] so, charmian and the fatal asp.
Oh, how I have longed to see a production of *Antony and
Cleopatra* where a great actress shall play the Evil Destroyer
and, Antony, the great warrior, the adoring lover is defeated

Dr. Rowse has shown in his article that Emilia Bassano
(1597) was deserted by one of her lovers as an 'incuba',
an evil spirit, and became the mistress of an elderly Lord
Chamberlain, 1st Lord Hunsdon, who had control of the
Burbage Players and so abandoned the gifted playwright for
a rich and power-wielding admirer. Unlike Octavian he did
not rebuff her. He was probably not a good actor, though
one feels that that is really what he wanted to be. How
odd it is that a first disappointment in his ambition forced
him to a second choice, the writing of plays and so gave to
England a great poet and a great genius. His Dark Lady the
incuba, played her part in his career. Who but she taught

369

LETTERS TO THE EDITOR

Cleopatra as the Dark Lady

From Dame Agatha Christie

Sir, I have read with great interest the article written by Dr A. L. Rowse and published by you on January 29, on his discovery of the identity of Shakespeare's Dark Lady of the Sonnets. She has always had a peculiar fascination for me, particularly in connexion with Shakespeare's *Antony and Cleopatra*.

I have no pretension to be in any way an historian—but I am one of those who claim to belong to the group for whom Shakespeare wrote. I have gone to plays from an early age and am a great believer that that is the way that one should approach Shakespeare. He wrote to entertain and he wrote for playgoers.

I took my daughter and some friends to Stratford when she was twelve years old and later my grandson at about the same age and also some nephews. One young schoolboy gave an immediate criticism after seeing *Macbeth*—"I never would have believed that was Shakespeare. It was wonderful, all about gangsters, so exciting and so real". Shakespeare was clearly associated in the boy's mind with a school room lesson of extreme boredom, but the real thing thrilled him. He also murmured after seeing *Julius Caesar* —"What a wonderful speech. That Mark Antony was a clever man".

To me Cleopatra has always been a most interesting problem. Is *Antony and Cleopatra* a great love story? I do not think so. Shakespeare in his Sonnets shows clearly two opposing emotions. One, an overwhelming sexual bondage to a woman who clearly enjoyed torturing him. The other was an equally passionate hatred. She was to him a personification of evil. His description of her physical attributes, such as, "hair like black wire"—was all he could do at that time (1593-1594) to express his rancour.

I think perhaps, that as writers do, he pondered and planned a play to be written some day in the future; a study of an evil woman, a woman who would be a gorgeous courtesan and who would bring about the ruin of a great soldier who loved her.

Is not that the real story of *Antony and Cleopatra*? Did Cleopatra kill herself by means of an asp for love of Antony? Did she not, after Antony's defeat at the battle of Actium, almost at once make approaches to the conqueror Octavian so as to enslave him with her charms and so retain her power and her kingdom? She was possibly by then tired of Antony, anxious to become instead the mistress of the most powerful leader of the time. But Octavian, the Augustus of the future, rebuffed her. And she—what would be her future? To be taken in chains to Rome? That humiliation for the great Cleopatra — never! Never would she submit; better call for Charmian to bring the fatal asp.

Oh ! how I have longed to see a production of *Antony and Cleopatra* where a great actress shall play the part of Cleopatra as an evil destroyer who brings about the ruin of Antony, the great warrior. She has finished with Antony.

Dr Rowse has shown in his article that Emilia Bassano, the Dark Lady, described by one of her lovers as an incuba—an evil spirit—became the mistress of the elderly Lord Chamberlain, the first Lord Hunsdon who had control of the Burbage Players. Presumably she abandoned the gifted playwright for a rich and power-wielding admirer. Unlike Octavian he did not rebuff her. In his mind Shakespeare kept that memory until the day that he wrote with enjoyment, and a pleasurable feeling of revenge, the first words of *Antony and Cleopatra*.

Shakespeare was probably not a good actor, though one feels that that is what he originally wanted to be. All his works show a passion for the stage and for comparisons with actors.

How odd it is that a first disappointment in his ambition forced him to a second choice—the writing of plays and so gave to England a great poet and a great genius. Let us admit that his Dark Lady, his incuba, played her part in his career. Who but she taught him suffering and all the different aspects of jealousy, including the "green-eyed monster"?

Yours faithfully,
AGATHA CHRISTIE,
Winterbrook House, Wallingford,

The edited version of Christie's letter as it appeared in The Times *on February 3rd 1973.*

him suffering and all the different aspects of jealousy, the
green-eyed monster.

Although the Notebook is clearly dated 'Jan. 26', the article
to which Christie refers was not published until three days
later on 29 January. It is entirely possible that, because of her
friendship with A.L. Rowse, she was aware of the forthcoming publication but it is more likely that she just wrote the
wrong date. These notes were, presumably, tidied up when
they were typed as the printed version is slightly different.
The letter was published in *The Times* on 3 February 1973 as
from 'Agatha Mallowan, Winterbrook House, Wallingford',
with three further responses three days later. One took
Dame Agatha to task for accepting 'interesting conjectures
as irrefutable proof' and reminding her that Hercule Poirot
would not have made the same mistake. Another challenges
her portrayal of Cleopatra as a 'cheap femme fatale'.

In his book *Memories of Men and Women* (1980), Rowse
has an affectionate chapter on his friendship with Agatha
and Max, a friendship which began through Max's election
as a Research Fellow in All Souls, Oxford, Rowse's own college. Recalling that she wrote him a 'warm and encouraging
letter' about his Shakespeare discoveries as being 'from the
mistress of low-brow detection to the master of high-brow
detection', he mentions her support with this letter to *The
Times* and her subsequent attendance at his lecture on the
subject at the Royal Society of Literature.

The Sixth Decade 1970–1976

'Thank God for my good life, and all the love that has
been given to me.'

◄O►

SOLUTIONS REVEALED
Nemesis

◄O►

In 1970 Agatha Christie celebrated her eightieth birthday;
with the employment of a little selective arithmetic, it was
also the year of her eightieth book. Extensive press coverage,
both at home and abroad, greeted the publication on her
birthday – 15 September – of *Passenger to Frankfurt*.

On the first day of the following year Agatha Christie
became Dame Agatha, to the delight of her global audience. As she worked in Notebook 28 on that year's book,
Nemesis, she wrote 'D.B.E.' (Dame Commander of the British
Empire) at the top of the page. A book more impressive in
its emotional power than in its plotting, *Nemesis* is, like its
1972 successor *Elephants Can Remember*, a journey into the
past where 'old sins cast long shadows'. And the last novel
she wrote, *Postern of Fate* (1973), is a similar nostalgic journey and the poorest book of her career (with the possible

exception of the curiosity that is *Passenger to Frankfurt*); one which, in retrospect, should never have been published. To counterbalance these disappointments, 1974 saw the publication of *Poirot's Early Cases*, a collection of short stories from the prime of the little Belgian and his creator, not previously published in the UK. (See Chapter 3, 'Agatha Christie's Favourites'.)

Coinciding with these reminders of the vintage Poirot, one of his most challenging cases, *Murder on the Orient Express*, was filmed faithfully and extravagantly by Sidney Lumet, working with an all-star cast. A massive critical and popular success worldwide, it became the most successful British film ever and created a huge upsurge of interest in the now frail Agatha Christie. Her last public appearance was at the Royal Premiere in London, where she insisted on remaining standing to meet the Queen. Her publishers knew that a new book would be unable to satisfy the appetite of the vastly increased Christie audience created by the success of the film. So Sir William Collins convinced Dame Agatha to release *Curtain: Poirot's Last Case*, one of her most ingenious constructions, written when she was at the height of her powers. Another global success followed its appearance in October 1975, heralded by a *New York Times* front-page obituary of Hercule Poirot.

On 12 January 1976, three months after her immortal creation, Dame Agatha Christie died at her Wallingford home. International media mourned the passing of, quite simply, 'the writer who has given more enjoyment to more people than anyone else' (*Daily Telegraph*); the perennial *Mousetrap* dimmed its lights and newspapers printed pages on 'the woman the world hardly knows'. She was buried at Cholsey, near her Oxfordshire home, and a memorial service was held in May at St Martin-in-the-Fields in London. *Sleeping Murder*, another novel from Christie's Golden Age, and the 'final novel in a series that has delighted the world' (to quote the blurb) was published in October and presented Miss Marple's last book-length investigation. Dame Agatha's *Autobiography* followed in 1977 and *Miss Marple's Final Cases*, a collection of previously uncollected short stories, in 1979.

Apart from the unparalleled success of *Murder on the Orient Express*, the much-underrated screen version of *Endless Night* had appeared in 1972. Despite Dame Agatha's objection to a love scene at the close of the film, this adaptation remains a faithful treatment of the last great novel that Christie wrote. The previous year the last Christie play, *Fiddlers Five* (reduced to *Fiddlers Three* in a subsequent version in 1972), was staged, but its lack of critical and popular success ruled out a West End production. In 1973 Collins published *Akhnaton*, her historical play, written in 1937 but never performed; and her poetry collection, called simply *Poems*, was also issued in 1973.

The final six years of Agatha Christie's life saw some of her greatest successes – her damehood, the universal successes, in two separate spheres, of *Murder on the Orient Express* and *Curtain* – but also the publication of some of her weakest titles. But by then it didn't matter. Such was the esteem and affection in which she was held by her worldwide audience that *anything* written by Agatha Christie was avidly bought by a multitude of her fans, many of whom had had a lifelong relationship with her.

Passenger to Frankfurt
15 September 1970

───────◄○►───────

Diverted by fog to Frankfurt Airport, Sir Stafford
Nye agrees to the fantastic suggestion of a fellow
passenger. On his return to England he realises that
he has become involved in something of international
importance – but what? A further assignation leaves
him little wiser. What is Benvo? And who is Siegfried?

───────◄○►───────

Published on her eightieth birthday, this was claimed to be
Agatha Christie's eightieth book and, despite the dismay with
which the manuscript was greeted by both her family and
her publishers, it went straight into the best-seller lists and
remained there for over six months. The publicity attendant
on the 'coincidence' of her birthday and her latest production certainly helped, but *Passenger to Frankfurt* remains the
most extraordinary book she ever wrote. Described, wisely,
on the title page as 'An Extravaganza' – the description went
some way towards mitigating the disappointment felt by
both publishers and devotees – and showing little evidence
of the ingenuity with which her name is still associated, this
tale of international terrorism and engineered anarchy is
difficult to write about honestly. Most fans, myself included,
consider it an aberration and, but for the fact that it is an
'Agatha Christie', would never have read it the first time, let
alone re-read it over the 40 years since its first appearance.
Like other weaker novels from the same era, it begins with a
compelling, if somewhat implausible, situation, but it degen-
erates into total unbelievability long before the end. Only
in the closing pages of Chapter 23, with the unmasking of a

completely unexpected, albeit incredible, villainess is there a very faint trace of the Christie magic.

The idea of stage-managed anarchy brought about by promoting student protest and civil unrest is not new in the Christie output. It reaches back as far as the mysterious Mr Brown in *The Secret Adversary* and also makes an appearance, 30 years later, in *They Came to Baghdad*. While both these examples demand some suspension of disbelief on the part of the reader, *Passenger to Frankfurt* demands a higher and longer suspension. The other echo from earlier works, and one that can be appreciated only now, after the publication of the alternate version of 'The Capture of Cerberus' (see *Agatha Christie's Secret Notebooks*), is the subterfuge about a fake/real Hitler character and the method of concealment. This element of the plot is identical in both the short story and the novel, written 30 years apart.

The other surprise about this novel, apart from the unlikeliness of the plot, is the fact that throughout her life Christie evinced little interest in politics. And yet the entire thrust of the novel is political, with politicians and diplomats meeting regularly and, it must be said, implausibly in attempts to maintain political stability. Such scenes are dotted throughout the book; although, despite these meetings and endless conversations, nothing happens. Most of the conversations, whether private or political, meander aimlessly and unconvincingly and swathes of the book could be removed without making any notable difference.

The character of Matilda Cleckheaton is, in many ways, a Marple doppelganger – elderly, observant, worldly-wise and devious. But her stratagem for dealing with 'Big Charlotte' is in the highest degree unlikely and unconvincing.

Passenger to Frankfurt was written in the year of publication and Notebook 24 has three dates, '1970', 'February 1970' and '16th February 1970', on pages 12, 14 and 17

respectively. Christie realised that the year of her eightieth birthday would inevitably involve publicity and that the
1970 'Christie for Christmas' would have to be finished earlier than usual for a September publication. Some selective
arithmetic had to be done to arrive at the significant figure
of 80 titles. Only by counting the American collections – *The
Regatta Mystery* (1939), *Three Blind Mice* (1950), *The Underdog*
(1951) and *Double Sin* (1961) – all of which contained stories
not then published in Britain, as well as the Mary Westmacott
titles, could this all-important figure be arrived at.

In an interview conducted shortly after the publication
of the book Christie denied that any of the characters were
based on real-life politicians and that her inspiration for writing the book was her reading of the daily newspapers. She
cited especially reports of rebellious youth and the fact that
youth can be more easily influenced than older people. She
was at pains to emphasise that, personally, she was 'not in the
least interested in politics' and that the novel was apolitical in
the sense that anarchy could originate from either the Right
or the Left. Much of this is echoed in the Introduction to
the novel where she also discusses her ideas and where and
how she got them. 'If one idea in particular seems attractive,
and you feel you could do something with it, then you toss it
around, play tricks with it, work it up, tone it down, and gradually get it into shape.' It is a sad irony that, of all her novels,
Passenger to Frankfurt is one where the ingenious ideas that
proliferated in other novels are notable only by their absence.

The opening gambit of the airport swap is one that, nowadays, would be practically impossible; in the less terrorist-
conscious days of the late 1960s, when the book was plotted,
it was just about feasible. But this feasibility does not extend
to believability: is it remotely likely that anyone would agree
to hand over their passport to a total stranger and then take
a drink with the assurance of that stranger that the drug that

it admittedly contained was harmless? This ploy is considered in six Notebooks with the earliest, in the first extract below, dating back to around 1963. As usual, details of names and airport locations were to change, but the basic situation remains the same:

Possibilities of Airport story (A)
After opening in central European airport (Frankfurt)
(Venice) – diversion of plane – substitution of girl for Sir D

Starts at European airport – woman, tall, sees a medium man wearing a distinctive cloak and hood. Asks him to help her – Sir Robert Old – she takes his place – he takes knock-out drops. Later woman contacts him in London. Thriller

D. Book
Starting at airport – substituting – Robin West –
international thinker type

B. Missing passenger

B. Passenger to Frankfort [sic]
Missing passenger – airport – Renata – Sir Neil Sanderson

B. Passenger to Frankfurt
Sir Rufus Hammersley – his cloak – med[ium] height –
sharp jutting feminine chin.

In Notebook 23 the first sketch above – 'Possibilities of Airport story' – continues at 'A.' below. But the scenario considered after the postcard and 'near escape' idea goes in a completely different direction from the one adopted in the novel. The 'Girl murdered' idea is rather similar to that of Luke Fitzwilliam's reading of the death of Miss Pinkerton following their meeting on the train in *Murder is Easy*. These notes appear on a page directly preceding the plotting of 1964's *A Caribbean Mystery* and this timeline is confirmed by the date of the proposed postcard, November 1963.

A. Advertisement?
Postcard? Frankfort 7-11-63 Could meet you at Waterloo
Bridge Friday 14th 6 p.m.
B. Sir D. is called upon by a rather sinister gentleman –
questioned about incident at Frankfort – D. is alert – non-
committal. Shortly after, a 'near escape' – gas? car steering
trouble? electric fault? Then a visit from the 'other side'
apparently friends of girl
Or
Girl murdered – her picture in paper – he is sure it is the girl
at the airport – it starts him investigating – he goes to the
inquest.

Notebook 28A contains the plot-line that Christie actually adopted and the following short paragraph, listed as Idea B, neatly encapsulates it. Although the calculation about the age of the supposed son would seem to place the writing of this note in 1969, Idea C on the following page is part of the plot of *Endless Night* (1967) and is followed a few pages later by extensive notes for *By the Pricking of my Thumbs* (1968). Unusually, here also is the exact title, spelling apart, of the projected book:

Passenger to Frankfort [sic]
Missing passenger – airport – Renata – Sir Neil Sanderson
London Neil at War Office or M.14. His obstinacy aroused
– puts advertisement in. Frankfort Airport Nov. 20th
Please communicate – passenger to London etc. Answer –
Hungerford Bridge 7.30pm

What is it all about? She passes him ticket for concert
Festival Hall. Hitler idea – concealed in a lunatic asylum
– one of many who think they are Napoleon or Hitler or
Mussolini. One of them was smuggled out – H. took his
place – Hitler – H. Bormann – branded him on sole of foot
– a swastika – the son born 1945 now 24 – in Argentine?
U.S.A.? Rudi Schornhorn – the young Siegfried

The following extract from Notebook 49 dates from the mid
1960s. Idea A on the same list became *Third Girl* and Ideas
C and D never went further than the four-line sketches on
the page of this Notebook. This outline tallies closely with
the finished novel although there is no mention of the ticket
and passport swap.

B. Passenger to Frankfurt
Sir Rufus Hammersley – His cloak – med[ium] height –
sharp jutting feminine chin. Fog in airport – flight diverted
– the young woman – not noticeable – thinks he has seen
her before – likeness – she will be killed – because of the fog
– diverted elsewhere – Miss Karminsky – passenger – he is
found in passage by loos – no money or papers
He gets money sent him – then asked to go to Intelligence.
He has a sixth sense and a feeling of partisanship. His
things searched. Advertisement – wants to see you again –
Hungerford Bridge – Nov. 26th Ticket at concert. What is it
all about

Probably because this novel did not involve clues and suspects and alibis, the usual components of a Christie detective novel, there is little in the way of notes or ideas that
were considered and discarded. In fact, it is fair to say that
there is little in the way of plot at all in *Passenger to Frankfurt*.
Apart from speculation about rearranging some sections,

the notes for the novel are mostly of the names of people and their countries and the interminable meetings that fill the book. The following early notes show uncertainty about the arrangement of some passages in the opening chapters. The seemingly odd reference 'Lifeboat' is to the name of the periodical used to conceal the safe return of Sir Stafford's passport.

> Chapter 3
> Car incident p. 51 – or keep it as original – or keep it on
> p. 46
> Last page rearranged – Start at breakfast – Interview at
> ministry. After ministry interview into Mrs. Worrit – clothes
> cleaned – man – panda?
> Rings Matilda – arranges to go down next week. Dinner
> with Eric – on way home car business – Lifeboat – passport
> – advertisement idea

A passage of considerable interest is the one concerning the antecedents of Siegfried, 'the young hero, the golden super-man' of Chapter 6. Chapter 17 of *Passenger to Frankfurt* contains distinct echoes of the 'new' version of 'The Capture of Cerberus', published in *Agatha Christie's Secret Notebooks*. Remarkably, after a 30-year gap, the central idea of the short story is recycled in the novel – the asylum with its many incarnations of famous, and infamous, people. In each case there is confusion about the 'fake' and the 'real' Hitler (Hertzlein in the short story) and the eventual release of the 'real' one. A major difference in the short story is that the newly released character has become a force for good and not evil, as in the novel.

> Are you suggesting he is Hitler?
> No, but he believes he is.

Statistics – Borman hid him there – he married a girl – child
was born – swastika branded on
child's foot – Renata has birth certificate [Chapter 17]

Some characters from earlier titles reappear. Mr Robinson, first mentioned in Chapter 3, and Colonel Pikeaway in Chapter 4, both appeared in both *Cat among the Pigeons* and Colonel Pikeaway also appeared in *At Bertram's Hotel*; these two shadowy figures would make a further reappearance in *Postern of Fate*. Matilda Cleckheaton's nurse, Amy Leatheran, on the other hand, is unlikely to be the same Amy Leatheran who narrated *Murder in Mesopotamia*; she is described in Chapter 20 of *Passenger to Frankfurt* as a 'tactful young woman'. Other interesting passages include a discussion, in Chapter 6, of *The Prisoner of Zenda*, to be discussed again by Tommy and Tuppence in *Postern of Fate*; an inadvertent naming of two Christie plays in a paragraph of Chapter 11; and a distinct reference, in Chapter 22, to the basis of the 1948 radio play *Butter in a Lordly Dish*. More personally, Lady Matilda's discussion of medicines in Chapter 15 is an echo of Christie's own description, in her *Autobiography*, of her work in the dispensary in Torquay.

Overall, the decline that began with *Third Girl* reached its nadir with *Passenger to Frankfurt*; the superb *Endless Night* beams out like a shining light among the last half-dozen novels. But there can be little doubt that the only reason that *Passenger to Frankfurt* was even published was that it had the magic name 'Agatha Christie' on the title page.

Nemesis
18 October 1971

---◄○►---

At the posthumous request of Mr Rafiel, from *A Caribbean Mystery*, Miss Marple joins a coach tour of 'Famous Houses and Gardens'. She must use her natural flair for justice to right a wrong. But she is mystified by a lack of clues – until one of her fellow travellers is murdered.

---◄○►---

Like its predecessors, *By the Pricking of my Thumbs* and *Hallowe'en Party*, and its successors, *Elephants Can Remember* and *Postern of Fate*, *Nemesis* is concerned with a mystery from the past. Retrospective justice is what Miss Marple is asked, by the deceased Mr Rafiel, to provide. And, similar to the letter received by Poirot at the outset of *Dumb Witness*, the posthumous correspondence from Mr Rafiel is very short on detail.

In one way *Nemesis* is the most surprising novel that Christie wrote in her declining years. As with most of the novels from her last decade *Nemesis* is rambling and repetitive, and it is disappointing as a detective novel. The coach tour, which promises much as a traditional Christie setting, is almost a red herring. And unlike the classic settings of *Murder on the Orient Express*, *Death in the Clouds* and *Death on the Nile*, where a mode of transport isolates a group of suspects, the vital characters in *Nemesis*, the three sisters, are all to be found outside the coach.

Yet, though it is not a great detective novel – clues to its solution are remarkable only by their absence – considered solely as a novel it is a revelation. Its theme is 'Love – one of the most frightening words there is in the world', according to Elizabeth Temple at the close of Chapter 6. The mainspring of the plot is the smothering, corrosive love of Clotilde Bradbury-Scott for the girl Verity. As a counterbalance to this claustrophobic situation there is the love of Verity for Michael Rafiel; but this love is also destined for tragedy. The doomed worship of Verity by Clotilde is the root cause of three deaths – the object of that love and the brutal killing of two innocent onlookers. This hitherto unexplored theme has powerful emotional impact, especially in the closing explanation which, unusually for Miss Marple, takes over 15 pages.

Like the novel itself, the notes for *Nemesis* are not very detailed. The bulk of them concern the crime in the past and its possible variations. The idea of the three sisters and the tomb disguised as a greenhouse seems to have been settled in the early stages of planning. This has distinct echoes of a similar plot device in *Hallowe'en Party*, where a sunken garden fills a similar role; and, earlier again, *Dead Man's Folly*, which features a folly as a grave. The notes for *Nemesis* are in four Notebooks and, as can be seen from the first extract below, work on it began just a year before publication. Note the incorrect name 'Raferty' instead of Rafiel:

Oct. 1970
Chapter I
Miss Marple at home reading Times – glances at Marriages
– then Deaths. A name she knows – can't quite remember.
Later in garden remembers Carribean [sic] – Raferty, the
dying millionaire.
Chapter II Letter from lawyer in London.

The Three Sisters – invitations to Miss Marple – Mr. Rafiel –
old manor house – a body concealed there
Clothilde

Lavender
Alicia
What kind of a house? What garden
A Greenhouse – wreathed over with polygnum – fell down
or collapsed in war

This list of characters from Notebook 6 reflects, with the
exception of the Denbys and Miss Moneypenny, that of the
completed novel.

People on Tour
Mrs. Risely-Porter (Aunt Ann) Elderly dictatorial a snob
And niece Joanna Cartwright (27)
Emlyn Price (Welsh and revolutionary)
Miss Barrow and Miss Cooke (spinster friends)
Miss Moneypenny (Cats) [possibly Miss Bentham or
Lumley]
Mr and Mrs. Butler Americans middle-aged
Colonel and Mrs. Walker (Flowers? Horticulture)
Mr Caspar (Foreign) about 50
Elizabeth Peters [Temple] Retired headmistress
Schoolgirl and brother – Liz and Robert Denby
Professor Wanstead

A section of Notebook concerning the murder of Elizabeth
Temple appears almost word for word in Chapter 11,
'Accident'. Details differ – the school is Fallowfield, not
Grove House Park, and it is Joanna Crawford and not Mr
Caspar who provides most of the details of the rock fall – but
in essence this extract is an accurate précis:

Death of Elizabeth Peters, late headmistress of Grove House
Park Girls' School – or is she in hospital? Does Miss M go
and see her?

Does Emlyn Price come and tell Miss Marple of accident?
She goes to local hotel to see other travellers – group talk
and chat. Either Miss Cooke or Robert Denby describe
what they saw – 4 or 5 boys climbing up – throwing stones
– pushing a rock – local boys. Mr Caspar later says that was
not what happened – it was a woman. Tells Miss Marple –
he was a botanist and had wandered by himself. Professor
Wanstead speaks to Miss Marple – mentions Mr. Rafiel –
suggests Miss Marple should go and visit her. He stresses
Rafiel told him about her

It must be said however that as a murder method, rolling a
rock down a hillside in the hope of hitting a moving target
is, at best, imprecise; 35 years earlier, on the banks of the
Nile, Andrew Pennington discovered this when his murder
attempt on Linnet Doyle failed, literally, to achieve its target.
And for a middle-aged murderess it is also very unlikely and
impractical.

The essence of the plot appears in Notebook 28 and, apart
from a few details – Gwenda and Philip are forerunners of
Verity and Michael – is reproduced in the book. It would
seem to have been written early in the plotting as it appears
directly ahead of a page dated 'Jan. '71'; and it is written
straight off with no deletions or changes. The ruse of the
'pinched' car and the obliterated body has familiar echoes
from *The Body in the Library*, 30 years earlier.

Elizabeth Peters 60 retired headmistress
A girl in her school – one of the 3 sisters had taken her up,
trip abroad art galleries. Girl had finally come to live with
her – girl was murdered by 19 or 20 years old young man –
picked her up in car (evidence that he did). Body found 20
miles away – face disfigured – identified by Miss C – says a
mole by elbow or above knee – a small silver cross or some

other trinket – pregnant – 6 weeks only. A scarf (Persian? or
Italian?) Red hair – auburn or black hair – Girl used to take
local bus to nearby Town – meet Philip there – C[lothilde]
finds out Gwenda and Philip – baby coming – going to
marry. Strangles her – hides body in garden – plans another
girl whom she knows – drugs her – drives her in car she has
pinched 20 miles away in quarry – obliterates features –
moles – jealous

Midway through Notebook 28 we find a touching note. In
the New Year Honours list for 1971 Agatha Christie became
Dame Agatha, a fact that she noted as she resumed work on
Nemesis. On a more practical note, this means that she was
less than halfway through the novel at the beginning of the
year, with the submission date three months away. And she
was 80 years of age.

> D.B.E. [Dame of the British Empire]
> Nemesis – Jan 1971
> Recap – death of Mr. Rafiel in Times – Miss Marple
> Point reached – Elizabeth Peters retired headmistress
> – accident as climbing – stones and rocks rolling down
> hillside – concussion – hospital
> Professor Wansted and Miss Marple

As she tidied the manuscript, to judge by the date, Christie
listed the characters again, this time with a few additions.
The final proofs were corrected by Dame Agatha while she
recovered from a broken hip in June/July 1971, at which
stage she also wrote the jacket blurb.

> Notes on 'Nemesis' March 18th '71
> Elizabeth Temple School Fallowfield
> Justin (?) Rafiel

Michael Rafiel – Verity Hunt
Miss Barrow – Miss Cooke – or Miss Caspar
The Old Manor – Jocelyn St. Mary
Clothilde Bradbury Scott – Lavinia – Anthea
Archdeacon Bradshaw Bradley Scott?
Emlyn Price
Joanna Crawford Mrs Riseley-Porter
Professor Wanstead
Broadribb and Schuster (Solicitors)

She also gives a proposed list of chapters, with some notes to herself:

Chapter I Births Marriages and Deaths
Chapter II Letter from Mr. Rafiel
Chapter III Note – a little cutting of this chapter?
Chapter IV Esther Waters
Chapter V Instructions from beyond – some cuts?
Chapter VI Elizabeth Temple
Chapter VII An Invitation
Chapter VIII The Three Sisters

This list is not exactly reflected in the novel, but the suggested title of the opening chapter here is surely better than that eventually decided upon. 'Overture' is not thematically inked with any other chapter, while 'Births Marriages and Deaths' is both accurate and intriguing.

Elephants Can Remember
6 November 1972

————————◄○►————————

At a literary dinner, Mrs Oliver is asked to investigate the double death years earlier of Sir Alistair and Lady Ravenscroft. Did he kill her and then himself or was it the other way round? Hercule Poirot journeys into the past to arrive at the truth.

————————◄○►————————

The adage 'Old sins have long shadows' runs like a motif through *Elephants Can Remember*, the last Poirot novel that Agatha Christie wrote. At its heart is a plot involving typical Christie ploys – mistaken identity, impersonation and misconstrued deaths – culminating in a last chapter reminiscent of the closing scene in *Five Little Pigs* with a group of people gathering at the scene of an earlier tragedy in order to learn the poignant truth. If it had been written 20 years earlier there can be little doubt that the plot would have been developed in a more ingenious fashion. As it is, the book is a series of conversations, with little action; and like its successor, *Postern of Fate*, the chronology of the earlier crimes will not bear close examination, a fault for which the elderly Christie's editors must accept some responsibility.

Old friends make reappearances: Mrs Oliver plays a large part and Superintendent Spence reminisces in Chapter 5 about *Mrs McGinty's Dead, Hallowe'en Party* and *Five Little Pigs*, all stories where Poirot investigates past crimes, the first two also in the company of Mrs Oliver. In Chapter 10 Miss Lemon, Poirot's secretary, appears briefly. Mr Goby, described in Chapter 16 as 'a purveyor of information', first appeared in *The Mystery of the Blue Train*, and also conducted enquiries on behalf of Poirot in *After the Funeral* and *Third Girl.*

There can be little doubt that it is Agatha Christie herself rather than Ariadne Oliver who muses throughout the first chapter on the difficulties of eating with false teeth, the horror of giving speeches, the difficulties of dinner-party companions and the unwarranted effusiveness of fans. And the passage in the same chapter in which Albertina remonstrates with Mrs Oliver about her diffidence is echoed in Christie's *Autobiography* when she describes how the wife of the British ambassador to Vienna had encouraged her to abandon her natural shyness and declare to reporters, 'It is wonderful what I have done. I am the best detective story writer in the world. Yes, I am proud of the fact . . . I am very clever indeed.'

There are fewer than 20 pages of notes, scattered over four Notebooks, for *Elephants Can Remember.* Notebook 5 contains six pages of notes but only the first few lines are relevant to the finished novel. In strong legible writing at the top of the first page of Notebook 5 we read:

Elephants Remember – Jan. 1972

Despite its incongruity in a crime novel it would seem that the title, or a slight variant of it, was settled from the beginning. The elephant motif recurs throughout the book – often in defiance of logic, for example the reference in the first chapter to Mrs Burton-Cox's teeth.

In the following extract Mrs Gorringe is the forerunner of Mrs Burton-Cox and, although their discussion about hereditary violence is not used, the last idea, a godchild and her fiancé, is. Details from this extract – Mrs Oliver's birthday and the 'bull in the field' memory – tally exactly with Chapter 1.

Mrs. Oliver – Poirot

Does a problem come to P? or Mrs. O? Lunch for literary
women – Mrs. Oliver – Mrs. Gorringe

Mrs G. 'Do you think that if a child had grown up she might
have been a murderer- murderess?'
Boys pull fly's legs off but they don't do it when they grow
up – just boyish fun. Are you very interested in these things?

Not really – it's just because of one particular thing – a god
child I've got – she's got a boyfriend – she wants to marry
him. (Interruption – Speeches) They go and sit and look at
the Serpentine.

All so long ago – everyone would have forgotten. People
don't forget things that happen when they were children
– Mrs. O remembers cows a bull in a field – a birthday
and something to do with an éclair. It's like elephants –
elephants never forget

After a brief detour to consider an alternative and to remind
herself to re-read an early Poirot short story with a very
similar plot, Christie outlines the opening of *Elephants Can
Remember* in Notebook 6, almost exactly as it appears in the
published novel:

Idea A
Husband and wife – she says her husband is poisoning her –
(wants to believe it) attracted to a young man who pretends
he is in love with her – actually is also courting niece tells
wife he is pretending this to deceive husband. Really, he and
niece are in on it. Re-read 'Cornish Mystery.'

Idea B
Mrs. O goes to literary lunch – bossy female buttonholes
her. I believe Celia Ravenscroft is your god-daughter? My
son wants to marry her. Can you tell me if her mother
killed her father or was it [her] father killed [her] mother.
Celebrated case – you must remember – both bodies on cliff
– both shot.

Mrs. O goes to Poirot or does she get Celia to come and see
her. Modern – violent – intellectual girl – says definitely of
course mother shot him – gives reason – story of what lay
behind it. Mrs. O gets interested. Talks to Poirot

A few pages later we find a mixture of ideas, some of which
found their way into the finished book. These notes are
somewhat confused and confusing – references to the wife/
sister are not always clear – but the underlying plot of two
sisters, one husband and lifelong jealousy ending in murder
and impersonation eventually emerged. There is an echo
of the Christie of old in the listing of alternatives, although
most of them are variations on a theme.

Further ideas

Is it actually Col. R has shot himself – wife is not his wife – a
sister in law – elder sister of wife – has been in nursing home
or mental Home for killing children – unfit to plead

Or Col. R's sister or his first wife – a tragedy in India – she
is paroled from mental home. Dressed in wife's clothes and
wig. Wife pretends to be sister – identifies body.

Sisters one is mental – kills children – unfit to plead – in
Broadmoor
or

Colonel's sister – devoted to him – jealous of his wife.
Paroled – comes to house – kills brother – wife shoots her
– dresses her in wig and clothes – stages it all – identifies
wife's body –
or
India Col. has wife/sister? – mental kills child – Ayah
accused – poisons herself. But was it the ayah? Could it
have been sister in law or the mother? [Chapter 7]

Story about Mrs. Ravenscroft sister in India – nervous
breakdown – killed a child – hushed up taken back to
England – nursing home.
Story – Wife and mother killed child
Story – Sister of Col – or Mrs. R – said to be accident. Goes
now to England in private mental home – released – lives
with a qualified mental nurse – nurse dies – sister in law
marries.

There is a reference to one of the ideas Christie regularly toyed with, that of the twins (see *Agatha Christie's Secret
Notebooks*); this motif does come into play in the novel,
although not exactly as Christie here speculated. And the
second reference below, from Notebook 6, is a plot very similar to the Marple short story 'The Case of the Perfect Maid';
apart from the idea of twins, it has little to do with *Elephants
Can Remember*.

Twin idea – 2 girls born same day – one girl tells her they are
identical – nobody knows them apart

Lalage and Lorna identical twins – born same day but really
not identical – look quite different – come from Australia or
New Zealand. Lalage plays part of both sisters – 3rd person
in house is Stephanie (really Lorna). Play part of maid or

one time au pair girl – foreign accent etc. actually looks like
her Aunt (mother's sister Francesca)

One of the ideas noted by Christie, however, appears in
Chapter 6 as a red herring:

Colonel R – is doing reminiscences of his days in India – girl
secretary comes – takes dictation from him ~~and~~ does typing.
Suggestion that there was something between them

Despite showing a glimpse in the final chapter of the Christie
of yesteryear, *Elephants Can Remember* remains a disappointment. Like the books published on either side of it, there are
too many rambling conversations that give the reader little
solid information but merely repeat what we have already
been told. The central idea has possibilities and there is certainly material for a long short story. It could have been a disappointing swan song for Poirot – but the Queen of Crime
had reserved a dazzling final performance, *Curtain: Poirot's
Last Case,* for the little Belgian.

∿✖∿

Postern of Fate
29 October 1973

While shelving books in her new home Tuppence
Beresford finds a hidden message concerning the
mysterious death of a previous inhabitant. With
the help of Tommy she investigates a mystery from
the distant past, unaware that new danger is very much
in the present.

Postern of Fate was the last book Agatha Christie wrote and the initial notes are clearly dated November 1972, almost exactly a year before publication. It is arguable that her agent and publisher should never have asked for another book after the previous year's *Elephants Can Remember*. Although H.R.F. Keating reviewed *Postern of Fate* charitably in *The Times* with the ambiguous phrase 'She stills skims like a bird', there is no doubt that it is the weakest book Christie ever wrote. The most interesting passages are those where we get a glimpse of the private Agatha Christie. Old Isaac's reminiscences in Book II, Chapter 2 ('Introduction to Mathilde, Truelove and KK') echo Christie's own memories of her childhood as described in Part I of her *Autobiography*. Many of the books mentioned by Tommy and Tuppence in the early chapters of the book – *The Cuckoo Clock, Four Winds Farm, The Prisoner of Zenda, Under the Red Robe* – are still to be found on the shelves of Greenway House, her Devon home. The description of The Laurels bears more than a passing resemblance to Ashfield, her beloved childhood home, even down to the monkey puzzle tree in the garden; and the first UK edition has on the jacket a photo of Bingo, Christie's own family dog and the inspiration for the novel's Hannibal. And when Tuppence complains about the effects of old age or the vagaries of workmen ('They came, they showed efficiency, they made optimistic remarks, they went away to fetch something. They never came back'), we can be certain that this is the elderly Christie speaking.

Interesting though these insights are – and they were to be superseded within a few years by publication of her *Autobiography* – they do not make a detective novel and there can be no argument that *Postern of Fate* is even a pale imitation of the form at which, for half a century, she excelled. The novel's intriguing opening premise, the coded message in the book, clearly shows that advancing age did not prevent Christie having ideas; what was missing was the ability to develop them as she would have even a decade earlier. All of the final half-dozen novels, from *By the Pricking of my Thumbs* onwards, begin with a fascinating idea – the disappearance of an elderly lady from her retirement home, the drowning of a child while bobbing for apples, the supposed double suicide of an elderly couple – but none of them is explored with anything approaching the ingenuity of Christie's yesteryear. As recently as two years earlier, *Nemesis* begins with a situation very similar to that of *Postern of Fate* – a message from the dead that demands an investigation. But the decline in those two years is all too evident and dramatic; the plot of *Nemesis* is coherent and reasonable and the action of the story moves forward throughout. All of these elements, sadly, are absent from *Postern of Fate*.

Not surprisingly this decline is mirrored in the two Notebooks, 3 and 7, which contain the plotting notes. There are fewer than 25 pages of notes and they vary between scattered jottings and complete paragraphs. Many of the notes are reminders to amend sections already written and there is none of the plethora of ideas normally associated with the Notebooks. Note that the page numbers below do not refer to the published version but, in all probability, to the proofs.

Continue next from P.120
March 9th [1973]
P.135 Letter or money in leather wallet
P.56 Name of village or market town? Must be mentioned in first chapter?
P.75 about M.R. Car accident? Change to illness

The book was completed by May 1973 and the editor at Collins wrote diplomatically in mid-June to say that he 'enjoyed your latest novel very much', remarking especially on the splendid character of Hannibal the dog and the wise comments on old age. He also mooted the idea of changing the title, despite the presence of the quotation, to *Postern of Death*, a suggestion that obviously was not well received. Further correspondence and phone calls were needed to rectify 'certain discrepancies' – whether references to the war refer to the First or Second World War, exactly who killed Isaac, and the splitting of some long chapters into shorter ones. With all of this clarification it is surprising that no one spotted the impossible chronology of the Beresfords' children. In *N or M?* Deborah, their daughter, is involved in war work; in Book III Chapter 16 of *Postern of Fate*, set 30 years later, she is described as 'nearly 40'.

Some old friends reappear – the mysterious Colonel Pikeaway and Mr Robinson – and there are numerous references to the Beresfords' earlier cases. They reminisce as far back as *The Secret Adversary* in 1922, their exploits as *Partners in Crime* in 1929 and their war-time spy adventure in *N or M?*. Oddly, although they remind each other frequently about these, neither of them mentions their most recent adventure *By the Pricking of my Thumbs*, a mere five years earlier. The murder method in *Postern of Fate*, foxglove leaves as poison, has echoes of the early short story 'The Herb of Death' from *The Thirteen Problems*. And note the reference, in Book II, Chapter 2, to the idea of taking pot-shots at departing visitors; this was the unsociable habit both of Richard Warwick, the victim in *The Unexpected Guest*, and Christie's brother Monty when he settled in Devon on his return from Africa.

For even the most devoted reader of Christie *Postern of Fate* is a challenge. Despite its intriguing premise – 'Mary Jordan did not die naturally. It was one of us. I think I know which' – the book never explores this enigma in any organised way. The investigation, such as it is, consists mainly of pointless and long-winded conversations, endless reminiscences and far too many inconsequential characters. What little plot there is would have benefited from the excision of at least 100 pages, but it is doubtful if even this ruthless exercise would make any overall difference. Yet the book went into the best-seller charts within weeks of publication – and stayed there. But there can be no doubt that at this stage fans automatically bought each new title just because it *was* the new 'Christie for Christmas'.

The opening of the book is almost exactly as sketched below:

> Notes for Nov. 1972 and Plans
> Opening suggestion for a book
> Tuppence says 'What a load of books we have.' Starts
> looking at books – takes some out – looks at them – laughs
> – finds a letter in book shoved behind shelf. Seems to
> indicate a murder

This is followed by speculation about the title, with 'Doom's Caravan' and a variation 'Death's Caravan' leading the field and heading the following page; and by the quotation that actually appears in the book:

> Book T[ommy] and T[uppence] Title?
> Doom's Caravan?
> Swallow's Nest
> Postern of Fate?

> Doom's Caravan

> Pass not beneath, O Caravan, or pass not singing
> Have you not heard
> That silence where the birds are dead yet
> Something pipeth like a bird?
> Pass not beneath, O Caravan, Doom's Caravan
> Death's Caravan

In the early pages of Notebook 3 Christie considers various ideas, some of which were discarded – a homicidal spinster aunt, a woman doctor – and some adopted – the census entries, hidden papers, Regent's Park. At this stage Mary is still a German spy.

> Points
> Death – accidental? – of Alexander. Horseradish picked by mistake was foxglove leaves
> Digitalin – Death from Heart –
> Who picked them? Who cooked them (a) Cook (b) Girl helping (c) Woman doctor? Goes round garden with one of the children. Aunt or perhaps mother of illegitimate child – who grown up as her nephew – in army or navy. Mary Robinson (governess) German girl, very beautiful, is German spy – takes plans to London – Regent's Park – Queen Mary's garden. Tommy by reason of some of his contacts (in N or M) – Census entries – who was in the house those 2 (?) dates
> Spinster Aunt – she poisons German Mary R
> Simon a school friend staying there – Recognises M.R. – pointed out to him as a woman by an Army god father or an older friend – or a foreign officer an [Australian] who in 1921 or thereabouts has a cottage a place like Dittisham [a village near Agatha Christie's Devon home] – (Reason – papers might be hidden there)

A list of characters from Notebook 7 includes a Miss Price-Ridley, who is surely a relative of Mrs Price Ridley, Miss Marple's neighbour in St Mary Mead; a character bearing this name does make a brief appearance in *Postern of Fate*. This is the sort of irritating mistake that an editor should have spotted.

Points Doom's Caravan
People
Dorothy called Dodo – Miss Little – big woman –
nicknamed The Parish Pump
Griffin – old – full of memories
Miss Price Ridley
Mrs Lupton – supports herself on 2 sticks – remembers the
Parkinsons, [the] Somers – also Chattertons
Place called Hallquay [Book I, Chapter 5]

And, inexplicably, in the middle of Book III, Chapter 7, after
a discussion of their adventures in *The Secret Adversary* and *N
or M?*, we find Tommy and Tuppence having the following
conversation. The version below, from Notebook 7, is reproduced almost exactly in the novel:

Swallow's Nest said Tuppence 'That's what the house was
once called.'
'Why shouldn't we call it that again'
'Good idea', said Tuppence
Birds flew from the roof over their heads
Swallows flying south, said Tommy. 'Won't they ever come back?'
'Yes they'll come back next winter through the Postern of
fate', said Lionel

This is followed by brief mention of Isaac's death, the most
casual murder in the entire Christie canon. The sang-froid
with which his murder is greeted is rivalled only by the casual
attitude to, not to mention the implausibility of, the shooting
of Tuppence.

Isaacs Death
Inquest – after inquest – Isaac's household – a niece or
wife – Nellie – a lodger who has not been there very long –

An extract from Notebook 7 and the plotting for Postern of Fate. *Note the legibility of the handwriting.*

2 lodgers perhaps. Mention by Nellie of Cambridge or an envelope on which Cambridge has been written – Boat Race that day – a bet made [Book II, Chapter 4]

In Notebook 28 Christie considers some scenarios for the opening chapter, eventually settling on C below. The reference to Harrison Homes is to the real-life charity, providing accommodation for the independent-minded elderly, with which she was closely involved:

Large numbers of books – Tuppence is going to sort them out – take some to hospital? Or Harrison Homes – some old lady knows something
A. Is there something in a book – 2 pages stuck together

B. or is there some letters or print which spell out words – a
message
C. Such a sentence as 'Mary Robinson did not die naturally.
It was one of us – I think I know which one.'

This is followed by a careful working out of the code found by
Tuppence in her copy of R.L. Stevenson's *The Black Arrow*. The
extract is from Chapter 5 of that novel and although it starts out
accurately, judicious editing has been done to avoid writing out
the entire extract. Eventually, isolated words only are used and
sense and logic are lost, a sentiment echoed by Tommy when
Tuppence shows him her discovery. Note, however, the change
of the name from Robinson here to Jordan in the published version; and the incorrect spelling of 'naturally' as 'naturaly' in the
code even though it appears correctly in the body of the note.
Very little of this working out appears in the published novel.

The Black Arrow R. L. Stevenson
Matcham could not restrain a little cry and even Dick
started with surprise and dropped the windac from his
fingers but to the fellows on the lawn this shaft was an
expected signal. They were all afoot together tightening
loosening sword and dagger in the sheaths. Ellis held up his
hand, the white of his eyes shone – let . . . . the men of
the Black Arrow had all disappeared and the cauldron and
the ruined house burning alone to testify . . . . Not in time
to warn these one from (from) upper quarters I have these I
and striking I will / Duckworth and Simon red with / Is the
arrow hurry ellis whistle / Space their house and dead
MARY/ROBINSON/DID/NOT/DIE/NATURALY/IT/WAS/
ONE/OF//US/I/THINK/I/KNOW/WHICH/ONE

It is touching to imagine the 83-year-old Queen of Crime
carefully copying and underlining her code; and to remember that it was the last ingenious idea she was to devise.

UNUSED IDEAS:
FIVE

The final Unused Idea is a very special and surprising one . . .

THE EXPERIMENT

The following notes all appear in lists of ideas for both short stories and novels. The first is Idea E on an 'A to J' list dated January 1935, which includes the original ideas for 'Problem at Sea', *Sad Cypress* and *They Do It with Mirrors*.

> The Experiment   Mortimer – How does murder affect the character?

The following item is the first idea on a short list that includes *A Pocket Full of Rye* and *They Do It with Mirrors*, indicating a late 1940s date:

> Mortimer – his plans – first killing and so on – his character gradually changes

This next jotting appears a few pages ahead of the notes for *Curtain* and a page of corrections for *The Body in the Library*, indicating a time-frame a decade earlier:

> Man (or woman) who experiments in murder (goes queer)

And the final short note is probably slightly earlier, as it appears alongside notes for *The Moving Finger* and *Sparkling Cyanide*:

> Mortimer – experimental murder

Although these four jottings were all written during her most productive and inventive period, it was not until the final year of her creative life that Christie elaborated on this plot. Perhaps she had been doing what she wrote of in her *Autobiography*, 'looking vaguely through a pile of old note-books and [finding] something scribbled down'; or perhaps the inspiration resurfaced from somewhere in her subconscious. The idea, as evidenced by its four Notebook appearances, was obviously one that attracted her and one that she had never tackled in any way in her published work; yet, at the time of the early notes, it would have been almost impossible for her to have attempted it with Collins Crime Club waiting for her annual 'whodunit'. It was not until the twilight of her career that she (and they) felt comfortable publishing titles like *The Pale Horse*, a murder-to-order thriller with supernatural overtones, and *Endless Night*, a psychological suspense story with a dark secret. And this idea would have fitted into the same category.

In Notebook 7 Christie began developing the idea. Here Mortimer has disappeared, to be replaced first by Jeremy and later by Edmund:

> Jeremy – discusses with friends – murders
> What difference would it make to one's character if one had killed someone?
> Depends what the motive had been – Hatred? Revenge?

Gain? Jealousy?

No – No motive – for no reason just an interesting
experiment. The object of the crime – oneself – would one
be the same person – or would one be different. To find
out one would have to commit homicide – observing all the
time oneself – one's feelings, keeping notes.

Needed a victim – carefully selected but definitely not
anyone that one wished dead in any way. 'I have killed –
now am I the same person I was? Or am I different – do I
feel – fear? regret? pleasure? (surely not!)

People to imagine and [in]vent

The victim

Various suggestions. A woman who has cancer or a heart
condition. It can suggest itself as a mercy killing.

The killer

Man? Woman? Possibly woman get excited, she too decides
to try the experiment also. Man (Jeremy) does not realise
what she is doing

Afterwards J finds he is excited, nervous – doctor or nurse
is suspicious. J begins to lay clues of who the culprit may be
and some reason why. J begins to feel he might do another
murder – Lay the clues

Edmund (Harmsworth) Murdock debates with friends –
Murder – How would it feel to be a [killer?]

Girl or woman – tells about shoplifting or stealing – or
falsifying accounts.

Edmund and Lancelot go away debating

Points to be safe – victim – man or woman

Who should be obliterated – ('unfit to live') (no motive no
advantage to be gained) (Someone must gain and profit)

Feelings of operation must be closely studied – will X's
character alter (no one must share knowledge)

Book?

Edmund (Harmsworth) - Murdock?

Debates with friends - Murder
How would it feel to be a —?
Girl or woman — tells about shoplifting or
stealing — or falsifying accounts —

Edmund + Lancelot go away debating.

Points To be safe — Victim — man or woman
who should be obliterated — ("unfit to live")
(no motive — no advantage to be gained
(Someone must gain and profit—)

Feelings of operation must be closely
Studied — Will X's character alter?)
(no one must share knowledge)

Someone at original Conversation might be
(although not suspected) be actually involved —
possibly even (guilty) Final Surprise?
                              or has planned the
whole thing —

*From Notebook 7 this is one of the last pages Agatha Christie wrote when
she was too frail to develop this fascinating sketch into one final Christie
for Christmas.*

By any standard *Postern of Fate*, the last book that Agatha Christie wrote, is a sad end to a wonderful career. Amazingly, the notes above are for the novel to appear in 1974. The page in the Notebook immediately preceding them is unequivocally dated 7 November 1973, just after the publication of *Postern of Fate*. As can be seen, this outline is far superior, both in concept and approach; even the notes read better than those for *Postern of Fate*. Here, at the age of 83, Christie was experimenting with a novel totally different from any she had written before. Sounding somewhat similar to Meyer Levin's *Compulsion* (1956), which, in turn, was based on the infamous Leopold and Loeb true-life murder case, where two college students murdered a small boy solely as an experiment, this would have been a radical departure. It seems remarkable that after the previous half-dozen weak novels Christie should be even planning something like this. Whether she had the ability, at this stage, to carry off such a demanding concept is debatable but these notes confirm, once again, that it was her powers of development, and not her powers of imagination, that were waning.

And lest there be any lingering doubt, the devious hand of the Queen of Crime is very evident in the last phrase, with its final – absolutely final – Christie twist:

> Someone at original conversation might be (although not suspected) actually involved – possibly even (guilty) final surprise? Or has planned the whole thing

13

Agatha Christie's Booklists

'I read enormous quantities of books . . . '

————————◄○►————————

A look at some of the booklists that Agatha Christie's scribbled down in her Notebooks confirms that her interests were eclectic and wide-ranging. While crime novels make up a proportion of each list, the appearance of historical novels, biography, history, philosophy, short stories and very British novels confirm a catholic taste. Interestingly, the crime fiction titles venture into areas other than her own sphere. Simenon's Maigret and the American noir, *Detour*, as well as the detective novels of some of her 'rivals' – Dorothy L. Sayers, John Dickson Carr, Michael Innes and Elizabeth Ferrars – make for an assorted collection. Apart from the short 'Books read and liked' list below, it is difficult to tell what these lists represent. They may be titles to be read, to recommend, or even to give as presents. I opt for the first possibility; the consistent dates seem to indicate that the lists were drawn from publishers' catalogues of forthcoming titles. And the evidence of the Notebooks suggests that an orderly list of 'Books Read and to be Recommended' would be out of keeping with the overall approach.

The following pages are a selection of booklists reproduced from the Notebooks. In some cases tracking down the title proved impossible, due usually to an illegible or incorrect word, or words; these I have omitted. Where a title is ambiguous, for example *The Clock Strikes Twelve* from the final selection, I have taken the publication nearest to the year of the surrounding titles.

The following short list from Notebook 39 appears on a half-page in the middle of the plotting for *Evil under the Sun*. All of the titles date from 1938/9 and this timeline tallies with the receipt of that manuscript by her agent in February 1939:

Booklist
The Valiant Woman Sheila Royde Smith
They Wanted to Live Cecil Roberts
Death in Five Boxes [Carter Dickson]
Revue Beverly Nichols
The Case of the Shoplifter's Shoe [Erle Stanley Gardner]
Case with No Conclusion [Leo Bruce]

Half of the titles are crime novels – a Perry Mason novel by Erle Stanley Gardner, a Sergeant Beef novel by Leo Bruce and a John Dickson Carr writing under his alter ego Carter Dickson. Dickson Carr's *The Burning Court* is a clue in Chapter 8 i of *Evil under the Sun*. Three very British novels make up the rest of the list.

Also from the same period, but this time from the opening page of Notebook 62, the next list contains only one crime title, from fellow crime queen Ngaio Marsh. Perhaps significantly, *Overture to Death* was Marsh's first title for Collins Crime Club. The page following this has the corrections for *Curtain* so, again, the timeline is correct. One minor mystery on this list is the appearance of a novel with a background of the American car industry, *F O B Detroit*.

Books read and liked
The Long Valley [John Steinbeck, 1938]
F O B Detroit [Wessel Smitter, 1938]
Overture to Death [Ngaio Marsh, 1939]
Black Narcissus [Rumer Godden, 1939]
The Patriot [Pearl S. Buck, 1939]
The Woman in the Hall [Marguerite Stern, 1939]
The Power and the Glory [Graham Greene, 1940]

Notebook 56 has a listing of historical novels, many of them titles from the previous century and some of them well-known classics – *The Black Arrow, Ivanhoe* and *Kidnapped*; others – Henty and Weyman – are mentioned specifically in Christie's *Autobiography*. Some of these titles are on the shelves of Greenway House to this day:

Historical Novels . . . Penguin Series
Unknown to History (Elizabethan) [Charlotte M. Yonge?]
Shadow of a Throne (French Revolution and Directory) [F.W.
    Hayes?]
In the Reign of Terror ([G.A.] Henty)
Cat of Bubastes (Henty)
In the King's Name [George] Manville Fenn
Under the Red Robe
The Red Cockade Stanley Weyman
The Castle Inn
The Long Night
One Last Hope (Seton Merrimen)
Kidnapped ([R.L.] Stevenson)
The Black Arrow (War of Roses)
Dickon (Marjorie Bowen)
Ivanhoe ([Walter] Scott)

Just inside the cover of Notebook 52 we find the following list of reading material, all dating from 1961/2. This date corresponds with the contents of the Notebook, which contains the notes for *The Mirror Crack'd from Side to Side* and *The Clocks*. I have rearranged the titles for ease of discussion but am unable to explain the '+' or '++.' 'D' seems to indicate that the title is a detective/crime novel – Waugh, Payne, Garve, Innes; and the '?' probably indicates uncertainty on the part of Christie. HB indicates hardback, but why some titles are crossed through and some not remains a mystery (Received, Read, Enjoyed, perhaps?). Where an author's name has not been included in the Notebook I have inserted it, using the 1961/2 guideline where there is ambiguity.

The first five titles are crime novels, the Garve and Blake titles from the Crime Club series, while Waugh is an American crime writer.

+ D ~~The Nose on my Face~~ [Laurence Payne]
+ D ~~The House of Soldiers~~ [Andrew Garve]
D *Silence Observed* [Michael Innes]
D ~~The Worm of Death (Nic~~[holas]~~ Blake)~~
~~D The Night it Rained (?)~~ [Hilary Waugh]

The non-fiction titles are mainly biography (Stalin, Cranmer, Ivan the Great), but travel (Durrell) and true crime (*Airline Detective*) also feature:

HB Books
HB *Morning Glory* (Autobiog) [Mary Motley]
HB *Stalin* [Isaac Deutscher]
Thomas Cranmer [Jasper Ridley]
HB *Ivan the Great of Moscow* [J.L.I. Fennell]
Every Night and All (Glasgow) [William Miller]
~~George (Emlyn Williams Autob)~~

(Legends etc.) ~~The Twelve Days of Christmas~~ [a Christmas
miscellany by Miles and John Hadfield]
+ ~~Airline Detective~~ (Useful?) [Donald Fish; published by
Collins]
++ ~~The Whispering Land (G. Durrell)~~

The list of novels and short stories ranges from the well-
known – Muriel Spark and Paul Gallico – to the forgotten
– Morel and Brent – but also includes the challenging –
Calvino and Narayan:

++ ~~The Prime of Miss Jean Brodie (M. Spark)~~
– ~~Miss Bagshot Goes to Tibet~~ [Anne Telscombe]
Confessions of a Story Teller (Paul Gallico)
+ ~~Exit~~ [Peter Ludwig Brent]
~~Autumn Fair~~ [Dighton Morel]
? History *Manila Galleon* [F. Van Wyck Mason]
+ *The Borders of Barbarism* [Eric Williams]
+ *The Non-existent Knight* [Italo Calvino – two short novels;
published by Collins]
The Man Eater of Malqudi [R.K. Narayan]
The Far Road [George Johnston; published by Collins]
+ ~~Roll of Honour (Eric Linklater)~~
? SS *Spine Chillers* [ed. by Elizabeth Lee]

The heading on the following titles ('to buy?') would seem to
indicate that the earlier titles were to be supplied, perhaps by
Collins. The sole non-fiction title was one written for those
with little scientific knowledge to help them understand new
scientific discoveries; and Christie was in her seventies.

Penguins to buy?
Fire Burn (John Dickson Carr)
Medicine Today [David Margerson]

The Wild Palms W. Faulkner
Pigeon Pie (Nancy Mitford)

The following is a two-page list from Notebook 35 and the titles (with one inexplicable exception) date from 1939–40. I reproduce them complete with crossings out and unexplained Xs but I have inserted explanatory notes and, where necessary, accurate titles, and have rearranged them for ease of discussion.

All of the following are 1939 crime titles by a mixture of US (Rawson, Chambers) and UK (Michael Innes, E.R. Punshon) writers, chosen from the well-known (Sayers) and the forgotten (Armstrong, Fethaland). Only Eberhart was a fellow Crime Club author.

Murder at Charters [John Fethaland]
Brief Return [Eberhart]
Murder in Stained Glass [Margaret Armstrong]
Murder Abroad (Punshon)
D *Stop Press* (Innes)
D *Some Day I'll Kill You* ([Dana] Chambers)
D ~~Detour (Tough American)~~ [Goldsmith]
~~In the Teeth of the Evidence (D. Sayers)~~
+ *The Footprints on the Ceiling* (Merlini) [Clayton Rawson]

Also included is an eclectic selection of novels and short stories from the same year:

~~Flight from a Lady~~ (~~[A.G.] MacDonnell~~)
+ *Before Lunch* (Angela Thirkell)
+ *My American* (Stella Gibbon[s])
+ *The Nazarene* [Sholem Asch]
+ *Household Gods* (Winifred Duke)
The Dark Star [March Cost]

John Arnison [*Introducing the Arnisons*] (Edward Thompson)
The Death Guard (Wellesian fantasy) [Philip Chadwick]
Nanking Road (Vicki Baum)
The Ghost of a Rose [Norman Davey]
~~*The Temple of Costly Experience*~~ [Daniele Vare]
Twenty-four Short Stories (Graham Greene – James Laver)
~~*By the Waters of Babylon*~~ ~~(R. Neumann)~~

And scattered in between are some non-fiction titles, a miscellany of music, art, travel, biography and history:

Ancient Greece ([Stanley] Casson)
Caroline of England [Peter Quennell]
Escape with Me (Osbert Sitwell)
Portrait of Padrewsky [The Paderewski Memoirs]
Dismembered Masterpieces [Thomas Bodkin 1945, about the restoration of damaged paintings]

Perhaps because the other books were to be supplied, a 1939 book by T.S. Eliot has a specific note:

Buy *The Idea of a Christian Society*

The opposite page of the same Notebook lists 1940 titles, including one by Crime Club author Elizabeth Ferrars and a slightly incorrect Maigret title. The third title below seems to be a collection of 14 ghost stories rather than the Miss Silver detective novel of the same name, which was not published until 1945.

Give a Corpse a Bad Name [Ferrars]
Maigret Goes [*Travels*] *South* [Simenon]
The Clock Strikes Twelve [Wakefield]
Mr Skeffington [Elizabeth Von Arnim]
Maid no More [Helen Simpson]
Idle Apprentice [Joanna Cannan]
Good Night, Sweet Ladies [S. Frazer]
The Edge of Running Water [William Sloane]

APPENDIX 1

Agatha Christie Chronology

Dates of publication refer to the UK editions

1921
The Mysterious Affair at Styles

1922
The Secret Adversary

1923
The Murder on the Links

1924
The Man in the Brown Suit
Poirot Investigates:
   The Adventure of 'The
      Western Star'
   The Tragedy at Marsdon
      Manor
   The Adventure of the Cheap
      Flat
   The Mystery of Hunter's
      Lodge
   The Million Dollar Bond
      Robbery
   The Adventure of the
      Egyptian Tomb
   The Jewel Robbery at the
      Grand Metropolitan

   The Kidnapped Prime
      Minister
   The Disappearance of Mr
      Davenheim
   The Adventure of the Italian
      Nobleman
   The Case of the Missing Will
The Road of Dreams (poetry)

1925
The Secret of Chimneys

1926
The Murder of Roger Ackroyd

1927
The Big Four

1928
The Mystery of the Blue Train

1929
The Seven Dials Mystery
Partners in Crime:
   A Fairy in the Flat/A Pot of
      Tea

The Affair of the Pink Pearl
The Adventure of the
  Sinister Stranger
Finessing the King/The
  Gentleman Dressed in
  Newspaper
The Case of the Missing Lady
Blindman's Buff
The Man in the Mist
The Crackler
The Sunningdale Mystery
The House of Lurking Death
The Unbreakable Alibi
The Clergyman's Daughter/
  The Red House
The Ambassador's Boots
The Man Who Was No. 16

1930
The Mysterious Mr Quin:
  The Coming of Mr Quin
  The Shadow on the Glass
  At the 'Bells and Motley'
  The Sign in the Sky
  The Soul of the Croupier
  The Man from the Sea
  The Voice in the Dark
  The Face of Helen
  The Dead Harlequin
  The Bird with the Broken
    Wing
  The World's End
  Harlequin's Lane
The Murder at the Vicarage
Black Coffee (stage play)
Behind the Screen (radio serial,
  co-authored)

Giant's Bread (as Mary
  Westmacott)

1931
The Sittaford Mystery
Chimneys (stage play)
The Floating Admiral
  (co-authored)
The Scoop (radio
  serial,co-authored)

1932
Peril at End House
The Thirteen Problems:
  The Tuesday Night Club
  The Idol House of Astarte
  Ingots of Gold
  The Blood-Stained Pavement
  Motive v. Opportunity
  The Thumb Mark of St Peter
  The Blue Geranium
  The Companion
  The Four Suspects
  A Christmas Tragedy
  The Herb of Death
  The Affair at the Bungalow
  Death by Drowning

1933
Lord Edgware Dies
The Hound of Death:
  The Hound of Death
  The Red Signal
  The Fourth Man
  The Gypsy
  The Lamp
  Wireless

The Witness for the
  Prosecution
The Mystery of the Blue Jar
The Strange Case of Sir
  Arthur Carmichael
The Call of Wings
The Last Seance
SOS

1934
Murder on the Orient Express
The Listerdale Mystery:
  The Listerdale Mystery
  Philomel Cottage
  The Girl in the Train
  Sing a Song of Sixpence
  The Manhood of Edward
    Robinson
  Accident
  Jane in Search of a Job
  A Fruitful Sunday
  Mr Eastwood's Adventure
  The Golden Ball
  The Rajah's Emerald
  Swan Song

Why Didn't They Ask Evans?
Parker Pyne Investigates:
  The Case of the Middle-aged
    Wife
  The Case of the
    Discontented Soldier
  The Case of the Distressed
    Lady
  The Case of the
    Discontented Husband
  The Case of the City Clerk

  The Case of the Rich Woman
  Have You Got Everything
    You Want?
  The Gate of Baghdad
  The House at Shiraz
  The Pearl of Price
  Death on the Nile
  The Oracle at Delphi
Unfinished Portrait (as Mary
  Westmacott)

1935
Three Act Tragedy
Death in the Clouds

1936
The A.B.C. Murders
Murder in Mesopotamia
Cards on the Table

1937
Dumb Witness
Death on the Nile
Murder in the Mews:
  Murder in the Mews
  The Incredible Theft
  Dead Man's Mirror
  Triangle at Rhodes

Wasp's Nest (TV play)
Yellow Iris (radio play)

1938
Appointment with Death
Hercule Poirot's Christmas

1939
Murder is Easy
Ten Little Niggers/ And Then There
  Were None

1940
Sad Cypress
One, Two, Buckle My Shoe

1941
Evil under the Sun
N or M?

1942
The Body in the Library

1943
Five Little Pigs
The Moving Finger
And Then There Were None (stage
  play)

1944
Towards Zero
Absent in the Spring (as Mary
  Westmacott)

1945
Death Comes as the End
Sparkling Cyanide
Appointment with Death (stage
  play)

1946
The Hollow
*Murder on the Nile/ Hidden
  Horizon* (stage play)

Come, Tell Me How You Live
  (memoir)
1947
The Labours of Hercules:
  Foreword
  The Nemean Lion
  The Lernean Hydra
  The Arcadian Deer
  The Erymanthian Boar
  The Augean Stables
  The Stymphalean Birds
  The Cretan Bull
  The Horses of Diomedes
  The Girdle of Hyppolita
  The Flock of Geryon
  The Apples of Hesperides
  The Capture of Cerberus

Three Blind Mice (radio play)

1948
Taken at the Flood
Butter in a Lordly Dish (radio
  play)
The Rose and the Yew Tree (as
  Mary Westmacott)

1949
Crooked House

1950
A Murder is Announced

1951
They Came to Baghdad
The Hollow (stage play)

1952
Mrs McGinty's Dead
They Do It with Mirrors
The Mousetrap (stage play)
A Daughter's a Daughter (as Mary
    Westmacott)

1953
After the Funeral
A Pocket Full of Rye
Witness for the Prosecution (stage
    play)

1954
Destination Unknown
Spider's Web (stage play)
Personal Call (radio play)

1955
Hickory Dickory Dock

1956
Dead Man's Folly
A Daughter's a Daughter (stage
    play)
Towards Zero (stage play)
The Burden (as Mary
    Westmacott)

1957
4.50 from Paddington

1958
Ordeal by Innocence
Verdict (stage play)
The Unexpected Guest (stage play)

1959
Cat among the Pigeons

1960
*The Adventure of the Christmas
    Pudding:*
    The Adventure of the
    Christmas Pudding
    The Mystery of the Spanish
    Chest
    The Under Dog
    Four and Twenty Blackbirds
    The Dream
    Greenshaw's Folly
Go Back for Murder (stage play)

1961
The Pale Horse

1962
*The Mirror Crack'd from Side to
    Side*
Rule of Three (3 one-act plays):
    Afternoon at the Seaside
    The Rats
    The Patient

1963
The Clocks

1964
A Caribbean Mystery

1965
At Bertram's Hotel
Star over Bethlehem (poetry and
    stories):

Star over Bethlehem
The Naughty Donkey
The Water Bus
In the Cool of the Evening
Promotion in the Highest
The Island

1966
Third Girl

1967
Endless Night

1968
By the Pricking of my Thumbs

1969
Hallowe'en Party

1970
Passenger to Frankfurt

1971
Nemesis

1972
Elephants Can Remember
Fiddlers Five/Fiddlers Three (stage play)

1973
Postern of Fate
Poems (poetry)
Akhnaton (stage play)

1974
Poirot's Early Cases:
    The Affair at the Victory Ball

The Adventure of the
    Clapham Cook
The Cornish Mystery
The Adventure of Johnnie
    Waverly
The Double Clue
The King of Clubs
The Lemesurier Inheritance
The Lost Mine
The Plymouth Express
The Chocolate Box
The Submarine Plans
The Third Floor Flat
Double Sin
The Market Basing Mystery
Wasp's Nest
The Veiled Lady
Problem at Sea
How Does Your Garden
    Grow?

1975
Curtain: Poirot's Last Case

1976
Sleeping Murder

1977
An Autobiography (memoir)

1979
Miss Marple's Final Cases:
    Sanctuary
    Strange Jest
    Tape-Measure Murder
    The Case of the Caretaker
    The Case of the Perfect Maid
    Miss Marple Tells a Story

The Dressmaker's Doll
In a Glass Darkly

1982
(in *The Agatha Christie Hour*):
Magnolia Blossom

1991
Problem at Pollensa Bay:
Problem at Pollensa Bay
The Second Gong
Yellow Iris
The Harlequin Tea Set
The Regatta Mystery
The Love Detectives
Next to a Dog
(Magnolia Blossom)

1997
While the Light Lasts:
The House of Dreams
The Actress
The Edge
Christmas Adventure
The Lonely God

Manx Gold
Within a Wall
The Mystery of the Baghdad
Chest
While the Light Lasts

2008
(in *Hercule Poirot: The Complete
Short Stories*):
Poirot and the Regatta
Mystery

2009
(in *Agatha Christie's Secret
Notebooks*):
The Capture of Cerberus
The Incident of the Dog's
Ball

2011
(in *Agatha Christie's Murder in the
Making*):
The Man Who Knew
The Case of the Caretaker's
Wife

Alphabetical List of Agatha Christie Titles

4.50 from Paddington **1957**

A.B.C. Murders, The **1936**

Absent in the Spring (as Mary Westmacott) **1944**

Adventure of the Christmas Pudding, The (Short stories) **1960**

After the Funeral **1953**

Agatha Christie Hour, The (short stories) **1982**

Akhnaton (stage play) **1973**

And Then There Were None (stage play) **1943**

Appointment with Death **1938**

Appointment with Death (stage play) **1945**

At Bertram's Hotel **1965**

Autobiography, An (memoir) **1977**

Behind the Screen (radio serial, co-authored) **1930**

Big Four, The **1927**

Black Coffee (stage play) **1930**

Body in the Library, The **1942**

Burden, The (as Mary Westmacott) **1956**

Butter in a Lordly Dish (radio play) **1948**

By the Pricking of my Thumbs **1968**

Cards on the Table **1936**

Caribbean Mystery, A **1964**

Cat among the Pigeons **1959**

Chimneys (stage play) **1931**

Clocks, The **1963**

Come, Tell Me How You Live (memoir) **1946**

Crooked House **1949**

Curtain: Poirot's Last Case **1975**

Daughter's a Daughter, A (stage play) **1956**

Daughter's a Daughter, A (as Mary Westmacott) **1952**

Dead Man's Folly **1956**

Death Comes as the End **1945**

Death in the Clouds **1935**

Death on the Nile **1937**

Destination Unknown **1954**

Dumb Witness **1937**

Elephants Can Remember **1972**

Endless Night **1967**

Evil Under the Sun **1941**

Fiddlers Five/Fiddlers Three (stage play) **1972**

Five Little Pigs **1943**

Floating Admiral, The (co-authored) **1931**

Giant's Bread (as Mary Westmacott) **1930**

Go Back for Murder (stage play) **1960**

Hallowe'en Party **1969**

Hercule Poirot's Christmas **1938**

Hickory Dickory Dock **1955**

Hollow, The **1946**

Hollow, The (stage play) **1951**

Hound of Death, The (short stories) **1933**

Labours of Hercules, The (short stories) **1947**

Listerdale Mystery , The (short stories) **1934**

Lord Edgware Dies **1933**

Man in the Brown Suit, The **1924**

Mirror Crack'd from Side to Side, The **1962**

Miss Marple's Final Cases (short stories) **1979**

Mousetrap, The (stage play) **1952**

Moving Finger, The **1943**

Mrs McGinty's Dead **1952**

Murder at the Vicarage, The **1930**

Murder in Mesopotamia **1936**

Murder in the Mews (short stories) **1937**

Murder is Announced, A **1950**

Murder is Easy **1939**

Murder of Roger Ackroyd, The **1926**

Murder on the Links, The **1923**

Murder on the Nile/ Hidden Horizon (stage play) **1946**

Murder on the Orient Express **1934**

Mysterious Affair at Styles, The **1921**

Mysterious Mr Quin, The (Short stories) **1930**

Mystery of the Blue Train, The **1928**

N or M? **1941**

Nemesis **1971**

One, Two, Buckle My Shoe **1940**

Ordeal by Innocence **1958**

Pale Horse, The **1961**

Parker Pyne Investigates (short stories) **1934**

Partners in Crime (short stories) **1929**

Passenger to Frankfurt **1970**

Peril at End House **1932**

Personal Call (radio play) **1954**

Pocket Full of Rye, A **1953**

Poems (poetry) **1973**

Poirot Investigates (short stories) **1924**

Poirot's Early Cases (short stories) **1974**

Postern of Fate **1973**

Problem at Pollensa Bay (short stories) **1991**

Road of Dreams (poetry) **1925**

Rose and the Yew Tree, The (as Mary Westmacott) **1948**

Rule of Three (3 one-act plays) **1962**

Sad Cypress **1940**

Scoop, The (radio serial,co-authored) **1931**

Secret Adversary, The **1922**

Secret of Chimneys, The **1925**

Seven Dials Mystery, The **1929**

Sittaford Mystery, The **1931**

Sleeping Murder **1976**

Sparkling Cyanide **1945**

Spider's Web (stage play) **1954**

Star over Bethlehem (poetry and stories) **1965**

Taken at the Flood **1948**

Ten Little Niggers/ And Then There Were None **1939**

They Came to Baghdad **1951**

They Do It with Mirrors **1952**

Third Girl **1966**

Thirteen Problems, The (short stories) **1932**

Three Act Tragedy **1935**

Three Blind Mice (radio play) **1947**

Towards Zero **1944**

Towards Zero (stage play) **1956**

Unexpected Guest, The (stage play) **1958**

Unfinished Portrait (as Mary Westmacott) **1934**

Verdict (stage play) **1958**

Wasp's Nest (TV play) **1937**

While the Light Lasts (short stories) **1997**

Why Didn't They Ask Evans? **1934**

Witness for the Prosecution (stage play) **1953**

Yellow Iris (radio play) **1937**

Index of Titles

4.50 from Paddington 39, 49, 261,
272, 283, 303, 309, 319, 321,
325, 332

The A.B.C. Murders 31, 34, 37,
39, 40, 54, 55, 123, 138, 183,
186n, 209, 212, 332, 348
Absent in the Spring 192
'Accident' 70, 127
'The Adventure of Johnny
Waverley' 61
*The Adventure of the Christmas
Pudding* 282, 303
'The Adventure of the Christmas
Pudding' 330
'The Adventure of the Clapham
Cook' 98
'The Affair at the Victory Ball'
68, 362
After the Funeral 26, 31, 46, 56,
98, 170, 260, 262, 272, 281,
282–90, 295, 299, 304, 320,
321, 323, 330, 346, 350, 390
Akhnaton (play) 138, 374
And Then There Were None (play)
38, 48, 50, 53, 55, 66, 101,
122, 137, 190, 193, 210, 228,
233; *see also Ten Little Niggers*

'The Apples of the Hesperides'
211
Appointment with Death 31, 40,
49, 94, 98, 138, 163, 170, 182,
188, 213, 222, 260, 288, 309,
325, 366
Appointment with Death (play)
101, 193
At Bertram's Hotel 57, 331, 332,
348, 382
An Autobiography 26, 28, 36, 41,
67, 71, 73, 88n, 95, 109, 117,
125, 127, 128, 140, 150, 157,
163, 184n, 190, 194, 201, 217,
262, 297, 328, 333, 374, 382,
390, 395, 404, 410

Behind the Screen (radio serial)
16, 138
The Big Four 32, 36, 57, 59, 60,
61, 68, 119, 212
Black Coffee (play) 94, 101, 137,
138, 139, 161, 296
'The Blue Geranium' 365
The Body in the Library 31, 57, 98,
140, 141, 180, 190, 192, 194,
195, 200–208, 234, 239, 386,
403

The Burden 261
Butter in a Lordly Dish (radio play) 193, 382
By the Pricking of my Thumbs 66, 199, 267, 301, 331, 332, 354–60, 366, 379, 383, 396, 397

'The Call of Wings' 124, 125
'The Capture of Cerberus' 212, 376, 381
Cards on the Table 23, 40, 64, 182, 187
A Caribbean Mystery 23, 39, 49, 58, 94, 124, 178, 180, 309, 331, 332, 336, 337, 345, 346, 379
'The Case of the Caretaker/ Caretaker's Wife' 234-39, 240–58, 327
'The Case of the Missing Lady' 69
'The Case of the Missing Will' 39
'The Case of the Perfect Maid' 234, 235, 236, 260, 276, 393
Cat among the Pigeons 39, 57, 177, 230, 260, 261, 307–18, 336, 382
Chimneys (play) 98–108, 139
'The Chocolate Box' 213
'A Christmas Adventure' 330
'The Clock Stops' 338
The Clocks 39, 52, 232, 304, 308, 323, 330, 331, 335–45, 358, 411
Come, Tell Me How You Live (memoir) 190
'The Coming of Mr Quin' 70
'The Cornish Mystery' 179, 348
'The Crackler' 69

'The Cretan Bull' 178, 309, 346
Crooked House 22, 40, 49, 58, 119, 121, 123, 127, 192, 264, 284, 299
Curtain: Poirot's Last Case 31, 37, 40, 46, 49, 53, 189n, 190, 194, 208–28, 235, 366, 373, 374, 403, 409

A Daughter's a Daughter 261
'The Dead Harlequin' 104
Dead Man's Folly 179, 201, 303, 338, 384
'Dead Man's Mirror' 38, 101, 137, 159, 162, 169, 170, 222, 236
'Death by Drowning' 69, 124, 126, 127, 141, 200
Death Comes as the End 24, 50, 53, 93, 94, 125, 192, 309
Death in the Clouds 31, 54, 63, 98, 137, 170, 201, 229, 230, 260, 288, 304, 383
Death on the Nile 22, 24, 31, 41, 46, 48, 57, 137, 138, 150, 179, 180, 182, 188, 191, 193, 208, 212, 213, 223, 260, 274, 362, 383
Destination Unknown 39, 51, 233, 260, 261, 265, 267, 283, 291–6, 321, 322
'Detective Writers in England' 191
The Disappearance of Mr Davenheim (TV play) 333
'The Double Clue' 212
Double Sin 377
'The Dream' 38, 304, 305, 346
'The Dressmaker's Doll' 124, 125–6

Dumb Witness 36, 37, 46, 62, 101, 125, 127, 151, 182, 213, 238, 383

Elephants Can Remember 212, 346, 372, 383, 389–94, 395

Endless Night 24, 31, 37, 38, 39, 47, 48, 50, 55, 57, 66, 123, 137, 150, 179, 234, 235, 260, 274, 299, 301, 330, 331, 348, 360, 362, 374, 379, 382, 404

Evil under the Sun 31, 41, 46, 57, 119, 137, 150, 201, 275, 409

Fiddlers Five/Fiddlers Three (play) 230, 309, 374

Five Little Pigs 24, 37, 40, 55, 63, 64, 94, 101, 191, 210, 319, 320, 326, 332, 361, 389

The Floating Admiral 138

'The Four Suspects' 39, 62

Giant's Bread 137

'The Girdle of Hyppolita' 314

Go Back for Murder (play) 101, 332

'Greenshaw's Folly' 170, 260, 303–7, 343

'The Greenshore Folly' 303

'The Gypsy' 124, 151

Hallowe'en Party 179, 201, 321, 331, 332, 346, 348, 383, 384, 389

'The Herb of Death' 397

Hercule Poirot's Christmas 31, 38, 40, 52, 137, 161, 163, 188n, 283, 366

Hickory Dickory Dock 261, 283, 309, 323

The Hollow 31, 40, 41, 57, 63, 64, 93, 191, 192, 213

The Hollow (play) 101, 262, 275, 296

'The Horses of Diomedes' 211

The Hound of Death 32n, 62, 69, 98, 125, 127, 138, 151

'The Hound of Death' 151

'The House of Lurking Death' 58

'How Does Your Garden Grow?' 321

'How I Created Hercule Poirot' (article) 182-9

'In a Dispensary' (poem) 328

'In a Glass Darkly' 124, 125

'The Incident of the Dog's Ball' 101

The Labours of Hercules 29, 41, 65, 123, 178, 192, 211, 217, 309, 314, 346

'The Lamp' 124, 125, 151

'The Last Séance' 69, 124, 125, 151

The Listerdale Mystery 32n, 69, 138

'The Listerdale Mystery' 170

Lord Edgware Dies 31, 45, 48, 49, 61, 94, 137, 139, 151, 158, 162–8, 169, 174, 185, 282, 283, 330, 350

'The Lost Mine' 60

'The Love Detectives' 124, 126, 127, 141

Love from a Stranger (play) 70, 139, 193

The Man in the Brown Suit 23, 31, 37, 48, 54, 68, 94, 95, 109, 152, 261, 264, 291

'The Man in the Mist' 31, 52, 69, 304

'The Man Who Knew' 128, 129–35, 135–6

'The Market Basing Mystery' 31, 50, 365

'A Masque from Italy' (poem) 363

The Mirror Crack'd from Side to Side 38–9, 58, 94, 119, 229, 231, 233, 309, 319, 320, 323, 331, 332, 336, 337, 345, 411

'Miss Marple Tells a Story' 234

Miss Marple's Final Cases 374

The Mousetrap (play) 23, 31, 52, 193, 230, 233, 262, 263, 296, 298, 304, 332, 361, 373

The Moving Finger 64, 119, 123, 127, 174, 184n, 235, 236, 322, 404

Mrs McGinty's Dead 28, 37, 187n, 210, 222, 261, 272, 276, 295, 311, 388

The Murder at the Vicarage 31, 32, 33, 41, 57, 119, 126, 137, 140–50, 161, 200, 237, 239, 258

Murder at the Vicarage (play) 193, 261

Murder in Mesopotamia 38, 93, 138, 161, 233, 322, 382

Murder in the Mews 138, 159, 169, 222, 236

'Murder in the Mews' 31, 50, 62, 209, 365

A Murder is Announced 22, 46, 65, 93, 122, 126, 208, 229, 230, 239, 261, 263, 264

Murder is Easy 23, 40, 138, 174, 179, 201, 309, 323, 325, 379

The Murder of Roger Ackroyd 23, 31, 32, 34, 37, 40, 46, 47, 48, 49, 55, 67, 70, 122, 139, 140, 149, 163, 185, 213, 333

The Murder on the Links 67, 82n, 101, 135, 184, 185n, 223

Murder on the Nile (play) 101

Murder on the Orient Express 23, 31, 38, 46, 57, 110, 119, 123, 137, 163, 190, 210, 211, 213, 233, 373, 374, 383

The Mysterious Affair at Styles 22, 23, 29, 31, 36, 48, 52, 57, 58, 65, 67, 70–94, 98, 101, 124, 128, 135, 137, 150, 182, 183, 184n, 260, 274, 309, 323, 362

The Mysterious Mr Quin 62, 69, 127, 138, 362

'The Mystery of Hunter's Lodge' 39, 288, 305

'The Mystery of the Baghdad Chest' 164, 170, 267, 330

'The Mystery of the Blue Jar' 124, 125

The Mystery of the Blue Train 14, 23, 32, 67, 109–16, 128, 150, 170, 185, 186n, 260, 288, 389

'The Mystery of the Spanish Chest' 267, 303, 330

N or M? 190, 191, 192, 193–9, 200, 204, 235, 266, 345, 354, 397, 400

'The Nemean Lion' 41

Nemesis 63, 348, 372, 383–8, 396

One, Two, Buckle My Shoe 24, 31, 57, 119, 170, 229, 230, 283, 363

Ordeal by Innocence 31, 37, 56, 93, 123, 126, 127, 210, 261, 272, 308, 309, 362

The Pale Horse 39, 58, 59, 62, 127, 151, 177, 180, 309, 323, 331, 346, 356, 366, 404

Parker Pyne Investigates 32n, 138

Partners in Crime 23, 32, 52, 58, 61, 69, 152, 194, 263, 304, 397

Passenger to Frankfurt 21, 25, 51, 58, 157, 267, 309, 372, 373, 375–82

Peril at End House 14, 23, 32, 61, 127, 152, 161, 192, 213, 229, 230

Personal Call (radio play) 62, 263, 321

'Philomel Cottage' 70, 127, 139, 193

'The Plymouth Express' 110

A Pocket Full of Rye 31, 56, 58, 68, 121, 262, 273, 275, 284, 295, 299, 323, 324, 346, 363, 403

Poems 374

Poirot Investigates 39, 68, 72, 288

Poirot's Early Cases 68, 127, 362, 373

Postern of Fate 22, 39, 62, 96, 123, 354, 368, 372, 382, 383, 389, 394–402, 407

Problem at Pollensa Bay 32n, 159

'Problem at Sea' 403

'The Rajah's Emerald' 110

The Rats (play) 267

'The Red Signal' 98, 124, 125, 128, 135–6, 151

The Regatta Mystery 137, 377

'The Regatta Mystery' 310

Road of Dreams (poetry) 69, 329, 363

The Rose and the Yew Tree 192

Rule of Three (3 one-act plays) 267, 332

'S.O.S.' 124

Sad Cypress 37, 191, 211, 212, 222, 348, 366, 403

'Sanctuary' 119, 124, 126, 127, 239

The Scoop (radio serial) 138

'The Second Gong' 101, 137, 159–62, 170, 222, 236

The Secret Adversary 51, 68, 70, 152, 194, 354, 376, 397, 400

The Secret of Chimneys 23, 51, 57, 61, 68, 69, 95–109, 152

The Seven Dials Mystery 32, 59, 68, 95, 109

'The Sign in the Sky' 119, 234, 237

The Sittaford Mystery 13, 14, 61, 127, 138, 150–58, 161, 174, 292

Sleeping Murder 22, 65, 121, 127, 182, 190, 211, 222, 237, 348, 356, 373

Sparkling Cyanide 31, 49, 55, 57, 101, 170, 191, 195, 208, 229, 230, 233, 260, 283, 288, 323, 404

Spider's Web (play) 61, 102, 119, 231, 263, 291, 296, 297, 333

Star over Bethlehem 333

'The Strange Case of Sir Arthur Carmichael' 124, 151

'Strange Jest' 39, 236

'Swan Song' 124, 126

Taken at the Flood 31, 50, 57, 63, 151, 170, 260, 273, 288, 322, 366

'Tape Measure Murder' 234

Tea for Three (play) 70

Ten Little Niggers 65–66, 192; *see also And Then There Were None*

They Came to Baghdad 22, 24, 31, 51, 63, 93, 95, 152, 233, 260, 261, 264–72, 291, 292, 293, 322, 376

They Do It with Mirrors 31, 49, 260, 261, 272–81, 284, 295, 320, 321, 361, 362, 403

'The Third Floor Flat' 110, 274, 303, 365

Third Girl 23, 327, 330, 331, 343, 345–53, 380, 382, 390

Thirteen at Dinner 164

The Thirteen Problems 38, 39, 57, 62, 69, 100, 104, 110, 123, 126, 141, 152, 200, 234, 239, 363, 365, 397

Three Act Tragedy 31, 51, 54, 61, 65, 94, 119, 137, 139, 142, 164, 169–76, 185, 208, 229, 230, 238, 260, 288, 319, 320, 323, 330, 350

Three Blind Mice 377

Three Blind Mice (radio play) 23, 52, 193

Towards Zero 40, 55, 123, 191, 238, 322

Towards Zero (play) 263, 296

'Triangle at Rhodes' 180, 212, 223, 276, 327

'The Tuesday Night Club' 57, 69, 110, 140–41, 363

'The Unbreakable Alibi' 31, 61

The Underdog 377

The Unexpected Guest (play) 24, 260, 263, 296–302, 303, 397

Verdict (play) 263, 296, 297, 298, 327

Vision 72

'The Voice in the Dark' 62

Wasp's Nest (TV play) 139

While the Light Lasts 32n

Why Didn't They Ask Evans? 13, 14, 17, 48–9, 93, 95, 119, 137, 138, 152, 157, 158, 161, 164, 168, 170, 292

Witness for the Prosecution (play) 70, 101, 210, 231, 262, 263, 291, 296, 374

'Witness for the Prosecution' 23, 31, 37, 38, 127, 210, 330, 350

Yellow Iris (radio play) 138

'Yellow Iris' 101, 234